WHY TO KILL A MOCKINGBIRD MATTERS

*What Harper Lee's Book and the Iconic
American Film Mean to Us Today*

TOM SANTOPIETRO

ST. MARTIN'S PRESS ⚏ NEW YORK

WHY TO KILL A MOCKINGBIRD MATTERS. Copyright © 2018 by Tom Santopietro. All rights reserved. Printed in the United States of America. For information, address St. Martin's Press, 175 Fifth Avenue, New York, NY 10010.

www.stmartins.com

Designed by Omar Chapa

The Library of Congress Cataloging-in-Publication Data is available upon request.

ISBN 978-1-250-16375-2 (hardcover)
ISBN 978-1-250-16376-9 (ebook)

Our books may be purchased in bulk for promotional, educational, or business use. Please contact your local bookseller or the Macmillan Corporate and Premium Sales Department at 1-800-221-7945, extension 5442, or by email at MacmillanSpecialMarkets@macmillan.com.

First Edition: June 2018

10 9 8 7 6 5 4 3 2 1

For Sarah

CONTENTS

CONTENTS

ACKNOWLEDGMENTS

My first thanks go to my agent, Malaga Baldi, and my editor, Michael Flamini. Their guidance and unwavering support proved to be of great help throughout all drafts of this book, and I feel fortunate to be in such good hands. Additional thanks go to editorial assistant Gwen Hawkes for her first-rate and prompt help with a multitude of details, as well as to publicist John Karle who has now done yeoman's work in helping to spread the word on two of my books. A particular thanks, as well, to copy editor Carol Edwards, production editor Kevin Sweeney, production manager Joy Gannon, proofreader Deborah Friedman, marketing gurus Brant Janeway and Beatrice Jason, and foreign rights managers Marta Fleming and Chris Scheina. Special thanks to Omar Chapa for his striking design, and to Michael Storrings, for a beautiful dust jacket that is better than anything I could have imagined.

I want to acknowledge Charles J. Shields's first-rate biography *Mockingbird: A Portrait of Harper Lee,* as well as his updated edition, *Mockingbird: A Portrait of Harper Lee, from Scout to Go Set a Watchman.* These remain the definitive biographies of Harper Lee and proved invaluable in providing background information on the reclusive author. Although his focus is on Harper Lee's life even more than the implications of the *Mockingbird* phenomenon, his in-depth research provided fascinating and helpful material. As always with any of my books, a special thank-you to film historian/author/professor Jeanine Basinger, whose knowledge of film history remains without equal.

Boaty Boatwright proved extraordinarily generous with her time and detailed recollections of casting the *Mockingbird* film, and I thank her for a fascinating afternoon. Pulitzer Prize–winning author Diane McWhorter was equally generous with her insightful observations regarding *Mockingbird*, Harper Lee, and growing up in Alabama.

Finally, thank you to a terrific group of friends and colleagues whose support and encouragement during the past year have been very much appreciated: Cara and Mark Erickson; Doris Blum Gorelick; Rheba Flegelman and Steven Zweigbaum; Nina Skriloff and Dan Mirro; Beth and Alf Blitzer; Nola Safro; Mary Gates; Don and Anne Albino; Robert Albini; Katherine Aucoin; Ruth Mulhall; Mimi Lines; Kimberly Anne Kelley; Peter Pileski and Bob Avian; Bruce Klinger and Frank Shanbacker; David Jackson and Peter von Mayrhauser; Alan Markinson; Marlene Beasley; Steve Schnetzer; Abe and Caitlyn Abraham; Lynnette Barkley; Jan Heise; Joan Marcus and Adrian Bryan-Brown; Brig Berney; Steven Sorrentino; Bill Cannon; Tim and Karen Lernihan; Brooke Allen; Eric Comstock and Barbara Fasano; Anton and Almerinda Coppola; Virginia Wade; Mary Lou Mellace; Janet Strickland; Carol Strickland; Debbie Lamberti; Greg Galvin; Larry Katen and Philip Rinaldi; Mark Henry; Mary Breilid; Simon and Nancy Jones; Michael Lonergan; Michael Wilkie; Scott and Jill Glenn; Wayne and Betty McCormack; Steven Brooks; Parker Tricarico; Ara Marx; Lynn Goldman; Mark Schweppe; Tracey O'Shaughnessy; Gina Barreca; Wally Lamb; Adriana Trigiani; Michael Riedel; Denis Ferrara; Gary Packnick; Bob Siegel; Susan Ladner; Susie Cordon; Wayne and Pat Yankus; Dianne Trulock; Tony DeSare; and Dan Kaufman.

To Kill a Mockingbird is a great book now, it was a great book yesterday, and it will be a great book tomorrow.

—James McBride,
National Book Award–winning author of *The Good Lord Bird*

To Kill a Mockingbird is the best of American literature because it tells us who we are, who we can be, and it paints the communities we lived in in vivid, truthful detail. I mean, if that's not art or our highest dreams for literature, for storytelling, I don't know what is.

—Adriana Trigiani, novelist and filmmaker

WHY TO KILL A MOCKINGBIRD MATTERS

INTRODUCTION

The one thing that doesn't abide by majority rule is a person's conscience.

—Atticus Finch in *To Kill a Mockingbird*

The two most important aspects of my father's life were when he met my mother and when, in 1961, Alan Pakula and Bob Mulligan sent him the book *To Kill a Mockingbird*. That became the defining role of his career.

—Cecilia Peck at the Academy of Motion Picture Arts and Sciences tribute to her father, Gregory Peck

On the late afternoon of April 8, 1963, exactly six days after the Reverend Dr. Martin Luther King, Jr., launched a new nonviolent campaign to end segregation in Birmingham, Alabama, and four days before the future Nobel Peace Prize winner was arrested for leading a protest march, Gregory Peck stood in front of his mirror, dressing for the thirty-fifth annual Academy Awards ceremony. Nominated as Best Actor for his role as attorney Atticus Finch in *To Kill a Mockingbird,* the just-released film based upon Harper Lee's bestselling novel of the same name, Peck found himself at a once-in-a-lifetime juncture unusual even for a film star of his stature: Acclaimed by both critics and audiences for a role that managed to meld an already beloved fictional character with basic aspects of his own essential personality, he was starring in that rarest of films, one that had actually caught the zeitgeist.

To Kill a Mockingbird, it seemed, had tapped into a fervent national desire, at least outside of the Deep South, for a better, more egalitarian America, and, in the figure of Atticus Finch, presented a man Americans of every stripe wanted to believe reflected their own essential decency. It wasn't true, of course—no one outside of Gandhi himself actually possessed such rock-ribbed moral certainty—but that representational ideal had clearly and unequivocally begun to cast a longer and more powerful shadow with each passing week.

If, a scant seven months earlier, James Meredith, a twenty-eight-year-old black air force veteran, had tried to enroll at the University of Mississippi only to find the door blocked by Ross Barnett, the governor of Mississippi, and if, five days after that, Meredith arrived again, this time with 536 U.S. marshals as escorts/protection, then how and why had a slim novel and its small black-and-white film adaptation taken ahold of the national consciousness in a way few, if any, previous novels had managed? The furthest thing from epic, and the antithesis of *Gone with the Wind*'s romanticized view of southern cavaliers and genteel ladies as guardians of civilization, *Mockingbird*'s deceptively gentle, seemingly nostalgic evocation of a long-vanished southern childhood had ultimately proved nothing less than an indictment of the American character. Yet far from being put off, readers and viewers alike had embraced the material with a fervor that kept the novel at the top of the bestseller lists, floored Harper Lee, and infuriated several high-toned critics. What, exactly, had Harper Lee wrought?

For starters, a multigenerational national discussion of race in a way no one—publisher, author, and filmmakers alike—had ever anticipated. A discussion that seemed to gain, not lose, power with each passing week that *Mockingbird* continued to spend on the bestseller lists. A conversation that also slyly upended traditional notions of femininity, regionalism, and the very idea of what constitutes a "real" family. All this from a book that took Harper Lee the better part of a decade to write, found only one eager publisher, and initially elicited no interest from any of the major Hollywood studios.

Any such thoughts that might have flashed through the racing mind of the courtly, avowedly political Peck on this most important night of the year in Hollywood were quickly banished. Instead, the handsome actor adjusted his elegantly tailored tuxedo, called out to his beautiful wife, Veronique, that it was time to leave for the Santa Monica Civic Auditorium, and grasped the most important finishing touch of all: the gold pocket watch that had belonged to A. C. Lee, Harper's father and the unquestioned inspiration for the character of Atticus Finch. Glancing once more at the inscription on the back of the watch—"To Gregory from Harper"—Peck walked down the stairs and out to his waiting car.

A mere four hours later, his life would never be the same again, nor, in a not so insignificant way, would the discussion of America's original national sin: slavery. A change in the country's consciousness because of *To Kill a Mockingbird*? The ever-practical Nelle Harper Lee would have laughed at the mere idea back in the late 1950s, when her noticeably different, wildly uneven novel bore the name *Go Set a Watchman*. Back when she wanted to write—had to write—her way out of her small, beautiful, and stifling hometown of Monroeville, Alabama.

MONROEVILLE, ALABAMA

My book had a universal theme. It's not a "racial" novel. It portrays an aspect of civilization, not necessarily southern civilization. . . . It's a novel of man's conscience . . . universal in the sense it could happen to anybody, anywhere people live together.

—Harper Lee, the *Birmingham Post-Herald,* 1962

Monroeville, Alabama. Situated in the southwest corner of the state, due north of Pensacola and two hundred miles south of Birmingham, with Montgomery lying to the northeast and Mobile to the southwest. Isolated, with the nearest passenger train depot thirty minutes away in Greenville. Population thirteen hundred. The town into which Nelle Harper Lee was born on April 28, 1926.

Oak and pine trees surround a town square anchored by a two-story redbrick courthouse topped by a silver cupola housing a clock on each of its four sides. Several warehouses for the cotton and lumber industries which form the basis of the local economy dot the landscape, making the area, in *Mockingbird*'s fictionalized description as Maycomb, "a patchwork sea of cotton fields and timberlands." There is exactly one department store—Katz's, a purveyor of dry goods. The town's red clay streets will remain unpaved until 1935, and horses circle the town square as often as do automobiles. A small, drowsy southern burg that hadn't been wired for electricity until 1923, Monroeville remains without a public library, a town where the scoutmaster serves as the undertaker and "[p]eople moved slowly . . . A day was twenty-four hours long but seemed longer."

Seventy-year-old post–Civil War political compromises had resulted in a United States where towns like Monroeville, located below the Mason-Dixon Line, remained rigorously segregated, the laws of the South enforced in such a way as to protect white Americans at the expense of all others. The Ku Klux Klan, emboldened by their heroic portrayal in the well-made but staggeringly racist *Birth of a Nation* (1915) had, thanks to that remarkably effective recruiting tool, visibly grown in popularity during the decade after the film's release. With the myth of African-American intellectual and moral inferiority remaining codified in the very laws of the land, the end result was a town that lingered in the past, a slow-moving world where the black community provided the backbreaking labor underpinning the lumber and cotton industries, while remaining poorly paid and bereft of social privileges. A world where the threat of lynchings lay directly beneath a veneer of social respectability. The Billie Holiday classic "Strange Fruit" spoke of a reality with no redress in sight:

> *Blood on the leaves and blood at the root*
> *Black bodies swinging in the southern breeze . . .*

If Italian-Americans, also the victims of lynching in the South, could and did turn to the Mafia for a form of protection, the African-American community did not yet possess any powerful alternative to the flawed, racially biased court system; the NAACP, only seventeen years old at the time of Nelle's birth, was slowly making inroads, but it did not yet possess the power capable of mounting sustained legal actions on a widespread basis.

With the NAACP still finding its footing, membership in the Klan swelling into the millions, and Prohibition the law of the land,

America suddenly seemed awash in people dictating a national moral code.

Which is exactly what made Nelle Harper Lee's refusal to play by anyone else's rules all the more interesting. She proved a tomboy from the time she learned to walk, or more accurately, run, and in the traditionally house-proud matriarchal society of the time, it was actually her father, Amasa Coleman (A. C.) Lee, with whom she most closely bonded, in substantial part because of the periodic emotional upsets suffered by her mother. Frances Finch Lee, known as "Miss Fanny," was a gentle, somewhat overweight soul, described by her eldest daughter, Alice, in later years as having suffered from a "nervous disorder." Exhibiting streaks of obsessive behavior, she played the piano constantly, oftentimes in the middle of the night, and worked crossword puzzles incessantly.

Although never discussed publicly, it appeared that she had suffered a breakdown after her newborn second daughter, Louise, cried unceasingly for weeks on end. In the small, closed-off world of early-twentieth-century Monroeville, consulting an out-of-town medical specialist rated as a form of unusual behavior, but A.C.'s education allowed him to think and move beyond the town's circumscribed patterns of behavior, and together he and Fanny traveled to Selma to consult with a pediatric specialist. It was this specialist, Dr. Harper, who finally diagnosed Louise's problem and put her on a special formula, which very quickly stopped the crying jags. To express their gratitude, when Frances and A.C. subsequently had their fourth and final child, their daughter was christened Nelle Harper Lee.

Born a full fifteen years after her sister Alice, ten years after Louise, and a little more than five years after her brother, Edwin, Nelle, as family and friends alike called her, grew up a true child of the Depression, only six years old when Franklin Delano Roosevelt took office as president. With her father busy practicing law and her mother suffering periodic episodes of emotional distress, Nelle was often left to her own devices. Giving rein to her tomboy instincts, she had the full run of both the natural world and the adjacent school playground, exploring the world while, however unconsciously, assessing her own place therein. It all proved to be a loving yet slightly uneasy childhood, and if Truman Capote's years-later tale that Miss Fanny tried to drown Nelle in the bathtub proved to be yet another of his attention-seeking, mean-spirited fabrications, it seemed true nonetheless that Fanny was, at the very least, high-strung—in Capote's words, "the most uptight person I've ever met, pulled taut just like a violin string." Whatever the pain Fanny's difficulties caused Nelle, she never spoke about it, instead resolving the problem in the semiautobiographical *To Kill a Mockingbird* by simply removing Scout's mother from the scene: Atticus became a widower and Scout and Jem motherless children, the maternal role in the Finch family filled by Calpurnia, the African-American housekeeper.

If Nelle's childhood proved unusual in some respects, it was, nonetheless, rooted in a bone-deep attachment to a familiar place, Monroeville, and filled with the seemingly extraordinary (to them) events all children encounter while cautiously expanding their boundaries and exploring the world at large. In the end, none of those experiences proved to be quite as unusual or life-altering for Nelle as the arrival of Truman Streckfus Persons (the name Capote came in 1933, when he was adopted by his mother's second husband, Joseph Capote). Only four when his parents divorced, with a father never on the scene and a mother busy pursuing the high life in New York, Truman was sent to live with the Faulks of Monroeville, the very same relatives who had raised his mother. In the Monroeville of the early 1930s, the strange, effeminate, brilliant Truman landed next door to the Lees like a visitor from outer space.

The Faulks themselves were eccentric, three maiden ladies and a bachelor brother, and Truman gravitated toward the seemingly much more secure family life of the Lees, where he found, in Nelle, a kindred spirit. They were, in the words of Lee biographer Charles J. Shields, bound together by "a common anguish." In appearance and behavior alike, each seemed half boy and half girl; just as Truman eschewed any pursuit of the traditional rough-and-tumble boyhood world of sports and fighting, Nelle forged a path as far away as possible from what *Mockingbird*'s Scout refers to as the "starched walls of a pink cotton penitentiary" found in traditional girlhood. (Said Anna Quindlen in later years, "I think one of the reasons I became so obsessed with Harper Lee . . . is because everything she did convinced me she was a grown-up Scout who hadn't gone over to the dark side of being a girlie girl.")

Nelle proved unequivocally tougher and faster with her fists than Truman, always glad to make short work of anyone who dared treat him poorly. (When novelist John Knowles met the adult Harper Lee, he opined, "A very nice charming down to earth, masculine sort of woman.") She did not fit into conventional society, and neither did Truman, but more to the point, neither seemed to care much about it, accepting the fact that in the South of the 1930s, different did not mean special—it meant oddball. If both Nelle and Truman were made to feel separate—alone, even—then they would be alone together.

With his strange mannerisms stopping bullies dead in their tracks, Truman made his way in an often alien world by means of gumption and intellect, qualities shared by the equally singular Nelle. Firing popguns, fishing, and daring each other into the yard of the seemingly haunted Boulware house, the duo bonded in their companionable exploration of the town; even at a very young age, they shared a burgeoning love of words and books, and Truman kept the prized pocket dictionary given to him by Nelle's father in his back pocket at all times.

A. C. Lee may have been an attorney, but he was scarcely well-to-do, and with little money to spare, the two youngsters made their own entertainment, devising wild scenarios inspired by books, movies, and, most crucially of all for aspiring writers, their own imaginations. In 1964, in her last in-depth interview, Nelle bluntly and humorously stated, "That kind of [southern] life produces more writers than living on 82nd Street in New York City." In this she seems to share a striking similarity with Bruce Springsteen's musing that all art comes out of a "rambunctious gang feeling" born out of the neighborhood. Telling stories would not be good enough—no, it all had to be written down—the junior novelists thrilled when they acquired a solid black secondhand Underwood No. 5 manual typewriter, courtesy of A. C. Lee.

Truman, always the more fanciful of the duo, would dictate a story for Nelle to type, but on the next day, the roles of storyteller and typist would be reversed. True southerners, they were, at a very young age, mutually steeped in the southern storytelling tradition, creating stories as a way of exercising control as they tried to navigate the confusing world of adults. Said Nelle in later years, "We lived in our imagination most of the time." They remained outsiders, standing apart, observing southern society with an ironic, occasionally jaundiced eye while searching for the telling social clue. Why, they asked themselves, did different equal bad? Why were blacks treated as second-class citizens? Such powers of observation became instinctive, the two youngsters already the living, breathing embodiments of screenwriter Phoebe Ephron's dictum: "Everything is copy." All of the information they gathered was stored away for future use, eventually bursting forth in their own published work: Idabel Thompkins in Truman's 1948 novel, *Other Voices, Other Rooms,* was Harper Lee transferred to the page, as was Ann Finchburg ("Jumbo") in his beloved story "The Thanksgiving Visitor." Biding her time, Nelle stored away her own telling observations, all of which informed the endearingly oddball character of Dill in *Mockingbird.*

Truman moved to New York when his mother remarried Joseph Capote, but the friendship with Nelle endured, and for a time he returned in the summer for visits, always filled with fascinating, improbable tales of life in glamorous New York City. The visits dwindled, but the friendship remained intact as Nelle navigated her way through grammar and high school. A high-achieving student who eschewed the traditional societal norms—why bother with skirts and dresses when pants were so much more comfortable—and possessed of an original personality, Nelle graduated from high school in 1944, and then matriculated at the all-female Methodist Huntingdon College in Montgomery. Sharp-minded and possessed of a dry wit, not to mention a keen sense of the absurd, Nelle made no effort to fit into the frilly sorority mind-set of her peers, and instead wrote for both the school newspaper and the campus literary magazine. She proved tough but warm, a gimlet-eyed observer constantly moving away from the hidebound traditions of the past, and it was while at college that her first two stories appeared in print: "Nightmare," a tale of lynching, and "A Wink at Justice," the short story of a judge dealing with a group of black men accused of illegal gambling.

At the same time she was, in many ways, a typical member of her generation, the first for whom radios, records, and movies proved a given. Born at a time when there were tens of thousands of former slaves still alive, Nelle was now part of a generation for whom the world came into one's own home every day, the radios and newspapers bringing with them the different viewpoints heretofore invisible in the rural South. The Great Depression and World War II landed in homes with an immediacy previously unheard of, and as a result, Nelle, like so many of her generation, held a worldview forever shaped by those cataclysmic events.

If war always remains the single biggest disrupter of traditional mores and customs, then in its reaction to World War II, Nelle's generation proved no exception. For men fighting on foreign soil cheek by jowl with soldiers of every conceivable ethnicity, parochialism inevitably began to crumble; Hollywood's World War II combat films, which featured a veritable melting pot of ethnicities, presented this viewpoint to the nearly forty million weekly moviegoers on the home front. For women who now began working in jobs heretofore reserved for men, the sense of freedom, both economic and social, upended the traditional societal roles in which Nelle already held no interest. Ladies auxiliaries? Power in the form of gossip? Nonstarters. The difference with Nelle, however, lay in the fact that she never would attempt to fit the accepted mold, unlike her contemporaries, who did so, however grudgingly.

That refusal to play by the rules went hand in hand with an

increasingly liberal worldview, but Nelle's biggest act of rebellion lay a few short years away. She first attempted to make her father happy by following in her older sister Alice's footsteps; transferring to the University of Alabama in Tuscaloosa in order to study law, she dutifully plodded along, but found much greater pleasure in writing the "Caustic Comments" column for the *Crimson White* campus newspaper. She derived even more satisfaction from humorous articles written for the *Rammer Jammer* magazine, and in 1946 she was chosen the magazine's editor in chief. By now she was an established, original presence on campus—a young woman who swore, didn't bother with makeup, and cared little about approval from those in charge. Her succinct and rather prescient profile in the *Crimson White* read: "Lawyer Lee will spend her future in Monroeville. As for literary aspirations she says 'I shall probably write a book some day. They all do.' "

One biographer said that "she hated studying law—and that was the term she used, *hated*." Instead, she found true pleasure and genuine freedom when she spent the summer of 1948 enrolled in Oxford University's international graduates summer school. It was Oxford that gave Nelle a taste of the world at large, exposing her to vistas unimaginable in Monroeville, and she returned home with a newfound determination to become a writer. Realizing that further pursuit of the law was pointless, she dropped out of college in 1948, one semester shy of graduation.

Part of her still needed Monroeville and always would; she loved the sense of community and the feeling of roots, but small-town life had begun to feel closed off and ultimately stifling. If it was comforting to know that neighbors would always keep a sharp eye out for your welfare, it was also disconcerting to realize that they knew all of your business. Looking around Monroeville, sanctuary and prison all in one, she literally saw more of the same no matter where she gazed: no mountains, no oceans, just an endless flat vista.

Return home from Oxford she did, but only to waitress for a year in order to save money for her ultimate goal: life in New York City. Eleven hundred miles away and the center of the publishing industry.

Impersonal and bustling, where you saw "the other" every day, interacting on the subway, in the stores, and on the sidewalk, until those initially strange-seeming men and women ceased to be anything but fellow New Yorkers.

Nelle, of course, already knew that there was a chasm as wide as the nearby Gulf of Mexico between the promise of America and what it actually delivered. Like millions before her, she needed to escape and explore, all the while asking herself the eternal questions "Who am I?" and "Where do I fit in?" She'd never find the answers, never figure out her worldview, by staying in Monroeville, and if it took an act of will to leave her hometown and pursue a life of writing up north, so be it. She would move to the epicenter of American self-reinvention: Manhattan.

MANHATTAN

Give me such shows—give me the streets of Manhattan.

—Walt Whitman

If it took guts to assert herself in the hardest city of all, the very act of trying nonetheless liberated Nelle. Change was in the air: Wartime had disrupted the old social order, Rosie the Riveter had tasted freedom, and if many women were forced back into the home upon the return of the soldiers, traditional roles would and could never be the same again, a fact that suited Harper Lee just fine.

Settling in the heart of Manhattan's Upper East Side, she rented a walk-up cold-water flat at 1539 York Avenue and supported herself by working first in a bookstore and then as a reservations clerk for Eastern Airlines and the British Overseas Airways Corporation (BOAC). Writing at night on a makeshift desk—a freestanding door placed across two sawhorses—she slowly forged a path through the city, gaining a new family of friends along the way. Through Truman she met Joy and Michael Brown (Joy, a ballerina, and Michael, a composer/performer), a married couple with whom she formed an instantaneous bond even while still maintaining her long-sought-after independence. Reveling in her solitary navigation of the Manhattan currents, she was never so much lonely as, more accurately, standing alone.

And then a double tragedy. When her mother died of a recently diagnosed cancer in 1951, Nelle was only twenty-five. Returning to Monroeville for the services, she was faced, a mere six weeks later, with the death of her brother, Edwin; age thirty-one, he had suffered a brain aneurysm in his bunk at Maxwell Air Force Base in Montgomery, Alabama, leaving behind a wife and two small children. There was, for Nelle, a renewed closeness with older sister Alice, "Atticus in a skirt" in Nelle's fond description; practical and focused, Alice later explained that Nelle's way of dealing with her grief at this time was to stop writing and, instead, begin painting. A breather, time to restore, and when she began once more to write, Nelle felt herself informed by a new purpose.

She would write what she knew best—her own life—but move beyond it, re-creating her southern world from a distance of fifteen hundred miles and several decades. In detailing her own life, she would also address the country's overwhelming racial divide, which informed every aspect of southern life and increasingly played out in stories splashed across the front pages of newspapers. In 1954, in the case of *Brown v. Board of Education*, the Supreme Court of the United States ruled that "separate but equal" standards of racial segregation remained unconstitutional. In 1955, Emmett Till, a black teenager, was murdered for supposedly flirting with a white woman. And in the same year, seamstress Rosa Parks refused to give up her seat in the "colored" section of a Montgomery bus for a white passenger, and a nationwide furor erupted.

Nelle's home state of Alabama was looming large in the burgeoning civil rights movement, leading to anger, frustration, and a burning desire on Nelle's part to make sense of it all through words. Many thought they could write, some even possessed the talent, but very few had Nelle's determination and guts, the self-belief that kept her writing day after day, month after month in a willingness to face the blank page. She shared little about her progress, even among her new circle of Manhattan-based transplanted southern friends. A muttered sentence about her continuing efforts was all that could be pried out of her, leading one of her friends to shrug her shoulders with the blunt assessment "We didn't think she was up to much."

In November 1956, she took a selection of short stories to the offices of husband and wife agents Maurice Crain and Annie Laurie Williams, the agents agreeing to meet with Nelle because of her friendship with Truman Capote. Crain expressed interest in her work, but the fledgling author's struggle to balance the need to support herself with the limitation of being able to write only at night continued, until she received an unexpected and life-altering present at the holidays: Spending Christmas Day of 1956 with Michael and Joy Brown, Nelle sat happily with her friends, watching their children open their presents, until the Browns told her to go to the tree and find the envelope with her name boldly inscribed on the front. Inside lay a check with a succinct message: "You have one year off from your job to write whatever you please. Merry Christmas." Lee was overcome by both the gesture and her friends' belief in her. Said Michael, "No honey, it's not a risk. This is a sure thing." Lee did not accept the check as an outright gift, but, rather, treated it as a loan to be paid back with interest.

Freed to write full-time, in January Nelle returned to Crain and Williams with the first fifty pages of a novel entitled *Go Set a Watchman*. She continued to submit the novel in fifty-page increments throughout January and February, until the entire manuscript had been handed in by February 27, 1957. Crain and Williams glimpsed great promise in the work but nudged Lee toward continued revisions, which she completed by May 6. Still not satisfied, the agents insisted upon further rewrites, and Lee handed in a fully revised manuscript on August 19.

Going to work in an attempt to woo publishers, in April 1957 Crain had crafted a pitch letter that was part rah-rah cheer and part press agent pitch: "*Go Set a Watchman* will be an eye opener for many

Northerners as to Southern attitudes and the reasons for them in the segregation battle. Also and incidentally, Miss Lee can write. She's about 30 and bright as a button. Sincerely, Maurice Crain." Of the ten publishers who received the letter, exactly one—Lippincott, Philadelphia-based and quintessentially mainstream—expressed interest. A meeting between publisher and neophyte author was arranged.

Lee later admitted having experienced abject terror as she walked into the Lippincott editorial offices, but her determination trumped fear, and she soon found herself chatting with a short, thin editor and author (*A Ministry to Man: The Life of John Lovejoy Elliott,* 1959) whose name was the rather formidable Therese von Hohoff Torrey, known within publishing circles as "Tay Hohoff." Smoke curling above her head from an ever-present cigarette, the Brooklyn-born, Quaker-reared, gravel-voiced Tay (referred to by Lee in a 1990 letter with the phrase "known to the trade as the Quaker Hitler") seemed the opposite of the shy southern author, but the two bonded quickly as they began discussing the novel Nelle was, at the suggestion of Maurice Crain, now calling *Atticus.* The smart, experienced Hohoff counseled Lee: "This reads like anecdotes you've tried to push together—it's not a novel. But—it can be revised." Reflecting further in later years, Hohoff added, "It was real. A keen and witty mind was at work."

At this early stage, it was Lee's autobiographical central character of Jean Louise Finch—"Scout" to her family—who remained the linchpin of the story and to whom Hohoff reacted most strongly. As Lee had constructed the novel, the twenty-six-year-old Jean Louise, back in her hometown of Maycomb, Alabama, for a three-day visit, had to confront the fact that her beloved father, Atticus, was a racist; as the plot unfolded, interrupted by flashbacks to her childhood, Jean Louise attempted both to overcome her anger and to understand the world of her father, one wherein change and the search for racial equality had "got to be slow."

Hohoff thought these were all interesting and thought-provoking ideas, but the sections of the manuscript dealing with Scout's childhood struck her as far more immediate and memorable than those told in the voice of the adult Jean Louise. Lee's style, she felt, was an original one, which, with a great deal of work, might just manage the neat trick of turning a personal Depression-era childhood, one grounded in the specific rhythms, pace, and mores of small-town Alabama, into a tale of lost innocence and the revelation of universal truths. That was the book Hohoff wanted to read, and with agent Crain negotiating a small advance of "a few thousand dollars," on October 17, 1957, Nelle's novel was sold to Lippincott. Reflecting the already fluid nature of the work in progress, the contract did not specify a title for the novel, a fact that bothered no one. For now, a single key fact trumped all: Harper Lee was going to be a published author.

At which point, the problems began, because Harper Lee knew what she wanted to say but not yet how to say it.

Buoyed by the check from the Browns, Nelle set to work revising *Atticus*. As she wrote, present-day events seemed to mirror and sharply remind her of those from her own childhood: At the same time President Eisenhower signed the Civil Rights Act of 1957, sending federal troops into Little Rock, Arkansas, to guard black students entering previously all-white schools, Nelle was revisiting the even more virulently segregated times of the Depression. And it wasn't just her own sharp powers of observation that colored her concerns with the debilitating effects of racism, but also the family stories that predated her own birth, primarily her father's defense of Frank and Brown Ezell, two African-American men accused of murdering the white William Northrup; having lost the case, A. C. Lee was so shaken by the outcome that he never again tried a murder case.

Lee knew her themes: the simultaneous wondrous and perilous journey to adulthood. The southern sense of tradition placed alongside the pernicious effect of racism. A piece-by-piece deconstruction of the concept of "the other." A mix of events remembered from childhood with what others thought or said happened. Novel writing, in the years-later words of Mario Puzo, as the "art of retrospective falsification."

She would flesh out her characters by utilizing the essential personalities of those closest to her, beginning with A.C. himself, whose dignity would inform the character of Atticus Finch, a man for whom family came first and an attorney possessed of unflinching morality even in the face of unpopular causes. For decades after the novel's publication, Nelle would continue to deny anything more than a superficial resemblance between the two men, but when publicly praising her father, the resemblance would remain clear: "Then and now he has been ahead of his time. The only slogan he ever offered me was 'Equal rights for all and special privileges for none.'" A. C. Lee, on the page, in the oh-so-slightly fictionalized character of Atticus Finch.

Knowing she wanted her novel to turn on Atticus's defense of a black man unjustly accused of rape, Nelle looked beyond her father's own case and, according to biographer Charles J. Shields, drew upon elements taken from two additional cases: the infamous 1931 case of the Scottsboro Boys, in which a group of nine young black men was accused of raping two white women on a train, and a 1933 case of interracial rape in Monroeville, in which African-American Walter Lett was accused of raping the white Naomi Lowery. In Shields's view, it was by combining elements of all three cases that Nelle hoped to arrive at larger, overarching truths regarding justice and the true meaning and price of the American dream. (Lee herself, however, took issue with this interpretation in a July 2006 letter to close friend Wayne Flynt, irritatedly complaining, "Because the two [the Scottsboro and Walter Lett cases] took place at the same time TKAM was set, this is an easy, 'Harper Lee must have been thinking of . . .' sort of speculation so loved by academics.")

The heaviest lifting regarding the revisions Hohoff continued to request revolved around the character of Atticus; having agreed with her editor's advice to concentrate solely on the childhood years described in *Watchman,* Lee had to delete all of the passages from *Atticus/Watchman* in which Atticus revealed himself to be a notably complex, indeed racist, man of his southern roots and times.

Atticus, seventy-two in *Watchman,* was now morphing into a hale and fit middle-aged man. Gone was the adult Jean Louise, who responded to Atticus's casual racism by internally insisting, "Don't you ever call me that again. You who called me Scout are dead and in your grave." Jean Louise's younger self, the tomboyish Scout, would dominate the action, with Jean Louise now supplying only the connective tissues of memory and hindsight. Atticus's racist attitudes, which proved so abhorrent to Jean Louise, would now be espoused by the poorly educated, abusive Bob Ewell. A. C. Lee, lawyer, editor of the local newspaper, and a state legislator who had once been urged to run for governor, would now evolve into a kinder, gentler version of Atticus Finch, a man who also just happened to be a lawyer, editor, and state legislator.

The harshest judgments of Atticus's character would be tabled, and Lee's view of her father, which at its best moments toppled from fervent belief into near worship, helped her channel Scout's young reverential voice regarding Atticus. Reflecting on A.C.'s soft-spoken, reserved dignity, she mused: "My father had genuine humility. He had no ego drive so he was one of the most beloved men in the region." Atticus and Amasa Coleman Lee would remain nearly interchangeable.

Yes, Lee wanted the autobiographical elements to serve as the building blocks for the novel's structure, but a lightly fictionalized autobiography could never reach a big audience, and she was after big game here. The tomboyish Scout certainly resembled the tough young Harper Lee, but so, too, did elements of the reclusive Boo Radley, a misunderstood and uncomfortable loner who simply wanted to be left alone. As a result, the presence of Boo began to loom larger and larger while the rewriting progressed, and Nelle spent increasing amounts of time experimenting with how best to convey the specter of this supposed "malevolent phantom," one who lurks in every child's imagination in a manner simultaneously scary and a little bit thrilling.

While fleshing out the character of Boo, she increasingly thought about the Boulware family of Monroeville, particularly the reclusive Alfred "Son" Boulware, a shy young man permanently kept at home by his father after getting into trouble at school. Largely kept out of public view, Son became the subject of fanciful neighborhood legends now brought back to life by Nelle, complete with half-forgotten details she embellished and polished down to their essence. If, as a child, she had half-believed that climbing over the wire fence surrounding the Boulware home meant that Sonny would stab you with a butcher knife, then the character of Boo Radley would also lurk dangerously in the dark—forever just out of reach.

Even more, in recalling Monroeville's stranger-than-fiction one-night mix of the young Truman Capote, the African-American community, Sonny's appearance at a costume party in town, and the Ku Klux Klan, Nelle felt certain she had now found key plot elements that could inform both Atticus's jailhouse defense of Tom Robinson and Bob Ewell's climactic attack on Jem and Scout.

As related by Truman's childhood friend Marianne Motes, that strange one-night maelstrom had begun innocently enough, with young Truman deciding to throw a big costume party, to which he invited his black friend John White. When word reached the local KKK that a young black man possessed the effrontery to think he could be a guest at a white costume party, a mass rally was organized. As the Klan marched toward the town square, they encountered a youngster encased in a series of silver spray-painted boxes meant to suggest the figure of a robot. The robot was, in fact, Son Boulware, but the Klan members concluded that the robot costume was being worn by Truman's young black friend, and they set off in pursuit of the by now desperately fleeing figure. In his panicked flight, Son tripped and fell down in the Lee's front yard, at which point, recalled one observer, Mr. Lee, in his undershirt, "was wading out through these sheet-covered Klansmen on the street. He was a big dignified man, and he was slinging people out of the way. The Klansmen didn't give him any resistance." Sonny, scared and crying, hair in his eyes, cowered as A. C. Lee addressed the Klansmen: "Look at what your foolishness has done. You've scared this boy nearly to death because you wanted to believe something that wasn't true. You bunch of grown men should be ashamed."

After this incident, Son Boulware rarely left his house, and certainly never in the daytime, turning into a full-fledged recluse who began a custom of leaving presents for the Lee children in the knothole of a nearby tree; it was a touching, sad bid for connection, the best the traumatized and scared Son could manage, and one that would, decades later, inform both a key plot element of *To Kill a Mockingbird* and the opening titles of the film.

Nelle never did admit that Sonny Boulware inspired her creation of Boo Radley, but other townspeople noted the unavoidable resemblance. Said one Monroeville resident in later years, "I did see him one time later on—he was about six feet tall—so white because he didn't go out in the daylight." By now rendered virtually invisible, Son lived on for several more decades, until he died from tuberculosis in 1952, at the age of forty-two. Upset over the basic similarities between Son and Boo, after publication of *To Kill a Mockingbird* the Boulware family threatened to sue for defamation of character, but the suit never came to pass.

Even with the character of Boo shaping up into the sought-after mix of monster and savior, Nelle continued to struggle in her search for the proper mix of nostalgia, regret, and social criticism. Frustration increased until, on a cold winter night in 1957, she threw the entire manuscript out the window before calling Hohoff in tears to report that she had given up. The editor uttered soothing words and gently suggested that Nelle go outside to recover those lost pages— immediately.

Hohoff settled Lee down, and although in later years Lee told her good friend, Pulitzer Prize–winning author Diane McWhorter, that she had originally written two chapters in the contemporary setting of the 1950s and two in the past ("I just felt that what I had to say could best be said in that flashback"), Hohoff suggested that the novel's time frame now be compressed to a three-year span covering only the summer of 1932 through Halloween of 1935. Rewriting and excising, Lee's constant revisions became, in the words of Hohoff, a never-ending process of "writing and tearing up, writing and tearing up."

Hohoff said, "It's no secret that she was living on next to nothing and in considerable physical discomfort while she was writing *Mockingbird*."

Even as the story elements slowly fell into place, Nelle labored to mix the sought-after tone with the proper narrative voice, ultimately rewriting the novel three times. In the first full revision, the entire tale was narrated in the third person, a style that she ultimately realized proved too distancing for such an intimate story. In the second attempt, she wrote entirely in the first person—an improvement, but a decision that negated the distanced perspective of the adult Jean Louise. Finally, in the third draft, she mixed two narrators—Scout the bright six-year-old tomboy, and her twenty-six-year-old grown-up self, Jean Louise Finch—in the process successfully blending the two into the singular voice of a wised-up child. Just as Nelle herself aged from six to nine from 1932 to 1935, so, too, would Scout. At the same time, the adult Jean Louise's role narrowed, until she appeared only occasionally, subtly drifting into focus in order to provide a seemingly nostalgic, yet in reality sharp-eyed, gaze that mirrored Nelle's own.

It was difficult to shift between the two narrative voices—one misplaced emphasis and credibility with the reader flew out the window—but the shifting viewpoint slowly and surely began to fit Nelle's increasingly lyrical style. In the words of Tay Hohoff: "After a couple of false starts, the story-line, interplay of characters, and rise and fall of emphasis grew clearer, and with each revision—there were many minor changes as the story grew in strength and in her own vision of it—the true stature of the novel became evident."

Lee painstakingly excised entire sections and at times seemed to struggle over every single word, but as the book came into focus, the Alabama of 1932 came alive, immersing even the most casual of readers in the slow rhythms of everyday life: "Ladies bathed before noon, after their three-o'clock naps, and by nightfall were like soft teacakes with frostings of sweat and sweet talcum." One shimmering sentence that adhered, and the reader was now on the front porch with these women who moved languorously yet didn't miss a trick in their observations of small-town life. The pages mounted, but progress veered uneasily between steady and glacial, and a May 1958 deadline for submission of the manuscript came and went with nary a page submitted.

When the novel finally did near completion, Lee asked her revered teacher Miss Gladys Watson—by now Mrs. Gladys Burkett—to read the manuscript. Reading carefully, Gladys made extensive notes, to which Lee paid strict attention before making her final revisions. With the third draft finally completed to the satisfaction of both Nelle and Hohoff, in November 1959 Lippincott officially accepted the manuscript for publication in the summer of 1960.

Along with the final manuscript had come a new title, with the eye-catching, enigmatic *To Kill a Mockingbird* appearing for the first time in Crain and Williams's records on September 14, 1959. In the words of novelist Allan Gurganus, "It's really a perfect title. Now we all know what it is, but then it was puzzling in a good way." *To Kill a Mockingbird,* by Harper Lee. Not Nelle Lee, not Nelle Harper Lee, but Harper Lee, the byline she had used on articles written for the University of Alabama newspaper. Hometown friends all called her Nelle, which came out as "Naille" when uttered in a southern drawl, but so wary was the new author of her first name being mispronounced as "Nellie" that she made a bold decision: Family and friends would continue to call her Nelle, but to the general reading public, Harper Lee it would be. Now thirty-three years old, she was, for better or worse, about to acquire a new public identity.

Prospective dust jackets were submitted before publisher and author alike settled upon a design by Shirley Smith. The central image on the cover would be that of the tree where Boo Radley leaves presents, its angular black branches bearing lacy green leaves, all of it silhouetted against a red clay background. The title would be placed in bold relief, the green-tinted words *To Kill a* all on one line, with *Mockingbird* written in white letters on a separate line beneath. In the empty red clay–colored space beneath the branches lay the simple words "A novel by Harper Lee." The front flap of the dust jacket would hold a green-inked blurb from Truman Capote: "Someone rare has written this very fine first novel: a writer with the liveliest sense of life and the warmest, most authentic humor. A touching book; and so funny, so likeable."

With the original copyedited manuscript returned to her possession, Harper Lee took it to Monroeville for safekeeping. As for that original manuscript of *Go Set a Watchman*? Well, the reasoning ran, that novel would never see the light of day, so on January 3, 1961, Lippincott duly mailed the pages to Alice Lee, who placed them in a safety-deposit box back in the far reaches of the Monroeville bank, where they remained nestled under the original *Mockingbird* manuscript. Safe. Forgotten.

As Nelle awaited publication day, she grew restless. She wasn't ready to start another book, but she was not inclined to sit around doing nothing, so when Truman Capote proposed that she accompany him to Kansas to research a proposed article about the shocking murders of an isolated Kansas farm family, she immediately said yes. Departing for Kansas on November 19, 1959, the duo arrived in Holcomb, Kansas, six days later, a mere ten days after the commission of the crime Truman had first read about in *The New York Times*.

Capote's original intention was to report on how a small, isolated town reacted to the unthinkable: the brutal murder of a family with no known enemies. Upon Nelle's and Truman's arrival, however, it became clear that the townspeople did not know what to make of Truman and, as a result, were loath to give him information. With his strange high-pitched drawl and affected style of dress, he remained a vision of otherness, but Nelle was someone to whom the entire town seemed to respond instantly. While Truman flamboyantly swung into town, all off-putting whirling scarves and drawl-laden innuendo, Nelle simply approached the Kansas townspeople at face value: She was funny, trustworthy, and, said townswoman Dolores Hope, she seemed to manage Truman "almost like if you have a child who doesn't behave well." As Truman would launch into one of his tall tales, Nelle would signal that he was greatly exaggerating—and the townspeople immediately responded with their trust. Said Kansas Bureau of Investigation agent Harold Nye, "Absolutely fantastic lady. I really liked her very much. But I did not get a very good impression of that little son of a bitch."

Nelle understood exactly how farmers, the men and women of small-town America, moved through life. If Truman had, in fact, ever understood such a way of life, he certainly no longer remembered, and seemingly had no interest in doing so. Nelle made the inroads among the townspeople, took copious notes, and constantly encouraged her friend when he wanted to give up in despair: "Hang on. You will penetrate this place."

Notes were never taken during conversations with townspeople, but instead were re-created the same evening upon the duo's return to their hotel. Truman was excited; this story, he realized, could grow into an entire book, a blend of reporting and novel, which he thought of as a "nonfiction novel." By the spring of 1960, Nelle had typed up no fewer than 150 pages of notes for what came to be known as *In Cold Blood,* leaving Kansas and her close friend Truman only when she realized that she needed to return east: *To Kill a Mockingbird* was about to land in bookstores across America.

Machines had printed, stamped, and bound a total of five thousand copies. In Nelle's opinion five thousand copies seemed wildly optimistic, but, she figured, if Lippincott could sell even two thousand copies, that might be enough to whet their appetite for another book.

She'd soon find out. Judgment day was at hand.

3

PUBLICATION

I wonder what their reaction would have been if TKAM had been complex, sour, unsentimental, racially unpaternalistic because Atticus was a bastard. TKAM would have received great critical acclaim (which it did anyway) and not've had a second printing, but I'm content with patronizing opinions & mere popularity.

—Harper Lee, letter to close friend Wayne Flynt, July 31, 2006

Simple? Yes. A bit glib? Yes. But, to a young man in Texas it was the first glimpse of a heroism that I could relate to.

—Glenn Hawkins on *To Kill a Mockingbird*

July 11, 1960: publication day for *To Kill a Mockingbird*.

A new-style southern novel—traditional on the outside, subversive at its core. A consideration of the philosophy that the only way to leap over the past is to embrace it. No sex and no trace of a love story, except for the muted but discernible love between Atticus Finch and his two children. Comforting—until readers who settled in for the seemingly cozy read promised by the opening pages soon found themselves pondering interracial sex, rape, murder, and economic inequality, in other words, the entire bifurcated structure of American life. Where we came from as a way of understanding where we stood now. Because, as George Santayana had it, "those who cannot remember the past are condemned to repeat it." Or, perhaps even more accurately, Harper Lee had succeeded in proving Rudyard Kipling's dictum—"If history were taught in the form of stories, it would never be forgotten"— because in the story of Scout Finch's Alabama girlhood, she had managed to impart a substantial piece of southern American history.

What strengthened the book's appeal was the fact that the traditional/subversive dichotomy underlying its very structure landed in a United States in the process of rapidly changing beyond recognition. Senator John F. Kennedy was running for president, a vibrant, handsome man of forty-three who exemplified an entire generational shift in the nation's power structure: If elected, he would be the first U.S. president born in the twentieth century.

A new America, where the just released birth-control pill would quickly change the nature of sexuality, child rearing, and the very structure of the family itself. A new culture, where foreign films filled with increasingly overt expressions of sexuality and modern discontent were arriving on American screens in ever-increasing numbers. With televisions now a part of virtually every American household, and Elvis Presley's groundbreaking meld of rhythm and blues with white rockabilly on the radio, change was literally in the air.

To Kill a Mockingbird, it turns out, was the right book in the right place at the right time, a reminder of both how much was changing and at exactly what pace. A book that asked the same question being asked with increasing frequency in the post–World War II years: If America had helped make the world safe for democracy by defeating the fascist powers, when would the country ever live up to its own promise of liberty and justice for all? In its own way, *To Kill a Mockingbird* played out as a reminder of William Faulkner's aphorism: "The past is not dead. It's not even past."

By holding up a mirror to that past, Harper Lee had managed to help inform the national discussion about race in the South, a region where no matter the gains of the civil rights movement, there remained not just resistance but an ofttimes murderous counteroffensive to that movement. With fires set and protestors beaten, and with the threat of violence continually hanging in the air, it was a South where Nelle's good friend the Reverend Thomas Butts found himself targeted by the Ku Klux Klan simply because he had signed a petition to integrate the public transportation system. In a Monroeville where segregated schools, water fountains, and churches proved the norm, and where African-Americans were not allowed to use the public park next to the Vanity Fair underwear factory, a shy young woman writing just this sort of novel actually constituted a form of rebellion. It was, in the words of Andrew Young, "an act of protest, but also an act of humanity." A New Deal sensibility permeated the pages—and one could rest assured that Eleanor Roosevelt approved.

Publication in the summer of 1960 meant that *Mockingbird* was soon competing for readers' attention with books as diverse as *Rabbit, Run* and another soon-to-be-classic tale of the journey through adolescence, *A Separate Peace*. And although it was *Mockingbird* that struck the deepest chord of all, in truth Nelle's own hometown did not pay an inordinate amount of attention to the book at the time of publication—"local girl makes good by writing novel" proved to be the tenor of the local conversation. When Gregory Peck came to town two years later to soak up the local atmosphere—that's when the townspeople really did pay attention. But for now, life proceeded as usual in Monroeville. In other parts of the country, however, it proved to be a completely different story, because in cities and towns clear across America, *To Kill a Mockingbird* landed with a resounding splash.

Nelle Harper Lee, a completely unknown writer, was receiving reviews nothing short of ecstatic, with *Time* magazine rhapsodizing, "Author Lee, 34, an Alabaman, has written her first novel with all of the tactile brilliance and none of the preciosity generally supposed to be standard swamp-warfare issue for Southern writers." The *Chicago Tribune* termed it a "novel of strong contemporary national significance," and, most notably, in the all-important *New York Times*, Herbert Mitgang wrote, "It is pleasing to recommend a book that shows what a novelist can do with familiar situations. Here is a storyteller justifying the novel as a form that transcends time and place. . . . Miss Lee's original characters are people to cherish in this winning first novel by a fresh writer with something significant to say, South and North." (In later years, Lee characterized her reaction to the laudatory reviews as one of "sheer numbness. Like being hit over the head and knocked cold. I had expected a quick and merciful death at the hands of reviewers.") From the standpoint of social significance, the words that presciently pointed the way to the book's worldwide, decade-long impact were found in *The Washington Post*: "A hundred pounds of sermons on tolerance . . . will weigh far less in the scale of enlightenment than a mere eighteen ounces of new fiction bearing the title *To Kill a Mockingbird*."

There were naysayers, of course, with the esteemed Flannery O'Connor, perhaps the most noticeable of the negative voices, acerbically commenting, "For a child's book it does all right." No one remained in doubt as to where O'Connor felt Nelle's book landed in the skirmish between highbrow and popular literature. In fact, O'Connor's was not the oft-seen jealous push-back of an established author annoyed by the hype accorded a bestselling first-time novelist; Nelle had not received a big advance, and the advance publicity had been rather perfunctory. O'Connor simply didn't like the book. (Nelle did not seem to hold a grudge; in later years, she cited O'Connor as one of the writers she particularly admired, along with Truman Capote, Mary McCarthy, John Cheever, John Updike, and Peter De Vries, dubbing the latter "the Evelyn Waugh of our time.") The esteemed Eudora Welty, however, admired *Mockingbird* and told Wayne Flynt, the Welty Scholar at Millsaps College in 1993, that she was "intrigued" to learn more about Nelle, and regretted that a meeting between the two authors could never be arranged.

For all its popularity, *Mockingbird* even caused some controversy on both sides of the political spectrum, with the Left claiming the book was patronizing to African-Americans, and the Right treating the novel as a false portrait of the South that would serve only to inflame the passions of African-Americans. In truth, the book was not much read by African-Americans at the time, and many of those black readers seemed to dislike it almost as much as white conservatives did. Certainly some of that reluctance is understandable; more than occasionally, the black characters in the book feel one-dimensional— they are all such paragons of virtue that they cease to be fully human. Calpurnia is a housekeeper taking care of two white children and remains an unceasing fount of maternal wisdom and kindness. For spending her life taking care of a white man's children?

There was even a small but rather vocal group of critical naysayers who refused to accept the juxtaposed narration of six-year-old Scout and the adult Jean Louise, finding the parts narrated by Scout impossible to accept as the words of a youngster; Lee was skillful enough to evoke childhood beautifully, but, in fact, when she used phrases like "throughout my early life," the reader was instantly pulled away from the youthful world she had lulled the reader into so readily accepting. Those same naysayers criticized the novel as overly sentimental; that claim, however, seemed to confuse Lee's belief in honest sentiment— the love of a father for his children—with cloying sentimentality, while pointedly ignoring the fact that far from being sentimental, by the time of the novel's resolution, no fewer than three important characters have died: Mrs. Dubose, Bob Ewell, and Tom Robinson. If Lee had provided easy, clear-cut lessons on morality, then Boo Radley would simply have wounded Bob Ewell, not killed him, and Atticus would not have been forced to compromise his own most fervently held beliefs about the very nature of justice.

For the most part, however, the raves continued to roll in, starting a national conversation that turned the book into a phenomenon, a discussion that people needed to have but, in those markedly less worldly times, weren't really sure how to begin. Slowly but surely, the word spread— from neighbor to neighbor, from mother to daughter, from teacher to student. The sale of thousands of copies turned into tens of thousands and then hundreds of thousands—eventually, there would be twenty-two hardcover printings before the book ever appeared in paperback.

Mockingbird was soon chosen as a main selection by the powerful Reader's Digest Condensed Book Club, the British Book Society, and the Literary Guild. Then in May 1961, one month after the Confederate flag, national symbol of states rights and southern slavery, was placed above the capitol in South Carolina in celebration of the Civil War centennial, came word that Nelle had won the Pulitzer Prize for fiction. The prize proved a form of doubly sweet justice for Nelle, coming as it did in the same month that Senator E. O. Eddins, a well-known segregationist, attempted to stop an Alabama legislative declaration in praise of Nelle, because of what he found to be *Mockingbird*'s much too liberal stance on racial matters. Eventually, he stopped his protest "lest it make a martyr of the author." (Nelle, it turned out, was only following in the literary footsteps of *The Rabbits' Wedding*, a children's book that Eddins had tried to ban because the story line featured the marriage of a black rabbit to a white rabbit.)

As it was, *Mockingbird* rather quickly earned a very high place on the list of banned books in the United States, keeping company with *The Diary of Anne Frank, The Adventures of Huckleberry Finn,* and *The Scarlet Letter.* The practice of banning *Mockingbird* began almost immediately upon its publication, and while Lee rarely commented publicly on such actions, in 1966, when the Hanover County School Board in Richmond, Virginia, banned the book as "immoral literature," she penned a letter to *The Richmond News Leader*: "Surely it is plain to the simplest intelligence that *To Kill a Mockingbird* spells out in words of seldom more than two syllables a code of honor and conduct Christian in its ethic, that is the heritage of all Southerners." Lee's words barely made a dent. For many on the Right, *Mockingbird*'s treatment of race, rape, and interracial sex rendered its impact incendiary.

Lee did more than share the southern instinct for storytelling exemplified by authors ranging from Thomas Wolfe and Margaret Mitchell to Faulkner himself. Musing upon her southern roots, Lee declared, "I think we are a region of natural storytellers, just from our tribal instincts. . . . We simply entertained each other by talking. We have rather more humor about us—we're not taciturn or wry or laconic . . . Our whole society is geared to talk rather than do."

What Lee so skillfully managed here, however, was to refine such talk in her own stylistic manner, uncovering the essential, hard-earned truths squirreled away in the midst of fanciful tales. Said novelist Adriana Trigiani: "*To Kill a Mockingbird* is really the model for anyone who wants to write a story in the first person. . . . Harper Lee takes you inside the character, and then she takes you outside the character, and then she takes you back in again."

Within her own style, author Lee is pointing out that Maycomb's society is built on the underlying lies of racism and inequality, a house of sand that inevitably will tumble down. Change—difficult, painful, and inevitable—was coming, and even the most reactionary readers at the time of the book's initial publication, in 1960, realized that on some subterranean level. What allowed those readers to embrace the book, however, were two key factors: The first was that as a young white southern writer, Nelle Harper Lee passed the authenticity test held by the book's initially targeted audience of white southerners. The landscape of her childhood was imprinted upon her psyche, and when filtered through the character of Scout Finch in the town of Maycomb, a chord was struck: "What I did present as exactly as I could were the clime and tone as I remember them of the town in which I lived. From childhood on, I did sit in the courtroom watching my father argue cases and talk to juries."

Starting with selected autobiographical elements, Lee had, like any good writer, embroidered an increasingly convincing series of essential lies; in the words of novelist Wally Lamb (*She's Come Undone*), "You start with who and what you know by taking a survey of the lay of the land that formed you and shaped you. Then you begin to lie about it. You tell one lie that turns into a different lie and after a while those models lift off and become their own people rather than the people you originally thought of. When you weave an entire network of lies what you're really doing is trying to arrive at a deeper truth."

The second factor underpinning the book's acceptance in the segregated Deep South lay in the fact that while those readers may have lived in a completely segregated society without a second thought, they were able to accept the novel because of Lee's decision to set it in the 1930s; the gap of the three decades between the story's setting and the time of publication made the harder truths about racism found at the core of the story easier to accept, enabling such readers to experience a form of reassuring disassociation: "Oh, that's not me. . . . Look how much better things are now."

Perhaps it was that comforting disconnect that allowed readers to gloss over the tougher aspects of the story, because Harper Lee was after big game here: the racist attitudes found in the small town of Maycomb that allowed those in power, from the sheriff on down, to maintain their position. Readers caught up in the deceptively light-hearted childhood memories needed a moment to realize that Harper Lee was targeting a great deal more than just the pervading Depression-era racist attitudes; she wanted to slice open the class barriers, economic snobbery, and societal disdain for those less fortunate that pervaded every aspect of southern rural life. Even the church proved a target in Lee's prose; a sense of religion permeates *Mockingbird*, especially in relationship to the African-American community (Calpurnia takes Scout and Jem to her church; the Reverend Sykes presents a moral force second only to that of Atticus), but unlike the Book of Job, where hell is described as a place where no order exists, for African-Americans in the Deep South of this time, hell lay in the societal order of the day.

Without ever saying so explicitly, Harper Lee wanted to point out the fallacy in believing that America resembles a meritocracy; it was the very style of her writing that allowed audiences to accept these hard truths, because Nelle's novel seemed to contain dollops of the same charm Raymond Chandler found in the best of F. Scott Fitzgerald: "It's not a matter of pretty writing or clear style. It's a kind of subdued magic, controlled and exquisite."

Mayella Ewell, who, goaded on by her abusive father, Bob Ewell, would accuse the African-American Tom Robinson of a rape he never committed, tells a heinous lie that results in Tom's conviction, but Lee wanted to point out that the problem ran a great deal deeper than Mayella's desperate falsehood. Mired in poverty as she was, and looked down upon by all who labeled her "white trash," Mayella never had a chance. She may have shared a white Anglo-Saxon Protestant (WASP) cultural identity with those in Maycomb's "proper" society, but it's her economic status that mires her as "the other," a low-life redneck whose desperate attempts to better her lot in life can be seen in the pathetically few flowers she displays outside of the Ewell hovel located by the town dump. The Ewells are not stock villains; Lee supplies enough information for us to understand why we are both interested and repelled by them at the same time. They serve as a deliberately potent reminder that class, as well as race, remains at the very core of the American experience. The Ewells are simply the Depression-era manifestation of the conflicts between "white trash" and African-Americans that date back to the era of Reconstruction, as well as a reminder that we've ignored the poor throughout our nation's history; we pretend that, unlike the British, we're a classless society, but nothing could be further from the truth.

In so many ways, *To Kill a Mockingbird* is a novel that could have fallen completely off the rails. By 1960, readers across the country had been saturated with novels portraying southern towns, settings for fervid examinations of small-town hypocrisy and lust, told in overheated prose that only occasionally dwelled upon the racial animus underlying the region. But there was a difference at work here: Harper Lee, born and bred in Monroeville, understood the small-town southern rhythms in her bones. Fully schooled in the oral tradition of the South, she was at home in every one of the novel's settings: the church and courtroom, the classrooms and homes, all of it fueled by the long, leisurely tales told by older men and women slowly rocking on the front porch.

Her success was far more than a case of just knowing her way around this territory. Lee needed and possessed the instinct and talent to write sparely, to sketch in an entire universe as much by what was left unsaid as by what she made explicit. Said Hudson Strode, her professor from the University of Alabama, in a letter he wrote to her upon *Mockingbird*'s publication, "I think part of your success lies in the shock of recognition—or as the Japanese might say, 'the unexpected recognition of the faithful "suchness" of very ordinary things.'"

Lee herself never claimed to have written a masterpiece, but she had—a novel in three acts, constructed like a well-made play, with a structure that Horton Foote would emulate when adapting the novel for film:

Act One: Childhood—Introduction of characters and plot.
Act Two: Conflict leading to climax—The trial of Tom Robinson.
Act Three: Resolution—The two story lines, a children's world of play and that of the adults, merging when Scout finally meets Boo.

With its shifts between past and present, as well as between adult and child, the entire novel seemed to unfold at a gently flowing tempo—occasionally in blazing Technicolor, often in sepia-toned passages of memory, but always managing a direct hit to the emotions. In the words of acclaimed novelist Richard Russo, "Masterpieces are not flawless—they tap into something essential in us. The book never ages."

Mockingbird reflected the zeitgeist of the changing times, still innocent yet increasingly tough, and managed to capture a yearning for simpler times while also pointing out that such a past was never simple. That yearning carried over into a highly personalized reaction to Atticus Finch, a man in whom readers glimpsed an idealized reflection of how they liked to think of themselves: neighborly, standing up for principles, silent until pushed—a combination of Gary Cooper and John Wayne. Atticus, in fact, comes off in some ways as a print version of Cooper in *High Noon,* the embodiment of America's frontier myth, one man standing tall against a cowardly mob.

The ordinary citizen is rarely if ever so heroic, but when Atticus wades through the taunts of "nigger lover" so that he can hold his own head high, explaining that he wants his children to avoid Maycomb's usual diseases of racism and a closed mind, he represents the man Americans want to be, or, even more to the point, want to believe they hold within. Miss Maudie, the down-to-earth voice of reason, simply tells Aunt Alexandra, "We're paying the highest tribute we can pay a man. We trust him to do right. It's that simple." He is a moral exemplar, one whose actions anchor a book that, in the words of author Rick Bragg, "may not make you do the right thing, but at least you know when you're doing the wrong thing."

Placed against the backdrop of the increasingly loud Alabama-centered civil rights movement, Lee had struck a chord: Intentional or not, indeed desired or not, To Kill a Mockingbird began to operate as a symbol of the civil rights movement, at least for white America. The black community may not have initially been reading the novel in any great numbers, and as United Nations ambassador Andrew Young commented in later years, "There was too much horror around me at the time for me to absorb more." But, he went on to explain, "To Kill a Mockingbird actually gave us hope that justice could prevail." It was an impact that would resonate nationwide, indeed worldwide throughout the years, and in 1966, recognition of that impact came directly from the White House, when President Lyndon Johnson invited Harper Lee to the White House for dinner—a salute to Mockingbird's achievement in furthering the discussion of race in the United States. To the image-conscious Johnson, then only one year past the riots in Watts and still in the midst of pushing forward his agenda for the Great Society, Mockingbird had become a symbol of the civil rights movement itself.

More than one commentator has noted that Scout presents like a female version of Huckleberry Finn; in fact, it's not just The Adventures of Huckleberry Finn one is reminded of but The Adventures of Tom Sawyer as well, with both Mockingbird and Tom Sawyer prominently featuring a mystery man and a haunted house. But, it is in the semiautobiographical figure of Scout that Lee struck recognizable gold, creating a young girl defined by a winning combination of innocence and a willingness to mouth off. Said Oprah Winfrey, "I fell in love with Scout. I wanted to be Scout." Winfrey's reaction is emblematic of the intensely personal reaction readers had to the novel. They didn't just like the book but actually took it to heart, wanting to morph into Scout and live in the comforting presence of Atticus.

Girls like Oprah wanted to be Scout, while boys accepted her because she was the very antithesis of simpering, dress-wearing little girls. Scout pushed first and asked questions later. Her imperfections—her habit of getting into fights, her insensitivity to Walter Cunningham's different ways, her need to repeatedly apologize and ask to be forgiven for her mistakes—make for a flawed but highly appealing youngster who in some ways seems to stand alone against the world. It's a crucial reason why the book remains such a favorite of students; as commentator Lee Smith has pointed out, a stance of "kids against the world" presents a very appealing idea to young readers, representing, as it does, a singular pursuit of the freedom all people desire, the very embodiment of the eternal questions "Who am I?" and "Where do I fit in?"

In taking the book to heart, readers occasionally missed its near-subversive note regarding the very concept of family. At a time when the prevailing norm for family life lay in a two-parent household, *Mockingbird* includes only one two-parent nuclear family—that of Tom Robinson. Scout and Boo are motherless, Dill has no father or mother in sight, there is certainly no mother present in the Ewell household, and the list of nontraditional households even extends to the secondary characters of Atticus's brother, Jack, and sister, Alexandra (who is married but whose husband is nowhere to be found). In fact, it is an African-American woman, housekeeper Calpurnia, who functions as Scout's and Jem's maternal figure.

From a purely structural standpoint, Lee built her novel upon the soundest of building blocks, playing with several narrative archetypes, including that of the monster, here exemplified by Boo Radley. If all children are haunted by monsters, responding with both fear and a simultaneous attraction to the darkness they represent, Lee here turns the archetype on its head. Far from being the rumored bloodsucking ghoul who may or may not have stabbed his father in the leg, Boo is a damaged, gentle soul, imprisoned by his father yet in the end the savior of Scout and Jem, the exemplar of the fact that who and what we most fear can, in fact, be what saves us. Having Boo save Jem and Scout is an inspired piece of business on Lee's part because it runs counter to the mood and pace established throughout the novel, where, in Diane Mc-Whorter's apt phrase, the writing "induces in the reader that endless, expectant feeling of the hot summer day, a sense that anything can happen but usually doesn't—you know, Boo Radley doesn't come out of the house. Until he does, big time."

Lee, of course, is after more than one monster here, the biggest one being that of racism. If white southern society required the maintenance of the tissue of lies built upon the foundation of racial segregation—and it did—then Lee's most telling indictment of that society lies in her deliberate decision to seal Tom Robinson's fate as soon as he states that he feels sorry for Mayella Ewell. A black man feeling sorry for and superior to a white woman, even someone as bedraggled as Mayella Ewell? Not allowed. He has spoken a truth, one based on kindness and decency, and he is doomed as a result, a victim of both slavery's legacy and white America's fear regarding the true intentions of black men.

When the jury finds Tom Robinson guilty, it is, for the children in the book and young readers alike, a harsh first lesson in the discrepancy between the rhetoric that holds that in America all men and women are treated equally and the reality that Tom has been convicted simply because he is black. It is no accident that when, after Tom Robinson's conviction, Aunt Alexandra complains to Atticus that he should not have allowed Jem and Scout to observe the trial, Atticus sharply retorts, "This is their home, sister. We've made it this way for them, they might as well learn to cope with it." The jury has ignored the evidence, and by condemning an innocent man, it has acquiesced in maintaining the town's continued racism. Atticus is aware that by championing Tom Robinson, he may even be putting his children in harm's way, but he is determined that they understand what it means to be a fully engaged and morally constructive citizen. Even if providing scant consolation at the time of the trial, Atticus's actions will place him on the right side of history.

For adolescent readers just discovering that novels can operate on levels beyond an initial question of "What happens next?", reading the book often provides a sense of intellectual awakening, a firing of the imagination. In reflecting on his own first encounter with *Mockingbird,* Wally Lamb explained, "It was the first time in my life that a book had captured me. That was exciting. I didn't realize that literature could do that." Like the proverbial peeling of an onion layer by layer, the *Mockingbird* text often serves as an exploration of ever-increasing complexities. These adolescent readers understand that it's a sin to kill the mockingbird, which exists only to sing and give pleasure, but they now comprehend that beneath the surface lies the metaphorical treatment of two human mockingbirds: Tom Robinson, an innocent, hardworking family man, and Boo Radley, a shy, damaged soul; just as Mr. B. B. Underwood, editor of *The Maycomb Tribune,* "likened Tom's death to the senseless slaughter of songbirds by hunters and children," putting Boo in jail for killing Bob Ewell would, in Scout's words, be "sort of like shootin' a mockingbird, wouldn't it?" In absorbing these lessons, the reaction of young readers mirrors Scout's and Jem's own dawning adolescent realizations that people can do the wrong things for the right reasons. Speaking of his twenty-five years teaching *Mockingbird* in high school, Wally Lamb said, "It's a book they read because they wanted to, not because they had to."

For readers of all ages, questions abound, because in Atticus's acquiescence to the sheriff's appeal on behalf of Boo, he is willingly ignoring the search for justice that has governed his life and constitutes his personal code of morality. Throughout *Mockingbird,* Atticus has been presented as possessing a near reverence for the moral responsibilities handed down from generation to generation, with a reading of the law providing the most fundamental building blocks of civilization. Far from thinking "outside of the box," as everyone in the twenty-first century is so relentlessly urged to do, Atticus respects the institution of the law, subordinating himself to it in actions that have formed the essence of his own character; knowing the customs of both the law and the town of Maycomb is what has made Atticus such an integral part of his own community. Now, however, for the first time in his life, he is ignoring the law's demand to bring a "guilty" man to justice, and in Atticus's decision lies a further key question: Do the innocent black man, Tom Robinson, and the murderous redneck, Bob Ewell, really cancel each other out? Have we now ventured into the questionable territory of an eye for an eye? Are there two different standards of justice—one for Ewell, the racist, and one for Boo Radley? For that matter, which is worse: the actions of Bob Ewell, or those of the community that condones his actions?

Young readers certainly see themselves in the book, recognizing aspects of their own personalities in the characters of Scout and Jem, the shock of self-recognition constituting a step forward in the development of identity. Their intense reaction to *Mockingbird*, however, expands beyond a question of seeing elements of themselves, because in the pages of *Mockingbird* lie glimpses of neighbors and friends, and, above all, the realization that one's own feelings of bewilderment, wonder, and frustration are not unique.

Mockingbird, it turns out, remains a potent reminder that we are all a mass of contradictions—or as Montaigne put it, "I have never seen a greater monster or miracle in the world than myself." In its own deceptively straightforward way, *Mockingbird* successfully addresses the most basic of all adolescent concerns: the need to feel understood. Understand ourselves and we can begin to understand others.

All of these contradictions remain of great import in *Mockingbird* because in the end, for all its depiction of good versus evil, the novel does not conclude with a cleanly moral universe. Aside from the nigh onto perfect Atticus, no one is all good, and aside from Bob Ewell, no one is all bad. It is, for so many readers, a first taste of what is, in the words of Stephen Sondheim, a feeling of "Sorry-Grateful"—the world

in all its shades of gray and ambivalence. There are no solutions offered. Atticus has lost his case, and Tom Robinson is not only found
guilty and sent to jail but also shot to death for trying to escape from the
prison sentence he didn't deserve. Mrs. Dubose has kicked her morphine habit but dies at the same time, and Bob Ewell has been killed,
while his murderer remains unpunished. The attempts are made at
neatly squaring off these everyday events, but the patterns are insistently disrupted—just as happens in real life.

For all of these reasons, by the time *Mockingbird* had been in release for several months, it had begun to be talked about in terms even
more strongly cultural than literary. *To Kill a Mockingbird,* it seemed,
was now being discussed in terms like those afforded *Uncle Tom's
Cabin* in the 1850s: a novel that changed minds about the biggest issue
of the day, race in America.

In retrospect, the timing of the book's publication could not have
been more apt: On July 12, 1960, the day after official publication, the
Democratic National Convention adopted a strong civil rights plat-
form, but only over vociferous southern protests. In November of that
same year, hundreds of whites rioted in the streets of New Orleans in
protest against the very notion of integration, and in 1961, on the very
day that the hugely popular and influential *Life* magazine published
pictures from an extended interview/story on Harper Lee at home in
Monroeville, photos of Freedom Rider buses burning by the side of
the road in Anniston, Alabama, ran in newspapers across the country. Just as one protest would be shut down, another would pop up;
the protests had not yet reached the fever pitch they would in the mid-
1960s, but a corner had been turned and the national conversation
about race had forever shifted.

And with that shift in the conversation came a late-blooming
interest in the country's bestselling novel on the part of that most
American of all industries—Hollywood. In the pre-Internet, pre–
social media age, when a Hollywood big-screen adaptation could and
did serve as the ultimate seal of mass media approval and interest, the

major studios now came sniffing for the film rights, strewing cash and monumental promises in Nelle's direction. The offers kept escalating, but it was all for naught, because Nelle and her agent Annie Laurie Williams already had other ideas. Small ones. The right ones.

WHAT PRICE HOLLYWOOD?

For me, the adventure of making films is learning about worlds I've never seen before.

—producer Alan Pakula

I'm a traditionalist. I like telling a story and making it clear what's going on, but without spoon-feeding.

—director Robert Mulligan

In that curious, byzantine way in which Hollywood works, it was neither director Robert Mulligan nor producer Alan Pakula who discovered *To Kill a Mockingbird* as a potential film property. Rather, it was Pakula's friend Isabel Halliburton, who read the book and insisted that Pakula do the same right away. Said the producer, "If she hadn't done that we would not have made the film."

The low-key, Yale-educated Pakula, just then beginning his Hollywood career and far from a member of the Hollywood elite, responded to his first read of Nelle's book with great enthusiasm. So obvious was his respect for the novel that even without studio clout, he succeeded in obtaining a promise from Harper Lee and her dramatic rights agent, Annie Laurie Williams, that they would not sell the film rights until he and his business partner and director of choice, Robert Mulligan, had put together a concrete bid. Williams responded favorably to Pakula's scholarly bent and especially his passion for the material, agreeing to his long shot of a request, not only because of his love for the novel but also because of the fact that while Hollywood producers had in fact already come calling, none of the prospective suitors had been affiliated with deep-pocket major studios.

The first producers to express interest had been the team of Robert Richards and James Yarborough, with Richards floating the idea of Gary Cooper as Atticus; searching through further lists of A-list survivors of the then starting-to-crumble studio system, Richards also came up with the intriguing suggestions of Bette Davis and Ann Sheridan to play the roles of Mrs. Dubose and Miss Maudie. Williams listened with an open mind, but when Richards went on to suggest that the truly ideal casting for Atticus was the flinty, opinionated director/actor John Huston, Williams politely but firmly passed. Pakula, newly returned from a vacation in Acapulco, pressed his case, fully aware that it wasn't just Williams's and Nelle's own sensibilities that figured in acquiring the film rights, but also that of Alice Lee, the chief overseer of her sister Nelle's financial affairs. Yes, Williams and the Lees wanted a financially remunerative deal, but money wasn't all, or even the overriding concern: All three women wanted to make certain that Nelle's novel would end up in the proper, caring Hollywood hands.

The son of Polish immigrants, Pakula was only thirty-two years old at the time, and although affiliated with Paramount Pictures, he found that initially the major studios still evinced no interest in the book; in later years, he related that the conversation he had had with the studio about filming the book ran along highly predictable lines: "They said 'What story do you plan to tell for the film?' I said, 'Have you read the book?' They said 'yes.' I said 'That's the story.'" The studio's reaction was one of amused disbelief: a movie about kids that wasn't from Disney? A meandering episodic examination of childhood? Where was the through line? There was no love story, no showdown, and no chance. How, they asked, could such a distinctly regional film ever be marketed successfully to a nationwide audience?

The lack of interest in *Mockingbird,* in fact, served to illustrate the limits of Hollywood's newly changing outlook. American films may have been growing up by slowly following the lead of European films, with their more graphic depictions of sexuality and violence, but that change represented nothing more than a hope to sell more tickets. No one cared about art. Hollywood studios simply wanted to make money, and if exploring previously taboo topics provided a means by which to counteract the ever-increasing influence of television, so much the better. But a black-and-white film containing no sex, no rough language, no violence, and not even CinemaScope? A film where all of the action was in the talk and in the unspoken subtext? Where the dramatic high point of the story came in a long courtroom speech? Forget it. Besides, they reasoned, these quiet character studies never worked. Look at Carson McCullers's *The Member of the Wedding.* Frankie Addams, a figure of more than passing similarity to Scout, had been played by the extraordinary Julie Harris, and the movie, even when directed by the esteemed Fred Zinnemann, had been a big flop.

Pakula was not deterred in the slightest by such arguments, and just as *Mockingbird*'s continued perch atop the bestseller lists finally began to heighten major studio interest, he succeeded in meeting with Nelle at Annie Laurie Williams's office in the fall of 1960. Author and producer formed a near-instant rapport, with Nelle appreciating Pakula's love for her novel, as well as his cultured low-key approach. Pakula was not just full of empty Hollywood promises, but would, in fact, exercise great care with the source material, fulfilling Williams's advice/warning to him: "From the very beginning, everybody who had anything to do with the book had felt it was special, deserving the most thoughtful handling." The deal granting Pakula the film rights was closed in January 1961.

Having formed a business partnership with director Robert Mulligan after the two men collaborated on the surprisingly successful

Fear Strikes Out in 1957, Pakula had all along intended to utilize
Mulligan as the director of *Mockingbird. Fear Strikes Out,* the story of
baseball great Jimmy Piersall's battle with crippling fears, had succeeded largely due to the strikingly nonmannered performance Mulligan had coaxed out of Anthony Perkins, and Mulligan's grounded yet
sensitive approach seemed tailor-made for Nelle's quiet book; after
reading the novel, Mulligan bluntly informed Pakula that so great was
his interest in directing the film that "he was willing to pawn his belongings" if that would help secure him the job.

The street-savvy Mulligan nicely balanced the more soft-spoken
Pakula, who smilingly stated in later years, "The best of this business
is the collaboration and the worst of this business is the collaboration." What Pakula brought to the project was not just his love of the
material but also his visceral attraction to Scout's feistiness; little girls
had by now begun playing with the newly minted (1959) Barbie dolls,
but Scout, all dirty overalls and self-determination, spoke to girls who
were not interested in dolls or any stereotypically female behavior, as
well as to boys who did not fit the traditionally accepted notions of
masculinity.

In Pakula's long and heralded career, Scout represented the first
of his tough, headstrong heroines, independent yet in need of help—
think Meryl Streep in *Sophie's Choice* or Jane Fonda in *Klute.* Scout
was independent and resourceful, and Pakula understood her fish-
out-of-water reactions, having spent his youth at Bronx High School
of Science, where he "kept wondering what the hell I was doing there
when my interests were in music and art." He identified with Scout's
determination not to live anyone else's version of her life: "I have
known many people who have been so conditioned that they never,
even as old people, act as themselves—always acting in terms of 'How
am I expected to act by those controlling my life?'"

Pakula already wanted to break out and direct, but he was at this
stage still a "closet director" who had been sidetracked into producing.
In point of fact, he was simply not yet ready to put himself on the line
as a director, admitting, "There's the fear of final exposure." As a result,

in some ways his collaboration with Mulligan constituted a reversal of the usual roles, with director Mulligan protecting producer Pakula, and even providing him with a kind of directing apprenticeship. For now, however, actual directing would have to wait, in part because Pakula and Mulligan had developed such a solid and comfortable working relationship. Said Pakula, "If I hadn't worked with a director I respected and admired, I might have done my own work so much more quickly."

Mulligan's firm yet quietly sensitive methods grew directly out of his unusual background. A Bronx-raised Irishman, he had studied for the priesthood but left the seminary in order to enlist in the U.S. Marine Corps during World War II. After eventually obtaining a degree in radio technology from Fordham, Mulligan landed a job as a messenger boy at CBS, where he climbed the ladder before eventually directing some one hundred episodes of the *Suspense* television series. He won an Emmy Award for his direction of Laurence Olivier in *The Moon and Sixpence,* and his television work, which included *Billy Budd*, *The Member of the Wedding*, and *The Catered Affair,* proved to be fast, clean, high-toned, and without pretension. Moving from New York to Hollywood, after *Fear Strikes Out* he quickly directed a roster of successful A-list pictures: *The Rat Race, The Great Imposter, Come September,* and *The Spiral Road.*

Mulligan may have been an Irish kid from the Bronx, but throughout his career he gravitated toward films set in the South, their parochial sense of setting and tribal rituals dovetailing with his own Irish clan sensibility. In his words, "Coming from Bronx Irish is hardly Southern. But there was that sense of the Irish storytellers, the fairy tales." Mulligan found himself inherently drawn to Atticus, because in grappling with the fallout from a racially charged murder trial, Atticus is forced to change; it is in that change that Mulligan found a hook on which to hang the movie: "That's what I think is true in life . . . we are moved by events, by death, sudden, inexplicable . . . and we change constantly."

Trained in the headiest days of television social drama, Mulligan understood that in some ways *Mockingbird* represented a continuation of those kitchen-sink dramas, this time in the form of black-and-white realism colliding head-on with racial prejudice. He found himself even more excited by the biggest challenge he faced: Could he pull off the basic structural conceit of *Mockingbird,* that of conveying the world through a child's eyes but with an adult's understanding? Presenting such a narrative viewpoint rated as a difficult-enough task in a novel, where interior monologues wrap themselves into the reader's brain, but would prove even more difficult in the hyperrealistic medium of film, in which every last gesture played out thirty feet high on the screen.

Although Pakula and Mulligan now held the rights to a national bestseller, they did not possess the clout to finance the picture themselves. To ensure an adequate budget, they needed a star—a big star—one whose presence alone would guarantee not just financing but also distribution. Who possessed both the requisite big name and strong-enough acting chops to believably portray a small-town Alabama lawyer circa 1933? In Harper Lee's mind, only one actor: Spencer Tracy.

ATTICUS FINCH ON FILM

It's somehow fitting that the greatest movie ever made about father-hood is told through the eyes of a child. . . . children literally look up to their parents with the unquestioning belief that they hold all the answers. They seem 10 feet tall. To Scout Finch, her father seems even taller than that. And as played by Gregory Peck, he is.

—film critic Chris Nashawaty on *To Kill a Mockingbird*

Oh yes, Harper Lee certainly liked Spencer Tracy—"I can't see any-body but Spencer Tracy in the part of Atticus"—and although she had vowed to leave Mulligan and Pakula to their own devices, she soon sent a note to Tracy via the William Morris Agency. Tracy pos-sessed a quintessential all-American face, and as evidenced by his work in *Adam's Rib* and *Inherit the Wind* was clearly at home in court-room settings. Perhaps he was a bit old for the role, but the veteran actor was possessed of such naturalistic acting ability that everyone involved felt enthusiastic about his casting. The idea, however, proved a nonstarter, because after receiving Harper Lee's note, Tracy responded that he was busy filming *The Devil at 4 O'Clock* with Frank Sinatra and could not even read or think about *Mockingbird* at the present time.

Gary Cooper? With his inherent decency and strong, silent, un-wavering morality, Coop would be great, but the idea never proceeded past the discussion stage because the actor, who had so memorably portrayed small-town heroes in *High Noon* and *Mr. Deeds Goes to Town*, was sick with cancer; he died in May 1961, shortly after shoot-ing of *Mockingbird* actually began.

The month after Tracy's refusal, Nelle's literary agent Maurice Crain wrote Alice Lee to explain that Bing Crosby "very much wants to play Atticus." Although Crosby had proved himself a capable dra-matic actor in *The Country Girl*, his championship box-office days were at least fifteen years behind him, and who would really believe Bing as a deliberate southern lawyer? Crosby's diffidence would, it was feared, immediately undercut the hidden but essentially warm and loving lay-ers of Atticus's character. At that point, the name of Robert Wagner was floated, but the then thirty-one-year-old Wagner lacked the requi-site gravitas, and with Universal having signed on to distribute the film, the studio began exerting its own muscle in the casting process. Their first question was a simple one: How about the biggest star at Universal, Rock Hudson?

Hudson, riding high at the box office after appearing in a series of smash-hit Douglas Sirk films as well as wildly popular comedies op-posite Doris Day, had expressed great interest in playing the role. In fact, he would have brought a solid masculine gentleness to the role, but at heart he seemed to lack the personal heft required; in casting agent Boaty Boatwright's words, "Knowing Rock, he had the intelli-gence and good taste of his own not to fight for it, to know he shouldn't play it."

With Hudson out, producer Pakula now spoke up. There was really only one actor he had in mind for the role: Gregory Peck.

But would Peck—"the perfect Atticus," in Boatwright's words—be interested in a story that had no romance, no violence, and little action? Already an admirer of Pakula's and Mulligan's work on *Fear Strikes Out*, Peck agreed to read the by now much-talked-about novel. Sitting up all night, he read straight through to the end, later recalling,

"I called them at about eight o'clock in the morning and said 'If you want me to play Atticus, when do I start?' . . . I felt I could climb into Atticus's shoes without any play-acting, that I could be him." A devoted father himself, he felt a kinship in Atticus's relationship with Scout and Jem, and his own small-town childhood memories came flooding back: the one-parent household, the longing for home—Peck felt it all in his bones, instinctively knowing he was right for the part.

The Academy Award–nominated Peck carried far more weight and experience in Hollywood than either Mulligan or Pakula, and aware of the fine performance Mulligan had drawn out of Tony Curtis in *The Great Imposter,* and trusting the artistry of both producer and director, he agreed to sign on. Just as Nelle had formed her own company, Atticus Productions, as a tax shelter, Peck now incorporated his own production entity, Brentwood Productions, to function as one of the film's producers. In a move of even more import, however, because of his stature and power within the industry, he was able to demand that the final cut of the film reside with Mulligan and Pakula; it proved to be a key creative provision neither producer nor director would have had the clout to insist upon.

The thoughtful, analytical Peck did, in fact, fit Atticus like a glove—even his limitations as an actor worked for this role. He might have been entirely too dignified for the displays of mischief and free-wheeling lightness that made a Cary Grant or William Powell so beloved, but just as Atticus always seemed to be wearing a three-piece suit even when home at night, Peck himself often looked a bit stiff on film; somehow, if the scene called for him to appear shirtless, he still seemed to be wearing a coat and tie. The role of a thoughtful man of principle, however, fit into his wheelhouse beautifully. Says film scholar Jeanine Basinger, "The right man landed the role. Spencer Tracy was a marvelous actor, but he would have been a more shambling, ambling Atticus. Gregory Peck had a majestic, untainted quality, which suited the character perfectly." And true to his own character, he would not just help produce the film but also have a say in casting, sign off on the script, and all along the way display his creative muscle, albeit in the most gentlemanly of fashions.

GREGORY PECK

He was so wonderful. He'll always be my Atticus.

—Mary Badham

I was sitting next to Gregory Peck at a luncheon for Quincy Jones. I didn't know what to say. I finally turned and said: "So how's Scout doing?" Because it's in my brain—because he will always be Atticus to me.

—Oprah Winfrey

In many ways, Atticus was the role for which Peck had been preparing his entire life.

Born in 1916, Eldred Gregory Peck had seen his parents separate when he was only two years old; the young Eldred lived first with his father and then with his mother, Bunny, who subsequently left him in the care of her mother, Katie. Katie represented the one stable aspect of his life in then small-town La Jolla, California, and he lived with her until he left for boarding school at age ten. She proved a loving, devoted grandmother, but even she could not shield him from life's harsh realities, causing the adult Peck to recollect: "I saw the burning cross in front of a house rented by a black family. . . . It was in the early 1920s, when I was about five years old, but I remember it well." The seeds of a lifelong liberal outlook were now sown.

Bouncing back and forth between Saint Louis and La Jolla, Peck endured a tough childhood, in which he hid his emotions and developed a love of both reading and the solitary sports of swimming and fishing. "I was lonely, withdrawn, full of self-doubt," he said. Interviewed in later years, he simply stated, "I don't care to talk about my childhood because it was so sad." He endured a series of schools—St. John's Military Academy, San Diego High School, and San Diego State Teachers

College—before landing at the University of California in Berkeley. Slowly shedding his introverted personality, he rowed crew and in the process learned the importance of teamwork, thereby forming a key component of his style as Hollywood icon: No matter how great his stardom, he understood that he was one part of a vast production team; belligerence and bellicosity never did become a part of his vocabulary.

It was while at Berkeley that the young English major was approached to audition for the campus production of *Moby Dick*. He proved stiff and awkward onstage, but with his deep, sonorous voice, great good looks, and commanding presence, he registered nonetheless. He had found his new home. "I think it had something to do with the fact that my childhood was a little bit unstable. So I think I reached out to that audience to try and make contact with them and to tell them a story I wanted to tell," he recalled.

After graduating from Berkeley, he moved to New York City to study at the Neighborhood Playhouse, but first he dropped the name of Eldred; henceforth he would simply be known as Gregory Peck. It was the Playhouse's esteemed acting guru Sanford Meisner who, in Peck's own words, taught him to convey "the story to the audience bit by bit with my mental and emotional processes going on underneath the words. What's underneath the words is more important than the words themselves because what's underneath produces the external effect." He proved to be an apt pupil—eager and, above all, driven; when, shortly after graduation, the fabled director Guthrie McClintic called the Playhouse to inquire about Peck's availability, the young actor hurtled down four flights of stairs, ran six blocks to the RKO building, took the elevator to the eighth floor, and burst into the room while McClintic was still on the phone talking to Meisner at the Playhouse.

His notices in the play *The Willow and I* (1942) proved so strong that his powerful agent, Leland Hayward, talked him into going to Hollywood to meet with studio executives about a potential film career. Peck, a certified theater snob, was not particularly interested, but he traveled west anyway, figuring he had nothing to lose. By now, he also had a wife to support, the five-years-older Greta Kukkonen, a cheerful blonde whom he had met while she was working as Katharine Cornell's hairdresser on *The Willow and I*. Off he went to Hollywood, where he quickly landed both a plum role in *Days of Glory* (1944), as well as critical acclaim upon the film's release.

What had become immediately clear was that the camera loved Peck. Because of his high cheekbones and a deliberate manner of speech that made his silences and mere presence all the more compelling, audiences sat up and took notice. So, too, did Hollywood executives, and when Darryl Zanuck viewed rushes from *Days of Glory*, he quickly offered Peck the leading role of a Roman Catholic missionary in *The Keys of the Kingdom* (1944). The result was Peck's first Academy Award nomination as Best Actor.

Besides Peck's innate talent, it was also his good fortune to have landed in the right place at the right time; he was a handsome man and seemingly tailor-made for a then flourishing Hollywood studio system, one that possessed the resources to build an actor into a larger-than-life star. The combination of his own Arrow collar profile and beautiful voice, as well as the efforts of the contract writers, studio directors, and press agents, turned Gregory Peck, like all golden age stars, into an extremely salable commodity.

Alfred Hitchcock now came calling, and when Peck was cast in the director's *Spellbound* (1945), he scored a second big hit, the typical rumors of a possible affair with costar Ingrid Bergman seeming only to add to his appeal. The world lay in the palm of his hand: a Hollywood career, a cute wife, and, in 1944, a son, Jonathan. And with fatherhood came a second key component in his worldview: a burgeoning determination to create the stable family life he had never known as a youngster.

One major film followed another, most notably David O. Selznick's bloated but interesting *Duel in the Sun* (1946), and with each film came a growing mastery of his craft: "I was a stagey kind of actor not really getting it—how to relax and concentrate in front of that machine. I thought I finally got ahold of it in *Duel in the Sun*." And then a hit movie with children, playing the paterfamilias in Clarence Brown's 1946 adaptation of Marjorie Kinnan Rawlings's Pulitzer Prize–winning *The Yearling*. Said young star Claude Jarman, Jr., "He was very patient, just very easy to get along with, made things very easy for me." The anxiety wrapped inside love felt by every father was beautifully captured, and so, too, was another Academy Award nomination. In retrospect, the role of Pa Baxter plays almost like an audition for Atticus, with Pa's impassioned speech to his son resembling a backwoods version of Atticus's posttrial talk with Jem: "A man's heart aches seeing his young'uns face the world. Knowing they got to get their insides tore out the way his was tore."

His screen persona was now coming into focus: the dignified American man of principle, with the emphasis landing on the word *American*. Even when portraying an Englishman in Hitchock's *The Paradine Case* (1947), he remained resolutely, uncontrovertibly American.

Gentleman's Agreement (1947) found him playing crusading journalist Phil Green, who assumes a Jewish identity for a series of articles exposing anti-Semitism in the postwar years. It proved to be a smash hit, and in some ways reads as yet another tryout for Atticus, with the character of Green undertaking the very Atticus-like action of stepping into another's skin. There were, however, clashes with director Elia Kazan, whom Peck found aggressive and highly strung, and the disconnect proved mutual, with Kazan finding Peck "very closed off and rigid. . . . He didn't have an artist's nature. . . . He was logical . . . cooperative. But it was hard to light a fire in a guy like that." When the action called for Green to explode in anger, Kazan found it impossible to coax Peck into punching the wall in rage. Peck was, it was clear by now, in control at all times.

But *Gentleman's Agreement* proved an essential film in establishing the Peck persona as a man of principle, that image reinforced in the audience's mind by Peck's increasingly well-known offscreen liberal beliefs. His talent was solid but quiet; there were no displays of dazzling technique as with Olivier, but, rather, an ability to paint beautifully within circumscribed lines. Further displaying his knack with children, *Gentleman's Agreement* included superb scenes with his son, nicely played by Dean Stockwell (although Stockwell opined in later years, "I got the idea that Gregory Peck didn't like working with a kid. . . . For that reason I didn't feel much warmth from him.").

The film won the Academy Award for Best Picture, and landed Peck another Oscar nomination; while the passage of decades has not treated the film's overly earnest sentiments particularly well, with the story now playing like a Stanley Krameresque message film, at the time it proved to be strong medicine for the mass moviegoing public. With journalist Phil Green—passionate, intelligent, dignified, and, above all else, principled—the mold for Atticus Finch was taking shape.

So, too, were the liberal political sympathies, and in the midst of the Red Scare, the by now top-tier Hollywood star was even named by some as a Communist sympathizer. Refusing to give in to the hysteria of the time, he kept up his friendships with those targeted by the House Committee on Un-American Activities. Although he was not among those who flew to Washington as members of the liberal-leaning Hollywood Ten, he publicly stated, "I hold no brief for Communists, but I believe in and will defend their right to act independently within the law."

Twelve O'Clock High (1949) found him playing a World War II officer dealing with a crisis of conscience, the cracks in the macho military facade exposed to interesting effect. The result was another nomination for Best Actor, which he followed up with a surprising and first-rate turn in *The Gunfighter* (1950), in which he portrayed an exhausted hired killer waiting for one final showdown. For all his success in films where he operated in full-tilt movie-star mode (*Captain Horatio Hornblower*, 1951), he was at his most interesting playing upstanding men of decency struggling to do the right thing; the frailties and neurotic underpinnings revealed under the heroic exterior in films like *Spellbound, Twelve O'Clock High,* and *The Gunfighter* were what kept audiences interested.

There was a touch of the melancholy about Peck, but that only enhanced his appeal and somehow made him more approachable, the perfect-looking exterior combined with interesting weaknesses. His solitary nature reinforced a certain core of sadness, as did stress at home. There were now three sons—Jon, Steve, and Carey—the standard star rumors of affairs with several of his beautiful costars, and ultimately a collapse in October 1950, in which, he admitted, "I felt like my head was going to go off, so I was turning to the booze and the drugs just to cool me down." He successfully stopped drinking and taking pills, and even with a nonstop work schedule, he redoubled his efforts to attend his children's school events and take family vacations. He was bouncing back professionally as well—both *David and Bathsheba* (1951) and *The Snows of Kilimanjaro* (1952) proved to be hits—and in a 1951 poll of fifty countries, he was voted "World Film Favorite."

He was off to Rome for *Roman Holiday* (1953) but first came a stop in Paris for an interview with *France Soir* reporter Veronique Passani. There was an instant attraction, he thirty-six, she twenty, but he was on his way to Italy in order to play freelance reporter Joe Bradley under the direction of the already legendary William Wyler. By now a seasoned pro, Peck quickly realized that his leading lady, newcomer Audrey Hepburn, was a star in the making, and in a move both gallant and practical, he told his agent to put her name above the title along with his: "If I don't I'm going to make a fool out of myself because this girl is going to win the Oscar in her very first performance." He was right—she did—and the film was a smash hit, scoring a nomination for Best Picture of the year. Equally thrilled by the handsome Peck and the gamine Hepburn, audiences around the world welcomed the film's lesson on the virtues of fairy-tale love. It was, in fact, that fairy-tale aspect of *Roman Holiday* that boosted Peck's appeal enormously. In the words of Kenneth Turan, "The two keys to Peck's success are he is unyieldingly dedicated to his work and women absolutely adore him." By now, moviegoers realized that Peck always held just a little in reserve on-screen—not so much an understated style of acting as his own essential persona showing through. In his own view: "Overacting is a self-indulgence, while underacting comes either through a lack of talent or a lack of courage."

There was another meeting with Veronique, and it was already abundantly clear that his marriage to Greta was finished. When their divorce was finalized at the end of 1955, he married Veronique the very next day, a marriage that lasted until the day he died. In the beautiful Veronique he had found a partner and protector, prompting Harper Lee to observe, "They run in rhythm. He doesn't begin to understand her feminine wiles, but he sure does appreciate them." Veronique ran interference on sets, her mission that of protecting her husband so that he could concentrate on his work. She could be charming, but, in the words of film composer Elmer Bernstein, she was also "formidable. I don't think she suffers fools gladly." Their marriage brought two new children, Cecilia and Tony, and if there was, perhaps, an occasional strain between Veronique and his three children by Greta (Carey's wife Lita Albuquerque told a friend that Carey was "not completely accepted by his stepmother"), life was nonetheless fulfilling, if complicated.

Peck played another returning veteran forever changed by his war experiences in 1956's *The Man in the Gray Flannel Suit*; as a disillusioned advertising executive, a man of action who had faced life-and-death situations in the war but now felt hemmed in by his suburban life and grinding daily commute, he struck a chord with Eisenhower-era audiences, his character becoming the very symbol of 1950s conformity. He followed it up with a complete change of pace, playing Ahab in *Moby Dick* (1956), but his relationship with director John Huston was strained; the two fell out after Peck discovered Huston originally wanted Orson Welles to play Ahab, and had talked Peck into undertaking the role only in order to secure financing. The personalities of the two strong-willed men never quite jelled, with Peck revealing to critic and writer Dennis Brown that if someone was using him for their own gain he would "simply . . . separate myself from them."

Aside from the directorial conflicts, what *Moby Dick* had made clear were the limits of Peck's talent. As Ahab, he appears overly

stiff—it's too far a leap from Peck's basic personality to portray obsession. Said screenwriter Ray Bradbury, "Greg Peck is never going to be
a paranoid killer or a maniac devourer of whales." Peck himself acknowledged the limitation: "I wasn't mad enough, not crazy enough,
not obsessive enough. I should've done more. At the time, I didn't
have more in me." To be sure, he could be self-critical, but he also possessed a full sense of his own talent, noting of fellow actors, "I've seen
them all, Olivier and Burton and Gielgud and the rest. Most of them
are simply vocalizing. It's fancy speaking and declaiming."

Buttoned-down characters full of repressed emotions and impeccable moral beliefs—pillars of rectitude—were his strong suit and
what audiences wanted from him. Having survived his own painful
childhood, he had, like so many actors, developed a deep desire to be
loved, and in an uncharacteristic bit of soul baring, he ruminated on
the very idea: "That desire to be loved may have led in the direction of
playing heroes, of people who wanted to make the world a better
place." In many ways, that desire to be loved had merged with a sense
of insecurity, and when combined with his nearly flawless exterior, it
made him all the more compelling on-screen. In the words of his son
Stephen, the uncertainty seemed to stem from a "fear of being revealed
as the person he was before he became a star. But I like that person. I
see not only a man who dreamt what he wanted to be and became it
but also a man less imposing and more vulnerable than his thirty-foot
image on the screen."

The hits continued, but after four Oscar nominations in the
1940s, there had been none in the 1950s. Best Picture nominee *The
Guns of Navarone* (1961) proved a big hit, as did a turn as the terrorized
family man in *Cape Fear,* but where, Peck wondered, was his career-
defining role? It was at just this point that Alan Pakula sent him a copy
of *To Kill a Mockingbird.* It seemed a perfect match of star and character, and in the words of Pakula himself, "I must say the man and the
character he played were not unalike."

Peck's reaction to the role? "God was smiling on me . . ."

The pieces had fallen into place. Atticus Finch would not represent a new Peck, but, rather, the culmination of the on-screen Peck persona. This was not a transformation, but a confirmation.

Now all he needed was a script.

6

ENTER HORTON FOOTE

A writer has an inescapable voice. I think it's inherent in the nature, and I think that we don't control it any more than we control what we want to write about.

—Horton Foote

As a gentle period piece, *To Kill a Mockingbird* would of necessity rely on atmosphere, tone, and texture in its transfer to the screen, and certainly no one knew the source material better than Harper Lee herself. Was she interested in a job as a screenwriter? Question asked, the negative response indicated indifference, which quickly shaded into noninterest: "After all I don't write deathless prose." Anticipating Lee's refusal, Pakula and Mulligan already had a second choice in mind: playwright Horton Foote, with whom Mulligan had worked three times on television's Philco-Goodyear Television Playhouse. Foote had never worked with Pakula, but after meeting with the producer, he felt reassured, indeed "very sympathetic towards his ideas about plays and films."

Soft-spoken and courtly he was, but Foote also possessed a sure sense of his own talent. A native of the small town of Wharton, Texas,

Foote certainly understood the world of *Mockingbird*, yet he represented, in many ways, a calculated risk for Pakula. Aside from his screenplay for the Cornel Wilde film *Storm Fear* (1955)—a small film that Foote humorously recalled as having been filmed on a "very low, low, low budget"—his writing for the screen had been almost entirely for television programs filmed in New York City. His Hollywood résumé was scant, but Pakula and Mulligan remained convinced, certain that Foote's quiet but effective ability to limn the atmosphere of small-town America made him the ideal choice. Even better, Harper Lee already admired Foote's writing for both theater and television, and felt quite certain that his distinctly southern vision would ensure a sensitive adaptation of her novel. Just one problem remained: Horton Foote wasn't interested in the job.

Having adapted William Faulkner's *Old Man* for television just one year earlier, Foote remained leery of being branded with the identity of "adaptor," and was, in his own words, "grousing as I usually do." Hard at work on his play *The Day Emily Married*, he was interested in establishing his own voice. Another adaptation would, in his estimation, mean marking time, nothing more.

In his own ever-growing oeuvre he had already begun fictionalizing the small town of Wharton, Texas, just as Harper Lee had done with Monroeville, Alabama, a similarity that made his lack of interest all the more frustrating for Pakula and Mulligan; producer and director both instantly understood that with Foote's exquisite ear for spare dialogue and meaningful silences—the deep currents of emotion lying just beneath the surface of everyday events—he did indeed represent the ideal choice for transferring Lee's vision to the screen. Ten years older than Lee, he had been an adolescent observer of the very Depression years Nelle wrote about. Family and community, change and tradition—the issue of how to negotiate those complementary and contradictory demands represented terra firma for the playwright. His beautifully constructed plays consistently meditated upon these themes, trying, as did those of Tennessee Williams, to make sense of the past by ordering the elusive memories that came and went with dizzying uncertainty and unexpected force.

More to the point, Foote understood the difficulties of successfully capturing the bittersweet tone inherent in an adult looking back on a vanished world, in this case that bygone world being not just one of childhood but also that of the entire agricultural, rural, small-town South. The theme of a vanished world was one Foote would return to over and over in his work, one gracefully stated by the character of Carrie Watts in his 1953 masterpiece, *The Trip to Bountiful*: "Pretty soon it'll all be gone . . . this house . . . you . . . But the river will be here. The fields. The woods. . . . We're part of all this. We left it but we can never lose what it has given us." Family, memory, and place—the unending search for home.

A disappearing world and the inevitability of change—these concepts formed a significant part of Foote's very worldview. Years later, in a *CBS News Sunday Morning* television interview with Dan Rather, which played out on-screen as a virtual definition of the word *elegiac,* Foote toured his hometown of Wharton, Texas, and, with a note of astonishment and sadness in his voice, exclaimed, "The most extraordinary change is that the town itself is disappearing. That is the story of America. Build something and tear it down the next day."

In a fashion strikingly similar to that displayed by Lee in *To Kill a Mockingbird,* Foote's work reflected a concern with the resiliency of human beings, the ability to keep going no matter the obstacle. Heads of broken families, dreamers, "believers in the basic honor and dignity of all living characters"—these represented the pillars of Foote's fictional world.

And still, even with the similarities between his own worldview and that of Lee, Foote did not even read *Mockingbird* when it was first sent to him. His wife, Lillian, however, admired the novel greatly, telling her husband, "You better get to that book and read it." Okay, he admitted, the book was moving, but still he dragged his feet. Lillian insisted. And then, while reading R. P. Blackmur's review of *Mockingbird,* entitled "Scout in the Wilderness," one in which Blackmur compared *Mockingbird* to *Huckleberry Finn,* and Scout to Huck, the key turned. "Whatever R. P. Blackmur meant, I suddenly became very interested in the character of Scout and in investigating that." (In later years, novelist Wally Lamb mused, "Scout is sort of an extension of a Huck Finn character. She's very typically an American character in that she's poking at the boundaries of good taste, and what's proper.") Lee's straightforward narrative, Foote realized, held the potential to be far more than a sweet tale of Depression-era childhood. From a dramatic standpoint, he loved the idea of utilizing the trial of Tom Robinson to lay bare the murderous effects of racism, while in structural terms, he was intrigued by the idea that the hypocrisy of the seemingly friendly small southern town would be discovered "along with and through the eyes of the children."

A meeting with Harper Lee was arranged, and the rapport between the two writers proved instantaneous: "I must say, she sold me. I mean I just loved her; she is a wonderful woman. And I thought, 'Well, I'll enjoy this, if no more than getting to know her.'" Their bond, and the deal itself, was clinched when Foote courteously but firmly told Lee, "You know there's going to come a time when this has got to belong to me and I've got to take this over." The novelist replied that was precisely what she wanted: "Now listen, you are going to write this, and I don't want to hear another word about this. I don't even want to think about it till it's done. You go ahead and don't worry about me at all." She then added the final grace note: "Don't talk to me and don't ask me questions, because I am not going to answer anything."

Foote was now home free. Home, in fact, proved the operative word, because he did not want to uproot his family with a move to Hollywood, and insisted upon writing the screenplay at home in Nyack, New York. So happy were Pakula and Mulligan to have Foote on board that they readily agreed; for the time being, Pakula could easily commute from Manhattan to Nyack for continuing script conferences.

Foote's concern with interior events and feelings dovetailed smoothly with *Mockingbird*'s child's-eye view of the world, one in which children, lacking the vocabulary to make sense of ofttimes confusing events, retreat into a state of perpetual observation. But, two difficult questions remained. First, given the hyperrealistic nature of movies, how was it possible not to hit the audience over the head while dramatizing the great emotional linchpin of the novel: the one brief but very intense period when children are approaching the foreign shores of adulthood—testing the current as it were—but still looking to their parents for guidance? How could Foote bottle the essence of Maycomb at precisely the moment when Scout's innocence and feeling of inviolable security were slipping out of her grasp forever? Second, in what fashion could Foote dramatize the moral courage that remained the key to the character of Atticus Finch? Foote knew that the trial would provide the movie's most overtly dramatic moments, and that given Peck's status as producer and star, the trial would take up more space in the film than in the novel. But what of the quiet moments of parenting designed to show a moral courage of far greater import than that found in the shooting of a mad dog? How best to accomplish that task while ensuring that the audience discovers the corruption and crumbling innocence of Maycomb at the same time as do Scout and Jem?

In trying to answer those questions, Foote proved a diligent craftsman, going to work immediately on compressing the "sprawling" nature of the novel (an admitted part of its charm) for the sake of dramatic urgency. Events that unfolded during the course of three years in the book would now be shaped within one eventful year. In similar fashion, while characters in the novel moved about town and countryside alike, action in the film would be kept within the town itself, the better to underline the sense of the simultaneously charming yet oppressive atmosphere of Maycomb.

Fleshing out the leading characters, Foote quickly came to understand Atticus, Scout, and Jem. But Dill? The quirky little boy who seemed to have landed in Maycomb from another galaxy? Foote was stymied—until he heard from Nelle that Dill was based on Truman

Capote: "The minute she told me it was based on Truman Capote, my mind just went wild."

Foote's first draft, dated October 3, 1961, focused upon the youngsters' exploration of their secure but increasingly unsettled environment, one entirely defined by Maycomb yet containing intimations of the world at large. Sequences were written so that Mulligan could visually explore a world that simultaneously conveyed a yearning for freedom in conjunction with the certainty of the (largely unspoken) love expressed by a father. The sanctity of a home anchored by Calpurnia would be contrasted with the racial tensions permeating Maycomb, the contrast building steadily to the climactic trial of accused rapist Tom Robinson.

Foote knew that he wanted the seemingly separate spheres of innocent childhood and the darker world at large to intersect in the sudden appearance of Boo Radley—"the other"—in the final minutes of the film, childhood conviction upended in a new comprehension of the beauty and terror of life in all its uncertainty. The first draft now flowed quickly, but a major problem loomed: The script was too long, at 157 pages, much too long. Treating the Pulitzer Prize–winning novel with reverence, Foote the dramatist had sacrificed his trademark economy of words for the sake of an all-inclusive approach.

Ruthlessly efficient in his quest for a streamlined screenplay, Foote began a wholesale tightening, even if favorite set pieces from the novel had to be excised for purposes of dramatic impact. Interesting but peripheral characters like Miss Fisher, Scout's nemesis of a first-grade teacher, were completely eliminated. Flavorful characters who added texture but slowed the dramatic momentum—Mrs. Merriweather, the droning speaker at the Halloween pageant, as well as Aunt Alexandra's bigoted church lady friends—were dropped. Even several of the novel's more dramatic events—Miss Maudie's house catching fire, and Jem's destruction of Mrs. Dubose's garden—were cut in the interests of narrative speed. Yes, their exclusion meant the loss of a certain balance—no sight gags or belly laughs remained, leading to, at most, a very gentle humor about the foibles of children and everyday life—but the resulting sense of drive and forward momentum more than compensated.

Foote found the key to the film's opening by adroitly bridging two early paragraphs from the novel into a rueful and wondering voice-over spoken by the adult Jean Louise. The film's first black-and-white images of small-town life would slide by as Jean Louise murmured Lee's measured words, at once slightly distanced and yet somehow still in thrall to the past:

> *Maycomb was a tired old town, even in 1932 . . . when I first knew it. Somehow, it was hotter then—men's stiff collars wilted by nine in the morning. Ladies bathed before noon and after their three o'clock naps. And by nightfall they were like soft teacakes with frosting from sweating and sweet talcum. The day was twenty-four hours long, but it seemed longer. There's no hurry, for there's nowhere to go and nothing to buy . . . and no money to buy it with. Although Maycomb County had recently been told it had nothing to fear but fear itself. That summer, I was six years old.*

Drawing upon memories of his own 1930s southern childhood, an era still centered upon self-restraint and the tight boundaries of a small community, Foote also recalled the hours he had spent gathering information by listening in when adults remained oblivious to his presence: "That's how I heard all the news I wasn't supposed to hear as a child." The significance of those sense memories became clear when he created two sequences not found in the novel. The first came with a scene in which Atticus listens from the porch while his supposedly sleeping children talk in bed about the mother they barely remember. In this gentle yet highly emotional sequence, Foote managed to provide full texture and background regarding a significant relationship Lee had purposely not provided in the book. Of equal note was the scene in which Jem and Scout find out about the upcoming trial by listening from their bedroom as the sheriff talks to Atticus about Tom Robinson. There is no ham-fisted dialogue featuring the sheriff declaring, "Atticus, you must take on this difficult but important case." Instead, through a few well-chosen words, the children realize that their world is about to be upended in ways they cannot yet fully comprehend.

The fact that Peck co-owned the script and would star in and produce the film still did not influence Foote into writing specifically for Peck: "Although some writers are very skillful at this kind of intentional writing, it would stymie me." Instead, he rather quickly finished his revised first draft and flew out to California to further streamline the screenplay in consultation with Pakula and Mulligan; screenwriter and producer were both pleased with this draft, but director Mulligan saw definite room for improvement, offering a brief and telling criticism: "Too often you lose the point of view of the children."

Mulligan was right. Back went Foote for another draft. At which point it dawned on the screenwriter that he was, in fact, in very good hands with Pakula and Mulligan. Supportive yet unobtrusive criticism? A screenwriter being consulted about locations, sets, costumes, and casting? What more could he ask for? Content in his cocoon, he did bemusedly ask himself, "Why are writers so unhappy out here?" before adding ". . . Later I learned the answer to that all too well."

Second and third drafts followed, and eventually a fourth, one that was deemed fit for Peck's scrutiny. So fit, in fact, that after reading it, the actor commented to Pakula, "Come on now, is this really the first draft?" Well, the producer smilingly explained, it was the first "official" draft.

With star, screenwriter, director, and producer all happy, it was time to cast the rest of the movie, beginning with the roles of Scout and Jem. In many ways, the fate of the movie now hung in the balance: No matter how solid Peck's performance, without the right youngsters in the lead roles, the movie would inevitably crumble into a morass of sentimental attitudinizing. Were there any nonshowbizzy children left in the United States? And if so, where did they live, because they certainly did not reside in Los Angeles or New York. A decision was made: If a nationwide talent hunt was good enough for Scarlett O'Hara, why not for Scout and Jem Finch?

The search was on.

CASTING THE MOVIE

Alan, I don't think I can talk to anyone under thirty ever again.

—casting director Boaty Boatwright to Alan Pakula

Just as *To Kill a Mockingbird* began gearing up for production, Alice Lee "Boaty" Boatwright, a feisty, smart, aspiring agent from Reidsville, North Carolina, then working in publicity at Universal Studios, heard about the upcoming film and presented herself front and center to Pakula. "I was at Sardi's and Roddy McDowell was there with Alan Pakula," she recalled. "I had just finished reading *Mockingbird*, loved it, and basically threw myself at Alan's feet, saying, 'I'm part Scout. You must hire me!'" A nonplussed Pakula called a mutual friend to ask, "Who is this Boaty Boatwright?"

Southern-born and -bred, Boatwright felt the story of *Mockingbird* in her bones, loving not just the young Scout's narrative voice, but also the fact that the novel shone a light on the pervasive racism in the South that most white people of the time would just as soon have ignored. "I grew up in Reidsville, North Carolina—forty-five minutes from any airport," said Boatwright. "Reidsville was really like Maycomb in some ways back in the 1940s and '50s. And my father would sit on the porch and we would talk—a bit like Atticus and Scout. He'd try to help people in trouble. But even with my parents, who were relatively enlightened for the time—my father said he would never serve as a juror if capital punishment were a possibility—so many racial attitudes were unthinking.

"We certainly didn't live in a mansion, but we had what was referred to as 'colored help.' I distinctly remember being eight years old and watching 'the help' arrive and asking my mother, 'Why can't they just come through the front door the way we do?' My mother answered, 'Because they're colored.' It was such a part of the social fabric. The racism was so ingrained and awful. . . . I think the best thing that has happened in years is that the Confederate flag is no longer flying over the state capitol in South Carolina. The romanticizing of the Civil War and the Confederate flag—I hate all of that. Intensely. There is nothing romantic about racism or slavery."

Boatwright had never cast even the smallest Off-Broadway play, but after meeting with Pakula—"a most remarkable man"—for three hours, she succeeded in charming and cajoling her way onto the production team as director of child casting. She next met with Bob Mulligan, who signed off on Boatwright's participation but strongly admonished her, "I want children—no showbiz professionals!"

Armed with energy, savvy, and Mulligan's dictum ringing in her ears, Boatwright soon waded through hundreds of interviews. She began in New York but soon realized that the northern boys and girls "didn't have the rhythm, the poetry of growing up southern—it never would have worked." Southward she headed, interviewing Shirley Temple wannabes in Richmond, Winston-Salem, Charlotte, Nashville, Dallas, and Atlanta. None were right, but one thing remained constant: "The mothers were just as pushy in the South as they were in the heart of Manhattan."

Her style was intimate; she sat close to the youngsters, talking to them and asking them to read. "I tried to make them feel comfortable," she recalled. "I served ginger ale and cookies. I met some real characters; one of the little boys eating a cookie said, 'This tastes like my foot when it goes to sleep. . . .' " Some of the children wanted to audition, while others were present only because they had been forced by their parents, but the lines of potential Scouts and Jems seemed to grow by the day, with no end in sight. Feeling burned-out, and no closer to casting the roles, she called Pakula to moan: "Alan, I don't think I can talk to anyone under thirty ever again." Pakula further remembered her saying, "I'm locked in my hotel room. I haven't been able to leave it for twenty-four hours because of the crowds of mothers and children just sitting waiting for me in that lobby downstairs—I saw over a hundred children today . . . and they all began to look alike."

An exhausted Boatwright was no closer to casting either Scout or Jem, when in walked nine-year-old Mary Badham, clad in jeans and a striped T-shirt and sporting, in Boatwright's words, "a gamine haircut." Badham had arrived at the auditions courtesy of Boatwright's good friend Gene Watt Bagwell, with whom Boatwright was staying during her sojourn in Birmingham. It was Gene who told Boatwright that little Mary Badham might be worth an audition, and when the youngster walked into the room, an exhausted Boatwright slowly looked up and thought, "Hmmm . . . definitely not a Shirley Temple clone."

Smiling but nonchalant, Mary thought this acting business sounded like fun but was not particularly concerned about winning the role. It was her mother, the proper Mrs. Henry L. Badham, who seemed most interested in the idea. Having done some acting in her native England, most notably a radio version of George Bernard Shaw's *Saint Joan,* she liked the idea of Mary following in her footsteps, but Mary's audition almost never happened, because Henry Badham, a retired air force general, had no interest in a possible acting career for his daughter. He bluntly told Boatwright, "We don't think nice people work in show business."

In the baroque world of personal southern geography, however— a world so interconnected that on a flight from New Orleans to Birmingham, Alan Pakula told the social, friendly Boatwright, "If you speak to even one person you know on this plane, I'm going to kill myself!"—it turned out that a cousin of Boatwright's mother was related to the Badham family. This fact, combined with a push from Mary's brother John, finally convinced Henry Badham to acquiesce to the audition. In the words of Mary's mother, "What could be the possible harm? . . . Henry dear—what are the chances the child will get the part?"

Aside from playing dress-up and putting on skits for her parents, Mary had never acted, and she had prepared nothing to read for Boatwright. In later years, she did vaguely remember "something about chopping some wood"—but what caught Boatwright's immediate attention was the youngster's forthright personality.

"How old are you?" she asked the girl.

"Nine."

"You look younger and smaller than nine."

"Well, if you drank as much buttermilk and smoked as many cornsilks as I do, you might be smaller too."

Chatting with the youngster about her life—southern to the bone, Badham, in Boatwright's recall, "pronounced 'nine' in two syllables"— the casting director was even more delighted to learn that Badham possessed a die-hard Scout-like desire to always tag along after her brothers, insisting on taking part in every last one of their games. She even had two Calpurnias in her life in the figures of Beddie Harris and Frankie McCall. Nonchalant, winning, and resolutely non show-biz, Badham charmed Boatwright, who concluded the interview, ran to the phone, dialed Pakula, and excitedly told him, "I found Scout!" (One of Badham's classmates, Elizabeth "Bimi" Woodward, was also in the running for the role; evidently, the loss grated, as she told their mutual classmates that the director and producer really preferred her for the role of Scout but that her mother "had nixed acting as 'tacky.'")

Making her red-letter day even better, Boatwright found her ideal Jem that very same afternoon when Phillip Alford, a thirteen-year-old eighth grader, walked in for his audition. With a boy-next-door affect and, in Boatwright's words, "an angel face," Alford projected a polite but rather indifferent attitude toward the idea of acting in a movie. The son of a bricklayer foreman, Alford had actually appeared in amateur theater productions of *The King and I* and *The Man Who Came to Dinner,* but when it came to acting, he could take it or leave it. He was more interested in sports than acting, explaining that he wanted to be Tarzan, not Johnny Weissmuller. As it was, when the same James Hatcher who had told Mary Badham's mother about the auditions called Phillip's mother and suggested that Phillip audition as well, Phillip turned the invitation down—until he learned it would allow him to skip half a day of school.

Alford, it turned out, lived a mere three streets away from Badham, and although the two youngsters did not know each other, the combination of his looks, nonchalant boy-next-door persona, and southern working-class background (he lived in Birmingham but spent summers at his grandmother's house in the Maycomb-like small town of Piedmont, Alabama) heightened Boatwright's interest. Even more to the point, it was immediately evident to the casting director that Alford possessed genuine acting talent. Alford met with Boatwright for no more than five minutes, returned home, and promptly forgot about the audition.

Everyday life resumed until three weeks later, when Alford was asked to come to New York for a screen test. Heading north on the train because his mother was afraid of flying, Phillip stayed in Manhattan for three days while meeting with Mulligan and Pakula. Badham flew north at the same time with her own mother, and the two children were paired together for their screen tests. Mulligan was immediately struck by the fact that they looked like brother and sister, and the discrepancy in their sizes felt just right: Alford was four feet eight and seventy-six pounds, small enough to pass as Jem but big enough to lord it over Scout and Dill.

Mulligan, in fact, did not ask either youngster to read from the

Mockingbird script. Instead, he put them before the camera and asked them questions about their lives, the better to gauge how natural they appeared on-camera. Did they come across as genuine children, or as jaded seen-it-all veterans from a road company of *Gypsy*? The verdict: Both Mary and Phillip read on-screen as utterly natural. Said Mulligan, "They both had a quality I was looking for. They were bright. They were alive. They both seemed to have active imaginations." Mulligan purposely kept it all low-key—no hangers-on, no studio executives. "The only one they had to deal with was me. I made it as much play as I could," he said.

It all passed pleasantly, if vaguely, and Mary and Phillip returned to Birmingham, happy with their New York sojourn. Both youngsters may have assumed they were about to resume their normal routines, but Robert Mulligan now had other plans in mind. After their informal but carefully calculated screen tests, he felt certain that he had found his youthful leads, two unstudied, natural-sounding southerners who would react to the filming just like regular children—as an adventure. Calls were placed—by this time Mary's mother had overcome her husband's objections—and Mary Badham of Birmingham, Alabama, was officially and enthusiastically on board to play Scout. At which point, on New Year's Eve of 1961, the phone rang in the Alford residence and Phillip's father was asked to have Phillip in Los Angeles by early February for the start of filming. The role of Jem was officially Phillip's.

In the end, after traveling thousands of miles and conducting hundreds of interviews, Boatwright had found her Scout and Jem on the same day, in the same town. Two youngsters who lived a mere three blocks from each other had been chosen from nearly two thousand applicants spread across seven southern states. In Boatwright's view, "It was just miraculous—serendipity."

Next came the casting of Dill, aka the young Truman Capote. After considering and rejecting several other young boys, the choice came down to two youngsters: Draper Shreve, Jr., and John Megna. Decades later, Boatwright smilingly recalled Shreve's extraordinary self-possession at age nine; when asked what he wanted to be in life, he replied, "I want to be in oil—and also to be a movie star." Megna, however, ultimately seemed the stronger choice; born John Anthony Ingolia (the half brother of actress Connie Stevens), and having played on Broadway in both the Frank Loesser musical *Greenwillow* and the dramatic *All the Way Home,* at the age of ten he already seemed like a pro compared to the untested Badham and Alford. With his quirky looks and unaffected manner, Megna possessed exactly the kind of sangfroid Mulligan imagined Dill to have, and he remained, in Pakula's words, "a very unaffected kid and not a movie kid." (Even fifty years later, Boatwright can recall the difficulty she had in telling the young Draper Shreve that Megna, not he, had won the role of Dill. Said Shreve upon hearing the news, "Someday when I'm a big star, you'll be sorry.")

Who to play the pivotal role of Tom Robinson? With the limited opportunities then afforded African-American actors, there was no single box-office draw to immediately consider. Sidney Poitier was already a major star, but it was highly doubtful that he would take on a secondary role. Preliminary discussions eventually narrowed the list down to two actors: Brock Peters and James Earl Jones. Jones had an impressive list of stage credits, but Peters, who had made his film debut as Sergeant Brown in *Carmen Jones* (1954), had recently made a big impression as Crown in Otto Preminger's *Porgy and Bess* (1959). So powerful had his presence been in the Gershwin opera that even with the charismatic Poitier and Dorothy Dandridge on-screen, the viewer's eye instinctively traveled to Peters. For Mulligan, the realization that Peters had more than held his own on-screen with Sidney Poitier meant that he could do the same with Peck.

In fact, Peters was almost a victim of his own skill, having registered so strongly as the heavy in both *Carmen Jones* and *Porgy and Bess* that he had remained stereotyped as a villain in the minds of casting directors. Cognizant of Peters's inherent nobility—what Pakula termed his "godlike quality—that voice, that face"—Mulligan and Pakula saw past the on-screen stereotyping to the actor underneath.

Place him on-screen in the same frame as Bob Ewell and, they felt, the point as to character would be made without a single word of dialogue spoken.

Peters read for the part in New York City, emphasizing his versatility by smartly, and counterintuitively, wearing a suit to audition for the role of the country-bred Tom Robinson; his good looks, dignified bearing, and, above all, the ardent emotion visible just beneath the surface convinced Pakula and particularly Mulligan that Peters was the right actor for the role. Peters's delight at winning the role was only heightened when Gregory Peck awakened him with an early Sunday-morning telephone call right before shooting began in order to welcome him to the production. The star/producer of the film welcoming a supporting player? Peters was so surprised, he dropped the phone.

Casting the role of Boo Radley presented a completely different set of problems. Not seen until the last minutes of the film, his presence nonetheless haunts the movie. Where was the actor who could wordlessly convey a gentle but stunted character, a metaphorical ghost with the pallor to match: Boo the man-child who would save and bond with Scout the child-woman? No immediate candidate leapt to mind among the standard roster of Hollywood supporting actors; Horton and Lillian Foote, however, remembered the brilliant performance given by the unknown Robert Duvall as the alcoholic Harvey Weems in Foote's *The Midnight Caller* at the Neighborhood Playhouse. Duvall possessed virtually no film experience—a minuscule role as an MP in 1956's *Somebody Up There Likes Me* rated as his most noteworthy credit—but Lillian Foote in particular recalled his subtle and startlingly vivid performance in *The Midnight Caller,* and she urged Mulligan to consider the actor. Impressed by Duvall's versatility, Mulligan offered the relative neophyte the small yet pivotal role— and his big break.

When 'turning his attention to the role of the villainous Bob Ewell, Mulligan recalled seeing an intense performance given by

James Anderson in a play about Caligula directed by Charlie Chaplin. Warned that for all of his talent Anderson often proved difficult, Mulligan nonetheless scheduled a meeting with the actor. The two shook hands and immediately locked eyes; the director felt certain of Anderson's talent but less sanguine about his behavior, and confronted the actor directly about his reputation for drinking and arriving late on the set. After considering others for the role, Mulligan scheduled a second meeting with Anderson, offering him the role but with a firm proviso: "You and I will have to have a clear understanding—take my hand and shake it—you have to promise me that you will be sober, on time, not cause trouble for me or anyone, and do honor to this script." The two men shook hands. *Mockingbird* had its Bob Ewell.

Mulligan next drew up a list of young actresses he felt could convey both the pathetic vulnerability and lying desperation of Ewell's daughter Mayella, but found himself turning to Collin Wilcox, whom he had directed in a live television version of *The Member of the Wedding*. Young but already an experienced actress with multiple theater credits, the North Carolina native auditioned in character. "All the other girls trying out for the part were overly made up; they had curly clean hair and wore brassieres and high heels. . . . I wore a secondhand dress, tennis shoes with holes in them, and dirty little white socks. I rubbed cold cream through my hair—that's why my hair looked so dirty."

The part was Wilcox's.

For the role of Calpurnia, the rock-steady African-American woman who anchors the Finch home, Mulligan decided upon a near neophyte, Estelle Rolle Evans, a New York public school teacher with only one Off-Broadway credit on her résumé. It was, however, Evans's calm, centered presence that struck the director as exceedingly similar to that of Calpurnia, and scant credits or not, Evans was signed to play Calpurnia.

When it came to the smaller supporting roles, Foote's encyclopedic knowledge of New York City actors and Mulligan's inbred dislike of overt theatricalization informed their mutual decision that well-known Hollywood faces would be avoided. Instead, they would cast either stage actors as yet unknown to movie audiences, or under-stated journeymen character actors, half-recognizable but always believable.

Rosemary Murphy, who possessed theatrical credits ranging from *Look Homeward, Angel* to *Period of Adjustment*, and whose work Mulligan had noted on dramatic live television shows such as *Robert Montgomery Presents*, landed the role of the sympathetic Miss Maudie Atkinson, her believable accent impressing Mulligan all the more when he learned that she was a native of Munich, Germany. At the other end of the spectrum, the quirky Alice Ghostley, who had first attracted attention in New York while appearing in *New Faces of 1952*, struck Mulligan as possessing just the right touch of eccentricity to render her believable as Dill's aunt Stephanie.

No matter the size of the role, Mulligan was searching for actors who would impart a small but important presence that added to the texture of Maycomb; Maycomb was not southern gothic, but rather idiosyncratic and down-home, and was to function as a virtual char-acter in the film. Would the audience accept the actors cast as town citizens as recognizably authentic when they ambled down Main Street or walked into the courtroom? Mulligan wanted actors who could disappear into their roles, and eschewing any Hollywood standard-bearers—no Walter Brennan here—he turned repeatedly to veterans of the Broadway stage.

The role of prosecutor Horace Gilmer required an actor who could essay the unpleasant nature of the legal task at hand without descending into a mustache-twirling cartoon version of southern big-otry, and Mulligan and Pakula focused their search on the relatively unknown William Windom. Having worked steadily on radio and live television dramas, Windom had recently gained notice on the "Five Characters in Search of an Exit" episode of *The Twilight Zone*, but he was still two years away from the television stardom he would find on television's *The Farmer's Daughter*. Mulligan, however, responded to Windom's take on the character and signed the actor for his first-ever feature-film appearance.

The solid, steady Crahan Denton had worked in television (*Perry Mason*) and in films ranging from *The Parent Trap* to *Birdman of Alcatraz,* and possessed the down-home appearance crucial to the role of Mr. Cunningham; character actor Frank Overton, familiar to both Mulligan and Foote from his work on the New York stage, particularly Foote's own *The Trip to Bountiful,* proved their mutual top choice for the role of Sheriff Tate. With a lived-in, workaday face, he seemed to embody just the right everyman qualities necessary to convey the internal conflicts of a man who always does his job—even when unhappy with the called-upon task.

For the crucial and unseen role of the narrator, it was Foote who personally asked the brilliant Kim Stanley (often referred to as "the female Brando"), whom he had known since she starred in the television broadcast of his *A Young Lady of Property.* Since she was esteemed for her work on both stage and television, the last thing Kim Stanley needed was a voice-over job, but she readily agreed, as a favor to Mulligan and especially to Foote.

Stanley, in fact, was so much a part of Foote's conception of the film that he later admitted to hearing her voice in his head even while writing his first draft. Crucial in establishing the film's tone, hers would be the very first voice heard as the movie began. Her cadence, with its gentle but insistent lilt and the slight sense of distance imparted by the older Jean Louise looking back on her childhood, would prove decisive in establishing the film's interplay of past and present.

As Mulligan continued to finalize casting choices, he began preliminary work with his production designers and cinematographer. Turning to men and women with whom he had previously collaborated in winning fashion, Mulligan landed his first choice for each of those crucial positions. Whatever else happened on the journey from Pulitzer Prize–winning novel to neighborhood movie screens, the look of the film would be in the hands of the most talented professionals in

Hollywood, because joining production designers Henry Bumstead and Alexander Golitzen would be cinematographer Russell Harlan, costume designer Rosemary Odell, and editor Aaron Stell. Oscar winners. Team players. Amiable coworkers. When to begin?

Yesterday.

8

FROM PULITZER PRIZE TO
HOLLYWOOD DREAM TEAM

I have nothing but gratitude to the people who made the film. It seemed to me to be such respect for the material. I was delighted, touched, exceedingly grateful. It seemed to permeate anyone who had something to do with the film.

—Harper Lee, interview on WQXR radio, March 1964

Robert Mulligan was well aware that the production design for a period piece like *Mockingbird* could make or break the film. One false detail, one anachronistic dwelling, and the entire house of cards would collapse. But, the rising director realized, he was in the best-possible hands with both Henry Bumstead and Alexander Golitzen.

Born in 1915, by the time of *Mockingbird,* Henry Bumstead— "Bummy" to his friends and colleagues—had established himself as one of the premier production designers in all of Hollywood, with work ranging from the intimate *Come Back, Little Sheba* (1952) to two brilliant Hitchcock films, *The Man Who Knew Too Much* (1956) and *Vertigo* (1958); it was the latter film, increasingly referred to in twenty-first-century American and British Film Institute polls as the greatest film of all time, in which the Bumstead production design so enhanced the unfolding story that it virtually functioned as another character. Able to convey acres of knowledge about characters and their reaction to environment without a word being spoken, Bummy's work as production designer was sought after by every A-list Hollywood director of the time.

After twenty-four years at Paramount, he had just moved to Universal at the time of *Mockingbird*. It wasn't just his extraordinary skill that Pakula and Mulligan sought; along with that talent came a gentlemanly demeanor, making the designer a true—and rare—collaborator in all senses of the word. Was he interested? "Yes," the answer came back quickly. In Mulligan's assessment, their production designer was nothing less than "an absolute wizard—a charming man to work with." This sentiment was echoed by film scholar Jeanine Basinger: "Henry Bumstead was a delightful man—humorous, and possessed of energy to burn. He loved movies with a deep passion and knew how to create a complete world on film, whether realistic or one of fantasy. He was one of the greatest men in Hollywood history."

Making the team even stronger, Bumstead brought along the highly regarded Alexander Golitzen as co–art director, as well as Oliver Emert as set decorator. Golitzen's life story was itself the stuff of a Hollywood movie, the designer having been born Prince Alexander Alexandrovich Galitzine, a Russian aristocrat, before his family fled Moscow during the Russian Revolution in 1917. Emigrating to America at age fifteen, he thereafter earned a degree in architecture and began to climb the Hollywood ladder, working for MGM, Samuel Goldwyn, and Walter Wanger; by 1954, he had been named supervising art director at Universal. He was rightly acclaimed for his dazzling designs on color films like 1943's *Phantom of the Opera* (his first Oscar), while his work on Hitchcock's *Foreign Correspondent* (1940) and Orson Welles's *Touch of Evil* (1958) showed his eye was equally adept with the displays of shadow and light so crucial to the success of black-and-white films.

The Bumstead and Golitzen team was completed by the addition of set decorator Oliver Emert, who by the time of *Mockingbird* had amassed a list of credits ranging from the Douglas Sirk–directed

The Tarnished Angels (1957) to the Doris Day vehicle *Midnight Lace* (1960). Having worked with Golitzen, Bumstead, and director Mulligan on *The Spiral Road*, Emert understood both the detailed vision of small-town 1930s Alabama desired by the production designers, as well as Mulligan's relaxed yet highly focused style.

Bumstead and Golitzen began their work by studying the notes compiled by Pakula after his first trip to Monroeville; although that original location scout had made it clear that Monroeville had changed too much since the 1930s for the movie ever to be shot there, Bumstead himself now requested a trip to Monroeville in order to soak up the atmosphere and garner specific architectural details for the upcoming studio backlot re-creation of the town. Off went Bumstead and Golitzen to southwest Alabama, flying from Los Angeles to Birmingham, where they picked up a car for the drive to Monroeville along Highway 84, the El Camino East/West Corridor linking Alabama with Texas, Mississippi, Louisiana, and Georgia.

Taking their time, the two gimlet-eyed observers absorbed the architecture, the color of the sky, and the very land itself—the pastures full of cows, the beaten-down farmlands—gaining a hands-on sense-memory understanding of the rural South, which they would re-create back at Universal. Their rural southern surroundings couldn't have been farther removed from Los Angeles and Hollywood itself, but the two men were charmed by the countryside and, most notably of all, by Harper Lee herself.

Reporting back to Pakula in a November 1961 letter, Bumstead extolled Harper Lee as "a most charming person. She insisted I call her Nelle." Under her guidance, Bumstead began examining the older houses in the area. "Most of the houses are of wood, one story and set up on brick piles. Almost every house had a porch and a swing hanging from the porch rafters," he wrote Pakula. There were copious details to be stored away for re-creation on the studio backlot: potbellied stoves still heated the Monroeville courtroom, with the coal that fed the stove stored in nearby containers, a telling detail the two men would pass along to Emert. Dirt streets may have represented a well-known

Depression-era historical detail, but it was only because of the scouting trip that the design team learned that no lampposts could be utilized in their set design, since lamps in the Monroeville of the 1930s were simply hung from telephone poles. Mailboxes could not be shown on porches or front yards; to pick up mail, Monroeville residents of the time walked into town, made the trip on horseback, or occasionally drove, the trips providing another chance for socializing and a welcome reinforcement of community ties.

No detail proved too small for the design team's consideration. It was deemed essential that Boo Radley's house should not just be dilapidated but appear never to have been painted at all; Harper Lee herself gave Bumstead instructions that Mrs. Dubose's house should be seen as emblematic of hard times, all peeling paint and dark Victorian furniture, a family home wired for electricity but still lit by oil lamps.

Some accidents of geography proved fortuitous; in walking and driving through Monroeville and the surrounding area, Bumstead came to understand that the black section of town, which in segregated Alabama of the 1930s was exactly where Tom Robinson's home would have been located, was built into areas filled with pine trees, "so we could do this sequence on the upper lake section of the lot where we have pine trees."

Bumstead actually did find isolated buildings dating from the 1930s that were still intact, but they were scattered throughout the small town, and the omnipresent sight of television antennae negated the possible use of anything but the tightest of camera angles. Cars now sped by on streets paved with asphalt, supermarkets dotted the landscape, and a plethora of neon signs loomed throughout. Monroeville had entered the modern age, and the Depression-era agriculturally based world was nowhere to be found.

The redbrick building where A. C. Lee had practiced law, and where Harper wrote part of the novel, was still in place, but her childhood home on South Alabama Avenue, the inspiration for Scout's cozy home, was nowhere to be found. Bumstead could find the address, but what he was looking at was not a simple southern bungalow, but, rather, a new building called Mel's Dairy Dream. The house next door, where Truman had lived with his aunts? Nowhere to be seen. A plaque would eventually mark the spot, but because a fire in January 1940 had destroyed the home, all that remained was a vacant lot, accented by a very tiny part of the old stone fence that had divided the Lee home from that of Capote's aunts.

The physical world of Harper Lee's childhood may have disappeared, but Bumstead came away from the trip having made one invaluable design decision: The Monroeville courthouse, which anchored the town square, still stood intact as a perfect example of period architecture, so perfect, in fact, that Bummy not only took photographs of the building but also spent hours measuring the exact dimensions of the interior in order to re-create it on the studio soundstage.

The inability to film on location may have initially been viewed as a detriment, but thanks to the combined efforts of Bumstead, Golitzen, and Emert, it had, in some ways, turned into an advantage. The simultaneously comforting and oppressive small-town atmosphere could now be blissfully micromanaged in the controlled environs of a Hollywood studio. There would be no gawking bystanders, no threat from the weather, and no takes ruined due to nearby noise. Instead, a designer-dictated re-creation of a vanished world would serve the entire film, one all the easier for director Mulligan to control.

There were, to be sure, stumbles along the way. Golitzen and Bumstead first designed the Finch dwelling as a substantial home with pillars that looked more than a bit like Tara in *Gone With the Wind.* Horton Foote took one look at the sketches and emphatically told the designers, "My God Almighty! This is wrong, this isn't her house. . . . It's a cottage, it's simple." Foote further explained to the designers: "They [the Finches] lived in the kind of house I'm living in right now, that I've lived in my whole life. . . ."(Such are the vagaries of Hollywood that when Margaret Mitchell first saw the sketches for

Tara in *Gone with the Wind,* the design was so much larger and more romantic than her conception that she burst out laughing.)

With Foote's admonition in mind, Golitzen began sifting through the dozens of photos he and Bumstead had taken on their trip to Monroeville, at which point he had an inspiration: The few houses remaining in Monroeville from the 1930s strongly reminded him of the old clapboard cottages that were now fast disappearing from the California landscape. After discussing the similarity with Bumstead, Golitzen began canvassing wrecking companies, asking them if they knew of any cottages slated for demolition. For two weeks, the designers drove around Los Angeles, scouting out any and all possibilities, until they found exactly what they wanted in Chavez Ravine: twelve clapboard cottages that had been abandoned in favor of a freeway extension, all of them constructed in the very same style as homes found in the Depression-era southern United States. Built from the turn of the century until the 1930s, these cottages all featured rooms feeding off of a central hall, the resulting style known as "gunshot-hall houses."

The soon-to-be-demolished cottages were acquired for a mere $5,000, and after deciding that the porches could be stabilized, and casement windows and shutters added, Golitzen estimated that the cost of repairs would total no more than $25,000; if the cottages had been built directly on the set, he felt certain that they would have cost "at least $100,000." In the end, all of Maycomb was built on fifteen acres of the Universal backlot for the astonishingly small sum of $225,000.

While Bumstead and Golitzen began their preliminary sketches, Pakula and Mulligan began technical discussions with cinematographer Russell Harlan, whose hiring completed a creative team composed entirely of men and women born before 1930, all of whom carried actual sense memories of the Depression with them.

Born in 1903, Harlan had started his career as a stuntman, but by the 1930s he had left his stunt days behind and begun working as an assistant cameraman. His first solo credit came on the Hopalong Cassidy Westerns, and he soon became particularly well-known for his skill at capturing the expansive natural settings found in Westerns. Supremely versatile, he proved a favorite of the demanding Howard Hawks, who utilized his services on no fewer than seven films. By the time of *Mockingbird*, Harlan had compiled a mastery of varied settings equaled by very few: the beautiful black-and-white western landscapes found in *Red River* (1948), the gritty, tight *Gun Crazy* (1950), the tough urban setting of *Blackboard Jungle* (1955), the riot of color suffusing Vincente Minnelli's *Lust for Life* (1956), and the claustrophobic courtroom settings found in Billy Wilder's *Witness for the Prosecution* (1957), all of them expertly rendered by Harlan's camerawork. In his discussions with Mulligan and Pakula, Harlan made it clear that he felt just as strongly as they that *Mockingbird* would carry decidedly more power if shot in black and white, the better to convey the feel of a memory piece. To Pakula, the technically adroit and easy-to-work-with Harlan felt like just the right collaborator for both Mulligan and Bumstead.

To compose what Pakula and Mulligan already envisioned as a low-key atmospheric score, they turned to Elmer Bernstein, whose versatility had already proven capable of handling any genre. His jazz score from 1955's *The Man with the Golden Arm* had become one of the first film scores to prove popular as a commercial recording in its own right and had established Bernstein among Hollywood's premier composers; by the start of the 1960s, his credits already ranged from the biblical epic *The Ten Commandments* (1956) to the beautifully sour *Sweet Smell of Success* (1957), and ranged far enough afield to encompass the 1960 Western *The Magnificent Seven*.

Bernstein professed himself intrigued by the difficulties of providing the proper childhood-centric score, and felt secure that Pakula and Mulligan would allow him both the time and the necessary creative room to experiment. In later years, he explained, "The reason that they were able to communicate to a composer was a fine understanding of what their film was about. It wasn't just storytelling, it was a question of understanding all of the characters . . . how they related to their society."

With Bernstein signed, Pakula and Mulligan's attention shifted to the job of costume designer. First choice was the thirty-seven-year-old Rosemary Odell, whose own childhood had been exactly contemporaneous with those of Nelle and Scout. Unobtrusive, and with credits stretching from the Anthony Mann–directed *Thunder Bay* to the Doris Day sex comedy *That Touch of Mink,* Odell designed clothes that fit the characters, eschewing any attempt to draw attention to herself. Mulligan had happily worked with Odell on the very recent *The Spiral Road,* and when he asked if she would be interested in collaborating once again, the answer proved an emphatic yes.

Odell quickly began designing what turned out to be the two iconic costumes associated with the film: Scout's overalls and Atticus's white suit. Scout's first entrance into the film, swinging Tarzan-like into the frame, would find her clad in a tomboyish pair of overalls, her ease of character in those clothes all the more heightened when she very grudgingly appears in a dress for the first day of school. (The scruffy dark overalls and old sneakers that Scout and Jem sport throughout the film contrast vividly with Dill's always immaculate ensemble of shirt, white shorts, knee socks, and neatly tied shoes. If clothing makes the man, it here defines the child.) Similarly, Atticus's rumpled cotton three-piece suit, complete with buttoned vest even in the brutal non-air-conditioned Alabama summer, communicated his sense of propriety: He might just as well stroll naked as publicly appear in casual clothes. The suit might wilt, but Atticus never would. Sketching in myriad small details, it was Odell's idea that the nighttime mob of farmers that comes to the jail in order to lynch Tom Robinson would be dressed in overalls yet still sport fedoras. Hats, it seemed, were worn at even the most shameful of occasions.

To complete the team, Pakula and Mulligan approached editor Aaron Stell, who had recently begun work at Universal after a decade spent at Columbia Pictures. Like art director Alexander Golitzen, Stell had worked on the Orson Welles masterpiece *Touch of Evil*, and had already collaborated successfully with Pakula and Mulligan on *Fear Strikes Out*. Drawn to both the restraint and lyricism needed for *Mockingbird*'s story, as well as the chance to work with Pakula and Mulligan once again, Stell quickly signed on.

As all of the designers dove into their preproduction assignments, and with the start of filming only one month away, the citizens of Monroeville received a highly welcome dose of Hollywood glamour when Gregory Peck appeared right in the middle of their downtown in January 1962. Nelle's hometown may not have paid all that much attention to her book until the Pulitzer Prize was announced, but even that genteel fuss paled in comparison to the excitement caused by Peck's arrival. Accompanied by his wife, Veronique, as well as director Mulligan and his wife, Peck stayed at the La Salle Hotel and ate at the local Wee Diner, giving the town natives multiple opportunities to ogle the ever-congenial star.

Accompanied by a small crew that was documenting his appearance in the very town that had inspired the novel, Peck visited the Western Auto Store and toured the town square, causing a fuss wherever he stopped. His casual comment that he had never eaten a downhome southern meal resulted in basket after basket of food being dropped off for him at the La Salle Hotel; after one day of the flattering but unasked-for townwide attention, Peck and Veronique decided that they would no longer venture out of their room for meals, asking instead that the diner send food over to their room.

Peck's hands-on guide to Monroeville was Harper Lee herself, who personally escorted the actor to the courthouse that had inspired the trial sequence. Lee was smitten with the actor, commenting to a friend, "Isn't he delicious?" But the main point of the visit seemed to be the chance for Peck to meet A. C. Lee, the forty-five-year-old actor meeting the eighty-one-year-old attorney at the brick ranch house the Lees had occupied after their move from South Alabama Avenue following the deaths of Frances and Edwin in 1951. The two courtly men made polite conversation and in the process formed a genuine, if understandably distant, bond.

Peck, ever the observer, made note of A. C. Lee's mannerisms and gestures, storing away details for the next month's start of filming. The round glasses used by A.C.? Peck would appropriate the use of a similar pair as one of the keys to the appearance of a scholarly, thoughtful lawyer. Watching A.C. play with his watch while simultaneously pacing and talking, Peck began calibrating exactly how large his own repetition of those physical gestures should be, gauging the difference in scale between real-life actions and those observed on a thirty-foot-high screen.

Like thousands of others, the actor wondered exactly how closely the character of Atticus resembled that of A.C., and found himself in accord with Nelle's own explanation to the *New York Herald Tribune* that Atticus was like A.C. "in character and—the South has a good word for this—in disposition." It was an irony worth noting that A.C. still did not really see himself in the book, as Nelle pointed out: "He was surprised when people greeted him on the street with 'Hello, Atticus,' but eventually he began signing the book 'Atticus.'"

With the cast and creative team set and the Horton Foote script finalized, shooting on Harper Lee's Pulitzer Prize–winning *To Kill a Mockingbird* was set to begin. Could Gregory Peck attract an audience when playing against type as the decidedly nonromantic Atticus Finch? In his role as producer, could he put aside an actor's vanity for the sake of the film itself? Most important of all, could he establish any sort of rapport with Mary Badham and Phillip Alford—because without it, *To Kill a Mockingbird* would be dead in the water.

Harper Lee, Alan Pakula, and Robert Mulligan were about to find out.

MAYCOMB COMES TO LIFE

I put everything I had into it—all my feelings and everything I'd learned in 46 years of living, about family life and fathers and children. And my feelings about racial justice and inequality and opportunity.

—Gregory Peck on *To Kill a Mockingbird*

It was all so easy. I get lost in memories of how easy it was.

—Mary Badham on *To Kill a Mockingbird*

Even before the start of filming on February 12, 1962, Gregory Peck met with Mary Badham, both in order to rehearse and also to welcome her into his family circle. By inviting her to spend weekends playing with his own children, the actor not only wanted Mary to feel comfortable around him but also to provide fun for a nine-year-old girl living two thousand miles from home. It was, in retrospect, a very Atticus-like gesture, leading Badham to reminisce in later years, "Always that warmth, that smile, that deep marvelous laugh. It makes you feel so secure. . . . He's just Atticus."

Two weeks of rehearsal with the children passed swiftly, with neither Peck nor Mulligan imposing too much order or enforced closeness upon either Mary or Phillip, instead developing the youngsters' trust by letting them reach out on their own terms. Mulligan brought the camera into rehearsals, beginning the sessions with the camera positioned far away, then slowly moving it closer and closer, until it seemed like a normal everyday presence to the youngsters, one they could and did simply ignore. The director was not interested in endless readings of the script around a table. Instead, he encouraged the actors to get up on their feet quickly, to walk around the set, lie on the beds, familiarize themselves with the furniture, and sit on the porch swing—in other words, to feel that they were in their own home. It all unfolded so smoothly that even at this early stage, Peck enthused, "It does not matter about the children being stars. All children live in a world of make-believe and certainly if they are intelligent, they can make the movie. I am looking forward to working with them."

As the start of filming neared, the question of accents came into play. Peck, it had been decided, would use a watered-down southern accent, while Badham and Alford would speak in their own natural southern-inflected speech. For the supporting actors, there would be no special attempt made to employ southern accents, a decision that proved to be just fine with Harper Lee. "Nothing empties a Southern movie house faster than tin-eared actors," she once commented. The author pronounced herself content with Peck's speech pattern—decidedly less southern than her father's, yet still suggestive of a small-town Alabama lawyer's. Peck permitted himself, she later wrote, "one harmless indulgence, an unobtrusive Southern 'you.' There was a lesson here for all young screenwriters—when spoken, lines written in implacable Southern idiom create the illusion of Southern voices."

Invited to visit the set for the start of filming, Nelle traveled to Los Angeles by train; many interior scenes would be filmed at Revue Studios, but Nelle immediately headed to the Universal backlot, where she was staggered by the work of Bumstead, Golitzen, and Emert. Right there in front of her—surrounding her, overwhelming her—was the Monroeville of her childhood. Glancing around, she took in the sights and sounds of her long-vanished childhood—the weathered clapboard houses fronting on dirt-packed streets, the front porch rocking chairs, the mix of horses and cars, the faded clothes and lined faces of her southern neighbors. She had traveled back in time.

As Nelle arrived on the set, Gregory Peck was undergoing final wardrobe tests; much as Nelle liked, indeed admired, the actor, she still possessed a niggling doubt or two about his ability to fully inhabit the role of Atticus. The handsome, charismatic Peck as a small-town southern lawyer in the 1930s? As the embodiment of her own father? She wondered—until she heard the sound of a closing door, looked up, and saw Gregory Peck walking out of his dressing room and onto the street set. At that point, her remaining doubts vanished. Clad in a rumpled suit and vest, glasses framing his face, and pocket watch prominently displayed, Peck was, in fact, the living, breathing incarnation of Atticus Finch. Harper Lee was stunned. "It was the most amazing transformation I had ever seen," she said. "A middle-aged man came out. . . . He didn't have an ounce of make-up, just a 1933-type suit complete with a collar, and a vest and a watch on a chain. The minute I saw him I knew everything was bound to be all right because he *was* Atticus."

Peck's very physical appearance seemed tailor-made for readers' perception of Atticus: the kind smile—slightly quizzical but always understanding—his trim six-foot-two frame, the Arrow collar profile. But, even more so, it was the voice that clinched the deal, a reassuring sonorous baritone capable of conveying everything from moral certainty to outrage, and, above all else, understanding. Harper Lee relaxed. Her novel was in very good hands.

One question remained in the novelist's mind: Where, she asked herself, was Horton Foote? The puzzlement persisted until it was rather bluntly explained to her that in the Hollywood pecking order, the screenwriter didn't count. Universal, still seeming to treat the film as a low-budget afterthought, had refused to pay for Horton Foote's presence on the set. As far as the studio executives were concerned, the script was frozen. There was neither time nor money for rewrites and they had no intention of paying any travel or hotel expenses for a screenwriter. Pakula had pleaded with the studio brass, but to no avail. Mulligan and the actors were on their own.

Cast, crew, and author now readied themselves for the very first shot of the film: Atticus's return home at the end of the workday, his arrival marked by Scout and Jem running to meet him in front of Mrs. Dubose's house. Harper Lee planted herself behind the dolly tracks, and director of photography Russell Harlan glanced once more around the Maycomb street scene; secure in the knowledge that the entire shoot would prove much easier to control on the backlot than on location, he was still aware of how much could go wrong: weather, temper tantrums, inexperienced actors, children—even worse, the children's parents—the list of potential obstacles seemed endless. But, after their easygoing collaboration on *The Spiral Road,* Harlan knew Mulligan would run a disciplined yet genial set. All final decisions would be made by Mulligan—"the shooting, the editing, the use of music—all that represents my attitude towards the material"—but, Harlan knew, Mulligan was always open to collaboration, indeed encouraged it.

Having spent hours discussing the exact look of the film—realistic yet suitable for a memory piece—both men felt completely comfortable in their division of labor: Camera placement, blocking, the efficacy of acting choices—all these were decisions to be made by Mulligan. The lenses to be employed, the very texture of the light, the use of specific filters—those decisions would be made by the director only after extensive collaboration with Harlan. Mulligan did more than trust Harlan; he listened to the great cameraman's advice, encouraging a back-and-forth dialogue in pursuit of the slightly diffused look crucial to the lyrical style he sought for the film. Theirs was, in the director's mind, an absolutely crucial collaboration: "If that man isn't really into my head, knowing the mood and the style I want, I'm dead."

Their prep work done, director and cinematographer were ready, anxious even, to jump into the deep end. It was time.

Peck, Badham, and Alford readied themselves.

"Roll Camera."

"Action!"

To Kill a Mockingbird was under way.

Scout and Jem race over to greet their father, words tumbling out as Jem hoists his father's briefcase, the family stopping to talk to crabby Mrs. Dubose, and—

"Cut!"

No need for a second take: First day, first scene, first take, and it's a print. A grand-slam home run.

Gregory Peck, happy that the scene has played out so beautifully in front of Nelle, feels secretly pleased that he spied "a glistening on her cheek." When he ambles over to his friend, there are no sentimental tears, but instead Nelle's smiling observation: "Oh, Gregory. You have a little potbelly just like my daddy!" The star's laughing retort? "That's great acting!"

Harper Lee stayed on in Los Angeles for three weeks, leaving when she realized "everything would be fine without me." She took the train back to Manhattan, where, on April 15, 1962, she learned that her beloved father had died of a heart attack. While her own childhood of thirty years past was being reenacted on a Hollywood backlot, she returned to the actual scene of that childhood, Monroeville, to help her sister Alice. Reality had set in: Brother Ed had now been gone a little over ten years, and sister Louise was living with her family in Eufaula, Alabama. For now it was just the two sisters at home in Monroeville.

As shooting unfolded on the Universal backlot, whatever the everyday stresses and strains inherent in filming, Mulligan continued to treat the children gently, giving direction only by crouching down to their eye level; there would be no Olympian direction from on high, but, rather, a simple explanation of where the camera would be placed before he called "Action!" There was never an attempt to give the children line readings; Mulligan valued spontaneity above all, as Badham later confirmed: "How I delivered the lines was left to me." His direction of Badham, Alford, and Megna would be limited to encouraging their innate acting ability and the naturalness he had discerned in their screen tests. Not only did he avoid dictating vocal inflections and gestures but he actually encouraged the children to improvise. "Kids are marvelous at improvisation. Far superior to adults because adults begin editing their stuff. Kids are so open. They do it all by themselves."

Expecting Hollywood casual as the prevailing style of the day, a *New York Times* reporter visiting the set recorded his surprise at seeing Mulligan direct while clad in a tan three-button suit, complete with narrow tie and black horn-rimmed glasses. That occasional formality aside, Mulligan proved low-key and at ease with the children, as far removed as possible from the autocratic style of an Otto Preminger. Cast and crew copied his style, bonding with the children by conveying a sense of low-keyed commitment. Secure in their setting, genuinely happy with the director and their friends on the crew, the children relaxed, acting not for the camera, but for fun—for themselves.

Always foremost in Mulligan's approach to the material was his realization that the novel centered upon the powerful and enormous effect adults have on children—"not in the Dr. Spock sense, but in the unconscious effect we have on them by what they see in us." It was as if decades before Stephen Sondheim wrote his typically wise and doubled-edged lyric for *Into the Woods*'s key song, "Children Will Listen," Mulligan understood the stakes at hand:

> *Careful the things you do*
> *Children will see and learn*

Taking her cue from Mulligan's sensitive, genial approach, Badham never felt nervous, a fact she confirmed in later years: "How do you know to be afraid when you don't know what's going on? I was not a child of the movies and I had had very limited contact with much of anything at nine years old." She felt an occasional puzzlement over the film being shot out of sequence, but had no time to dwell on that. There was fun to be had, an entire make-believe village to be explored. Secure with her family off the set—her mother, aunt, and the family maid Frankie were all with her—and feeling equally safe with Peck and Mulligan on the set, it all played out as a marvelous vacation that she didn't want to end.

There was fun, sheer delight, in fact, when it came time to film Scout's first appearance in the movie. Swinging into the frame while hanging on to a rope, the overalls-wearing Scout is propelled smack into the middle of the frame. Ahh, Badham thought, can we do that again? The sheer joy of moving through space, unfettered, a seemingly limitless future stretching to the horizon . . .

Filming proved to be such a joy that Badham did not even mind her on-set schooling with Mrs. Crotke. "My guardian angel—just marvelous" was how she later described her teacher. Tutoring ran up to three hours per day, but school on a movie set proved to be a far cry from the confines of a school classroom in Alabama, and the three children enjoyed the fact that Mrs. Crotke was, if anything, stricter with Mulligan and Pakula than she ever was with them. Come 5:00 P.M., no matter what was happening at that moment, onto the set Mrs. Crotke would march, stepping right in front of the camera to announce, "That's it guys. We'll see you in the morning."

Like Badham, Alford felt full of the confidence unique to the young: "It never occurred to me that I couldn't do it. I wasn't afraid of it. It was going to be something new," he recalled. Ironically, he hadn't even read *To Kill a Mockingbird* and never did feel the need to do so until much later in life, but for now, he arrived in Hollywood fresh, a bit wary, but eager. It was impossible for Phillip to grow homesick, because his entire family had relocated to Hollywood for the duration of the shooting: his mother, father, and even his sister, Eugenia, who found work as one of Mary Badham's stand-ins. Having grown up in the South, with a pesky little sister like Scout and a tire swing in his backyard, filming *To Kill a Mockingbird* represented terra firma for Alford. The entire experience was playing out as an interesting adventure.

The bonds formed between the children and Peck during rehearsal only deepened at the start of filming, with Badham spontaneously crawling into the actor's lap between takes, intuitively responding to Peck's own sense of paterfamilias. He was by now a father of five who remembered his own difficult childhood and instinctively felt protective of any child. "The world never seems as fresh and wonderful, as comforting and terrifying, as good and evil as it does when seen through the eyes of a child," he commented. Said his son Stephen, "The man I see is still basically a small-town boy. He's shy and very sensitive to people's feelings. He doesn't want them to be hurt the way he was hurt."

Peck's deliberately casual manner relaxed the children; he allowed them to wander in and out of his dressing room, and taught Phillip Alford how to play chess. It all added up to a quiet and fatherly approach that suited the character of Atticus to a T. He was, on set and off, in the view of his friend Elmer Bernstein, "[a] great humanist. He believes in people. He always believes that things can be better and he's willing to help in various causes to try to make things better— and in a quiet way."

Watching Mary, Phillip, and John explore the set and experience the sheer joy of childhood freedom brought back the more pleasant memories of the actor's own bumpy childhood in La Jolla: the bike rides, the exploration of the surrounding countryside, even the excitement found in "climbing into spare tires and rolling down the street. It was just like *To Kill a Mockingbird*." Said the smiling star, "Acting with Mary and Phil is like living the part. They believe in their portrayals and they don't pretend. They play themselves no matter what the dramatic situation. It is the most refreshing experience I have had in a long time."

Teasing abounded—some good-natured, some, as in real life, containing more of an edge. Mary, quick on the uptake, began silently mouthing Phillip's and John's lines while she stood off-camera, her lips forming the words ever so slightly ahead of their own attempted speech. With her eyebrows constantly traveling up and down, she drove Alford to distraction, and the breakfast scene alone required no fewer than thirty takes. It would, Alford later commented, be years before he could even look at bacon and eggs again. In similar fashion, twenty-three takes and twenty-three partially eaten meals turned out to be required for the scene in which the Finches eat lunch with Walter Cunningham. Ironically, it may just be that focusing his enmity on Mary helped Phillip; utterly relaxed while shooting those twenty-three takes of the lunch shared with a syrup-pouring Walter, his naturalness helped diffuse any excessive focus on Atticus's potentially ponderous explanation of why it was a sin to kill a mockingbird.

Fed up with Mary, John and Phillip plotted revenge, their plan coalescing around the scene in which Scout rolls down a hill inside a tire. With the lighting setup completed, Mulligan shouted, "Action!" and the two young boys started the tire rolling, deliberately aiming it straight at an equipment truck. The tire crashed into the truck, but Badham emerged unscathed. Nonetheless, it was decided that in all subsequent takes, she would only be glimpsed climbing into and out of the tire, with the actual roll downhill now entrusted to a stunt double. Alford's years later assessment: "We tried to kill her, but we were too small and couldn't get the tire going fast enough."

Even these quarrels made the family dynamic displayed on-screen seem all the more real, and dustups aside, the three youngsters joyfully explored the twenty-acre set between takes, with Bumstead and Golitzen's extraordinarily detailed re-creation becoming their own personal playground. Running over the entire backlot, the children enjoyed such freedom of movement that a limit was reached only when they had to be stopped from fishing in a backlot pond. The reason? The pond had been designated a reservoir and placed off-limits by the California Fish and Game Commission.

Because all of the preproduction rehearsals had left the children utterly at ease in their surroundings, once filming began the action seemed to unfold spontaneously. Mulligan would rehearse the scene in question a few times, keep the instructions to a minimum, call "Action," and usually limit the takes to no more than two or three, in order that the acting remain instinctive. The director's mantra: Get something going in rehearsal, shoot it quickly, and move on to the next setup.

In his on-set discussions with Peck, Mulligan emphasized that Atticus Finch represented "an heroic man without any of the typical hero traits." There were no fistfights, gun battles, or physical stunts. Instead, at the center of the movie stood a man possessed of genuine conscience, one who quietly, and on a decidedly human scale, represented the proverbial knight in shining armor—a small-town southern lawyer who stands up to the prevailing evil of the day. A man of the segregated Depression-era South who, according to Mulligan, was working in his own quiet way "to establish the kind of justice toward the Negro that must exist if this nation is to fully realize its position as a free and democratic country."

Day after day, Mulligan, head down and deep in concentration, would walk around the set, planning camera moves and angles, only to look up and see the constantly rehearsing Peck pacing back and forth as he refined his interpretation. Never satisfied with his own efforts, Peck continually adjusted his performance, asking himself: How would Atticus walk? Does his body language change as soon as he steps onto the porch of his own home? Does he find reassurance by habitually running his hands over his pocket watch? Peck's goal: to flesh out Atticus so that he remained a real man rather than a secular saint.

When the time arrived for the emotional front porch scene in which Atticus explains the meaning and nature of compromise to Scout, Mulligan whispered one simple direction to Badham: "Think of something very, very sad—something that would really upset you." Badham tried, but it was hard. The nine-year-old was so extraordinarily happy at all times during filming that it took her some time to summon an appropriate memory; the scene was finally shot, Mulligan yelled, "Cut!" and Badham happily skipped over to the next setup, a nine-year-old girl possessing no idea that the just-snapped still image of Atticus Finch on a porch swing with his arm around his daughter would be seared into moviegoers' memories for the next fifty years. Without any of the participants realizing it at the time, they had just forever preserved on film the very image of an ideal, all-protective father: wise, discerning, and, above all, capable of quiet but uncondi-tional love.

So strong was the feeling among cast and crew of working on a very special film that even normal on-set tensions seemed to dissipate, the one notable exception being the perpetual difficulties that seemed to surround James Anderson, an ornery character at the best of times. Anderson's relationships with both Peck and Brock Peters remained fraught; was the tension between Anderson and Peters caused by the characters they were playing, their differing acting styles, or their own personalities? Even years after the fact, no one was really sure, but whatever the cause, the on-set tensions proved real, if mostly notice-able only to the two men. Said director Mulligan, "I heard that there was real hostility between Jim and Brock. I didn't know it." In Peters's memorable description of Anderson, the "malevolence that he carried around on his shoulders" was what caused Peters to exercise great cau-tion around his prickly costar. "I was really afraid I wouldn't be able to take much of the attitude he projected without getting into difficulties," he recalled. Mulligan himself admitted that he was never quite sure if Anderson's perpetual discontent was simply a by-product of staying in character, but the off-putting intensity remained, and throughout the entire shooting period, the director was the only person to whom Anderson would speak.

Things went from bad to worse with Anderson after Gregory Peck offered a suggestion during one of their scenes together; Anderson's snarled response to Peck was, "You don't show me shit!" A more ego-centric leading man than Peck might have forced an apology. Peck was the muscle on the film and Anderson possessed none, but Peck merely moved on, letting Mulligan take care of the matter with Anderson. Peck's analysis: "Jim despised me and I didn't think too much of him. He thought I was a leading man who couldn't cut the mustard and really create a character." As it was, Anderson's difficult personality

even extended to his interactions with the children; during the filming of Bob Ewell's climactic attack on Scout and Jem, he pulled Phillip Alford by the hair, yanking him around the wooded set throughout
two days of fighting, leaving Alford to recollect, "That was not fake. A
lot more was filmed than ended up in the movie."

It quickly came time for the filming of a second crucial father-
daughter scene, that of Scout reading aloud to Atticus in her bedroom.
The scene called for Atticus to listen gravely, intent upon his daughter's
progress, the love between father and daughter communicated simply
through the act of a young girl reading aloud and delightedly examining her father's pocket watch. The entire sequence possessed extraordinary freshness, flowing effortlessly as the line between actor and
character seemed to blur: Atticus Finch and Gregory Peck, men of
kindness, caring, and unimpeachable morality. Fathers possessed of infinite patience. For nine-year-old Badham, whether on-screen or off,
Gregory Peck remained a fantasy father figure. "It was something I
always wished my father would do with me. It was a warm, wonderful
scene to do," Badham later commented.

Peck's deliberate style, which had failed in *Moby Dick,* was here
perfectly suited to serve as both a check on the children's natural exu-
berance and as an extension of Atticus's own basic personality, in the
process pushing the character to the breaking point but never beyond;
when the judge asks Atticus to defend Tom Robinson, Peck takes a
very long time to answer, and just as the viewer starts to wonder
whether he'll actually respond, he does—simply, quietly, and in the
affirmative.

The entire shoot had by now led up to Tom Robinson's trial,
which would take two complete weeks to film. No detail in the sequence proved too small to analyze, from the look of the judge's bench
to the costumes of principals and extras alike. Discussions ensued
among Rosemary Odell, Collin Wilcox, and Bob Mulligan. Would
Mayella wear high heels in court? Yes, said Wilcox. No, said Mulligan. Yes, she would, replied Wilcox, but with socks. Back and forth
they went. Would the shoes even show? It didn't matter. It simply had

to feel right—for Wilcox and for a beaten-down, abused backwoods woman on her one day in the public eye.

By this point in the film, it is stifling in the courtroom and Atticus Finch is tired—from the heat, the lies, and the hostility of the entire town. He is bloodied but unbowed, and to emphasize that fatigue, Peck deliberately appears with less than perfectly groomed hair. It's a telling detail, given the actor's extraordinarily handsome appearance, drawing attention away from the combination of straight nose, intense gaze, and thick dark eyebrows that immediately draws the viewer's eye. Peck launches into Atticus's minutes-long summation, but halfway through, Mulligan cries, "Cut!"

Director and star confer, the former emphasizing that the material is so inherently emotional that the audience will feel overwhelmed and pummeled if all of the attendant emotions are channeled at the exact same time. Peck regroups, intently studying his handwritten script notes: "Don't hurry. Give it weight." Pull back. Begin again.

And—

"Action!"

It now flows like water off a duck's back. Said Peck, "It's like getting back on the stage. I'd rehearsed a lot at home. Would you believe two or three hundred times?" No matter how many times it was shot, no matter how many different angles employed, Peck relished every last take, shedding his occasional starchiness and thereby commanding the screen without ever trying too hard. So involved was he with the scene, so intense both his real- and reel-life bonds with Brock Peters, that when Peters, now on the witness stand, started to cry, Peck found himself choking up. "I had to stop myself," he said. "We couldn't have both the defendant and the lawyer blubbering all over the courtroom."

Peters, barely glimpsed in the rest of the film, is here transformed into the fulcrum off which the entire film pivots. Mulligan trusted the actor completely, simply leaning in right before the first take and whispering, "There is nothing I can tell you that you don't know about this man. I only know him secondhand, which is hardly any use to you."

There was, in fact, nothing of the victim in Brock Peters, and Tom Robinson's heroic stance in the face of a stacked deck—the verdict of an all-white jury was assured before the trial concluded—afforded his character an additional layer of dignity. Peters's recollection of the racism he had himself faced in life—"I've been kicked, beaten"—heightened his own awareness of the monumental injustice faced by Tom Robinson. "The anger, the isolation, the frustration was an easy place to get to and tap in my performance." The fear, resignation, and outrage felt by any black man railroaded toward injustice in the American South of the 1930s is all there in one close-up of Brock Peters's face.

In fact, for all the collegiality on the set, the trial scene occasioned one of the production's very few tense racial moments, when an assistant director charged with wrangling the extras cried out, "All the colored atmosphere upstairs; all the white atmosphere downstairs." Brock Peters pulled the man aside, talking to him about the offensive nature of his language, after which the direction became "Balcony atmosphere upstairs, please." That incident aside, in an era when racism still lingered in Hollywood, Peters felt at ease on the *Mockingbird* set, appreciating the dedication found in all departments, the silence that ruled without the need for continual shouts of "Quiet!" As Peters said, "It gave the working actor a sense of contributing something important." When commenting on the experience years later, he expanded on this theme: "We didn't know how successful the film would be, but somehow or other when we came onto the set, we all worked hard to achieve what we felt that story carried with it."

It wasn't just the actors who felt pride in working on a prestigious adaptation of a Pulitzer Prize–winning novel. Members of the crew felt they had been handed a chance to help make a film that spoke truth about life in twentieth-century America, and they reacted with an enthusiasm unusual among hardened Hollywood veterans. Harper Lee, fascinated by the sight of the crew bringing in huge trees and setting them in place for outdoor scenes, proved distinctly amused when Mulligan remarked, "We need a knothole in that tree," and an assistant director instantly piped up, "I've got one at home. I'll bring it in tomorrow." Even more than the fact of an assistant director having a false knothole lying handy at home, the novelist was astonished that a member of the production team so enthusiastically volunteered to bring in this highly unusual piece of set dressing. Where were the jaded do-the-minimum-and-nothing-more crew members she had heard about?

It came time to film the climactic scene of Boo's first appearance on-screen, and Duvall nailed the scene on the first take, underplaying by instinct. "Horton's work is very delicate . . . you can't push it along," the actor explained. In Boo's case, actions spoke louder than words, and Duvall's wondering, unguarded eyes conveyed acres of information without a single word being spoken. Duvall knew the scene worked well—better than well—with every element coming together in that rare sought-after moment when an actor completely subsumes his identity into that of his character. "As I touched the boy I had goose pimples and I knew I was on the right track. I could do nothing wrong," Duvall commented later.

When, near the end of Lee's novel, Boo whispers to Scout, "Will you take me home?", she holds out her hand and together they walk in companionable silence to the Radley house. On-screen, no dialogue is even necessary; Scout slips her hand into the crook of Boo's arm, and as she walks him home, his journey from monster to protector is now complete, the metamorphosis highlighted by Scout's momentary role as his guardian angel. For the first time, Scout now fully grasps Atticus's dictum that you can never really know a man until you stand in his shoes and walk around in them. Now and forever after, she understands that "just standing on the Radley porch was enough." She can guide Boo through her own house, and even walk him back to the Radley place, but, in her own words, "I would never lead him home."

Filming progressed nearly on schedule, but as Universal executives watched the dailies, they sent a stream of reports to Pakula reporting their displeasure. Peck was looking too old. Where was the handsome movie star who drew women to the box office? A rumpled suit? Glasses? The order was given: Make him look more like a movie star, for God's sake. He's Gregory Peck, not Slim Pickens. Bad enough that the movie contained no romance and virtually no action, but did Peck have to look so, well, awful? Pakula read the memos and never once relayed their content to Mulligan. The hell with the executives. Pakula thought the rushes looked great: funny, touching, and, in some cases, a straight shot to the heart.

In fact, the more Pakula looked at the dailies, the more excited he became over the manner in which Mulligan had shot the shocking events after the trial: When Atticus learns that Tom Robinson has been shot while trying to escape from jail, Mulligan avoids the temptation to milk the horrible news with reactions of outrage and crumbling body language. Instead, as Atticus delivers the news to others, the director filmed Peck from the back, the actor glimpsed only in partial profile. In Mulligan's words, the reverse perspective was "the only way that satisfied." The direct close-up is eschewed. The viewer will come to the character.

Pakula was happy—no, more than happy—he was as close to ec-static as his low-key nature would allow him to be. Key sequences now unfolded on-screen with even greater-than-hoped-for power; in Mulligan's hands, it's the judicious use of silent but telling small de-tails that tell the story and add texture. When Scout and Jem express astonishment at the unexpected discovery that Atticus, who holds no interest in guns (that most traditional southern measure of man-hood), turns out to be the best shot in the county, capable of dispatch-ing a mad dog with a single shot, Mulligan manages to find the precise visual equivalent of Lee's prose: When the mad dog appears on the street, there is no overt change in Atticus's speech, actions, or even his clothes. He merely drives home from work still dressed in his suit and vest, pushes his glasses up on his forehead, aims the shotgun, and dis-patches the dog with a single shot. The contrast between the dignified attire and the task at hand makes this unexpected turn of events all the more startling. Jem and Scout are flummoxed—their sober, suit-wearing father is a sharpshooter? Yes—but there is never any discussion about it. The ways of adults remain ever puzzling.

Harlan and Bumstead were, of course, responsible for the look of the film, but it was Mulligan's background in live television that proved invaluable in placing the near-palpable feel of Maycomb directly on-screen. In order to convey the essence of a town where personal secrets and racial animus bubble right beneath the surface, Mulligan deliberately uses pauses, empty spaces, and a periodic sense of remoteness from the actors that echoes the style of golden-age live television—in Mulligan's terms, a clean style of "staging long scenes and not being afraid of it." Scout's puzzlement over the distance between actions and words, her dawning realization that adults are often wrong and don't say what they mean, is skillfully—and silently—conveyed by means of the distances glimpsed on-screen.

While Mulligan directed, Pakula purposefully stayed away, occasionally coming onto the set to confer, but nothing more. Said Pakula, "I would tell actors, 'Look, when I come on the set, it's to talk to Bob; if I don't mention what I thought of yesterday's dailies, it doesn't mean I don't like them. Don't worry about me; forget about me. . . .' I made myself stay away from the set. I wasn't going to direct through Bob." In a stance directly opposite from that adopted by the legendarily obsessive David O. Selznick, producer Pakula offered advice but never interfered, and as a result, Mulligan trusted Pakula's opinions all the more. The rapport between the two men proved to be so easygoing that, according to Pakula, "One of my favorite parts of the day was to meet at the end of the day and just kibbitz about where we were. Free-associate and let the picture roll over us—where does it seem to be."

Weeks of shooting speed by, actors, director, producer, and crew all a part of what appears to be a beautifully oiled machine, until it is time to film the very last scene on the schedule: Atticus guarding Tom Robinson at the jailhouse. So caught up is Mary Badham in her cocoon of fun and belonging—of connection—that she purposely blows her lines in order to delay the inevitable end of filming. Cosseted, the center of attention, treated with kindness by Peck and Mulligan as well as the wardrobe ladies, gaffers, and propmen, Badham has acquired a new family she doesn't want to lose. Take after take is deliberately ruined, until her mother finally takes her off to her dressing room and lays down the law: "I don't know what's going on with you, but you better get yourself together. Do you know what the freeway is like at five o'clock? These people have to go home." After she tells Mary, "Let's get this done and get it over with. You're a professional now," the scene is shot one more time, Badham executes her lines flawlessly, and—

"Cut!"

Just like that, the filming of *To Kill a Mockingbird* is over. Over, that is, except for one last piece of business. Throughout the filming, Peck has actually allowed the children to spray him with squirt guns whenever costumes wouldn't be ruined, but now, after that final cry of "Cut," Peck steps aside and the overhead crew pours water onto the heads of the children, bringing laughter in the midst of their sadness—the Finch family is breaking apart forever.

Principal photography, which had lasted a mere twelve weeks, officially ended on May 3, 1962, only eight days behind schedule, and just in time to avoid problems resulting from Alford's growth spurt: From the day of signing his contract until the end of filming, he had grown from four eleven to five three, a spurt complete with an ever-lowering voice.

Pakula and Mulligan now went to work assembling a rough cut with editor Aaron Stell—"a man with a great passion for film," in Mulligan's admiring words. If, in Stell's hands, Scout's incredulous reaction to the syrup-pouring Walter Cunningham very quickly alerts the audience to the social and economic stratification found within the town, it is in the rough cut of the penultimate sequence where Stell's work shines even more brightly: When Scout first encounters Boo Radley and murmurs, "Hey, Boo," the effect is not just powerful, but even a bit breathtaking, a shorthand version of "We're all equal." Nine-year-old Mary Badham has captured all of the necessary emotion with a perfectly calibrated look of wonder as she encounters the bogeyman of her imagination in her very own house. Director Mulligan was thrilled with the result: "[I was] so happy with the 'Hey, Boo' moment that leaving dailies I wanted to run down the street like the kids!" Scout's realization that putting Boo in jail "would be like shooting a mockingbird" is underplayed beautifully, and a potentially saccharine moment of moralizing remains all the more powerful because of its understatement.

As editing progressed and scenes were refined—chopped here, elongated there—one stumbling block began to loom ever larger. The entire ten-minute sequence in which Jem reads to the morphine-addled Mrs. Dubose (Ruth White) as punishment for destroying her camellias, was causing unexpected problems. On the one hand, White was terrific, the sequence was appropriately atmospheric, and lent a bit of southern gothic to leaven the sentiment. For those examining the thematic underpinnings, the scene even raised the interesting question of whether Atticus has betrayed a client's confidence by telling his children that Mrs. Dubose is a morphine addict. But the sequence threw the film entirely off course. There was no time for this meandering side trip, no matter how flavorful the "love your enemies" lesson. The plot needed to build slowly, inexorably, to the trial, and this sequence now unbalanced the film; at a crucial moment in the story, Scout had disappeared completely. Stell looked at Mulligan, Mulligan at Pakula, and the decision was unanimous: The entire sequence had to be cut.

Ruth White's days of spending four hours in makeup had all been for naught, and eventually all that would remain of her performance was a quick shot of the cantankerous Mrs. Dubose yelling at the children. Mulligan gently explained the decision to White—a potential career-making opportunity had vanished. "She could have easily been nominated for supporting actress. . . . I was full of apologies for years whenever I saw Ruth," Mulligan recalled. Like the coveted cut scenes from Orson Welles's *The Magnificent Ambersons* or George Cukor's *A Star Is Born*, White's scenes have seemingly disappeared forever. The frustration *Mockingbird* fans felt over the lost footage only heightened the desire to find them; in the twenty-first century, they would be included as extras on a DVD, but in 1962 they were left on the cutting room floor.

Stell, Pakula, and Mulligan continued to edit, and found themselves particularly pleased by cinematographer Harlan's work. Utilizing softer lighting in the film's earlier sequences of the children at play, he imperceptibly darkens the look of the film until, when Atticus guards the jail, Maycomb is covered in harsh shadows. Harlan's feel for the South was instinctive—in *Ruby Gentry,* he had filmed the post–Civil War South in a meticulous style that vividly contrasted prosperity with poverty—and something in his eye inherently captured the languorous, dusted world of the small-town Depression-era South. Whatever else the merits of the finished film, Stell, Pakula, and Mulligan now knew that it would look absolutely authentic.

A rough cut was delivered to Peck on June 18, 1962, a mere six weeks after the end of filming, and after intently studying the film, the star/producer fired off a memo to both his agent, George Chasin, and Universal executive Mel Tucker, enumerating his forty-four points of concern. Most prominent among them: too much footage of the children and not enough of Atticus. "Atticus has no chance to emerge as courageous or strong . . . the cutting generally seems completely antiheroic where Atticus is concerned, to the point where he is made to be wishy-washy. Don't understand this approach."

A second cut was delivered by Mulligan and Stell. It was better. In fact, it was much better, but in a second memo, dated July 7, the actor still stated, "In my opinion, the picture will begin to look better as Atticus's story line emerges, and the children's scenes are cut down to proportion." Peck may have been a gentleman, but he was also a savvy star protecting his own territory. In the end, a compromise was reached; the first half of the film would tilt in favor of the children's story, but as soon as the movie gathered momentum and headed toward the trial, Atticus would take center stage. In mathematical terms, approximately 15 percent of the novel is devoted to the Atticus-centric trial, but in the film, that percentage would now more than double. The end result? The takeaway image from the film is Gregory Peck heroically standing in the courtroom, a white-suited principled man of the highest morality.

With a rough cut as his guide, composer Elmer Bernstein began working on the score, constantly starting and stopping as he struggled to find the right tone. He had utilized screeching brass to depict the jangled world of dope addict Frankie Machine in *The Man with the Golden Arm,* a solution that struck him as both obvious and winning, but how was he to convey the inner world of a six-year-old girl? He certainly trusted his instincts; in fact, when asked to score *12 Angry Men,* he quickly realized that since the dialogue heard in the jury room constituted virtually the entire film, the film didn't need any music, and as a result, he talked himself out of a job. On *Mockingbird,* however, he was faced with a different sort of problem; any sort of morality-thumping, "This is an important moment" score would instantly tear apart the fabric of the film. He remained stymied, writing and discarding various themes until, in a flash, he understood that he needed to focus on the "quiet magic of the children's world."

The proper notes came to him as a series of subtle, fragile, bell-like tones, beginning with one finger pressing down the keys on a piano, just as a child would pick out a tune. He started with the high registers on the piano, echoing their sound with the addition of woodwind and harp. With a spare use of strings, it played out as both pensive and memory-laden, and when supplemented by the humming of a child, it made for a lyrical sweet/sad score. Said Mulligan, "The first time I heard the theme I was home on a Sunday. Elmer called me and said, 'I want you to listen to something.' He played the theme over the telephone and I've never forgotten the sound of this theme over the telephone."

Bernstein utilized a variation of this main theme during Scout and Jem's wondering nighttime conversation about their mother, but he continued to switch tone and instruments for the more action-oriented sequences of the film; after a frightened but determined Scout knocks on the front door of the Radley home, she immediately runs away, while, in the nicely worded phrase of the soundtrack liner notes, "the trombones pursue her back to the safety of her house." An angry theme of foreboding for Bob Ewell, a churchlike string-laden passage at the announcement of Tom Robinson's guilt, dark, jangling, discordant notes as Jem and Scout are attacked while walking home alone at night—themes were laid in with great specificity as to the instruments in the forefront: piano for the children, solo violin for Boo, and clashing woodwinds for Bob Ewell. Excited by the beauty of Lee's story, Bernstein was drawing upon the full range of his compositional skills to craft a score that he forever after termed "one of my personal favorites . . . I continue to have tremendous feeling for the movie."

With Bernstein's work completed, the score was laid in over Stell's final edit, at which point Universal weighed in once again; the entire film had been budgeted at an astonishingly low two million dollars, and with the studio still looking upon the movie as a small art film, they wanted to make cuts in the final edit. They would have done so if not for Gregory Peck's contract, which contained the ironclad guarantee that Pakula and Mulligan had the right to final cut. Universal was stymied, and Horton Foote pronounced himself extraordinarily grateful to the star: "I think he saved the picture because Universal didn't like it much, but they couldn't touch it. I think they would have slashed it all to pieces."

Designs were drafted for an ad campaign, but there was difficulty in finding the one piece of art that captured the film's appeal at a single glance. One version after another was discarded until it was decided that the approach would be one of back to basics: The film's literary pedigree would be emphasized at the very top of the poster. Spelled out within a yellow strip that ran the entire width of the advertisement were words placed on two lines:

The most beloved and widely read Pulitzer Prize
Winner now comes vividly alive on the screen!

Directly underneath, against a brown background depicting the trunk of a tree, lay a jagged-edged cutout image of Gregory Peck as Atticus. Peck's image would be placed just above a torn-in-two children's drawing of a bird, with crayons and marbles placed right on top of the artwork. Beneath the children's drawing lay the words:

To
kill a
Mockingbird
starring
GREGORY PECK

A yellow band at the bottom bookended that at the top, this one filled with credits for actors, director, screenwriter, author, composer, and producer. The message was clear: loving, warm, serious. And a Pulitzer Prize Winner to boot.

Still not convinced of the film's box-office potential, Universal made plans to market it by releasing it into small theaters in large cities. Once again, Peck exercised his star/producer prerogative; eyeing a general release date of February 14, 1963, the star insisted that the film's premiere be held at the highest-profile theater in the United States, New York City's Radio City Music Hall, before spreading out into large-scale first-run theaters throughout the country.

First up, however, even before the film could open in Los Angeles on Christmas Day of 1962 for a one-week Academy Award–qualifying run, came a specially arranged screening for members of Congress and the nine justices of the United States Supreme Court. Hoping for a triumphant evening of enlightened liberalism, Pakula and Mulligan instead faced an artistic disaster when the lab that had processed the film handed Pakula a damaged print. Instead of beautifully textured scenes painted with light by Russell Harlan, the audience of political heavyweights was greeted with "a study in grays," all of which added up to a washed-out mess.

There was no way to salvage the evening, but with all future prints corrected, the filmmakers prepared the publicity machine for the fast-arriving release on Christmas Day of 1962. At which point, the intensely private Nelle Harper Lee did something completely unexpected and out of character: Professing herself absolutely thrilled with the respectful, loving attention lavished upon her novel—"I think it's one of the best translations of a book to film ever made"—she agreed to talk to the ever-invasive, sensation-seeking, fact-misinterpreting press. The question of whether or not the rest of the country would like the movie remained up for grabs, but for perhaps the first time in the history of the film industry, this was one Pulitzer Prize–winning novelist who remained thrilled with Hollywood.

10

ON SCREENS AROUND THE WORLD

I can only say that I am a happy author. They have made my story into a beautiful and moving motion picture. I am very proud and very grateful.

—Harper Lee

Nelle Harper Lee's willingness to speak to the press on behalf of the film was a surprise not just because she disliked attention from the press, but also because by now she had begun to actively shun it. Weighed down by the avalanche of publicity that had surrounded the publication of her book, she had stopped answering her fan mail months earlier, after just one day's delivery had brought her sixty-two letters. Replying to each one was turning into a full-time job, and Nelle wanted to begin writing again. Enmeshed in planning an entire series of new novels, she was simply no longer interested in granting interviews, a stance that caused Truman Capote to comment, "I wish she could relax and enjoy it more: in this profession it's a long walk between drinks."

By this time, Truman was exhibiting more than a little jealousy over Nelle's Pulitzer Prize, leading Alice Lee to state, "Truman became very jealous because Nelle Harper got a Pulitzer and he did not. . . . It was not Nelle Harper dropping him. It was Truman going away from her." In later years, Nelle herself simply stated, "I was his oldest friend and I did something Truman could not forgive: I wrote a novel that sold. (Never mind its content—I doubt that he ever understood what was in it.)" Writing to Alvin and Marie Dewey, their mutual *In Cold Blood* Kansas friends, Truman, in the most patronizing tone possible, referred to Nelle as "dear little Nelle." Learning that Nelle had agreed to publicize the upcoming film, he sniffed that she was doing so only because she owned a percentage of the profits. It was, he felt, highly undignified behavior for a serious artist. Never mind that Capote had made sure his own name was prominently mentioned in all publicity regarding the previous year's hit movie adaptation of his *Breakfast at Tiffany's*—no, it was Nelle who was behaving in undignified fashion.

Unaware of her friend's sniping, Nelle agreed to undertake a series of national radio and print interviews in order to let people know she was so pleased with the film that she had already seen it six times. Pakula and Mulligan were more than happy with her participation, but the two men still retained more than a few doubts as to the film's box-office reception. Not about the quality of the film—of that, they were more than certain. Instead, their uncertainty centered around the willingness of the American public to spend money on a film that would inevitably remind them of the present-day newspaper headlines detailing the civil rights struggle roiling the South.

Was their concern justified? Yes, and then some. When, in September 1962, James Meredith had tried to enroll at the University of Mississippi, protesting students had hung the Confederate Stars and Bars—symbol of southern pride and slavery—in place of the flag of the United States. Such was the tenor of the times that a scant four months later, on January 14, 1963—precisely five weeks before the film went into nationwide release—Governor George Wallace of Alabama thundered at his inauguration, "Segregation now, segregation tomorrow, segregation forever." So wide was the political and cultural divide that the Pulitzer Prize–winning author Diane McWhorter later recalled observing the use of fire hoses and police dogs on Birmingham protestors at the very same time that *To Kill a Mockingbird* was premiering in that city. Such behavior was not simply a manifestation of a few ignorant rednecks; it was, rather, mutely sanctioned by men and women of all social strata.

Pinpointing the game-changing principles at play through the prism of *Mockingbird*, McWhorter, who was a grade school classmate of Mary Badham at the time, explained the complicated reactions to watching the film at the time of its release: "By rooting for a black man you are betraying every principle you are raised to believe. What would my father think seeing me fight back these tears? It made me confront the difficulty southerners have in going against people they love." She admitted, "I was upset about being upset," and said in one interview, "I think other classmates had the same reaction, but there were aspects of the film we never really discussed, like the rape." In her book *Carry Me Home*, she wrote, "For the first time, we came face-to-face with the central racial preoccupation of the southern white psyche, the dynamics that justified and ennobled Our Way of Life: the rape of a white woman by a black man."

She told one interviewer, "We saw the movie over and over—after all, our classmate Mary Badham was the star! We saw the movie before we read the book—we were young girls at the time, but by memorizing the dialogue—particularly the scene where Atticus averts the lynch mob—this was our acknowledgment that on some level we really understood what we were seeing. It was a classic experience of cognitive dissonance for white children of the time. Things were not the same as we had been taught. We were becoming aware, one step at a time, and watching the movie provided us with several of those steps. Of course, the segregationists of the time simply doubled down rather than changed. They were like cult leaders who predict the apocalypse, and when it doesn't happen, they just proclaim it will be coming all the more loudly."

Civil rights proved to be the lead story on nearly every nightly newscast, routinely garnering the top spot over both the Cold War and the escalating conflict in Vietnam, and at a time when the movie's release guaranteed increased scrutiny of author Lee's own opinions, she did not shy away from expressing them: "I think Reverend King and the NAACP are going about it in exactly the right way. The people in the South may not like it, but they respect it." In the context of the violent, racially divided South of the early 1960s, these innocuous words proved rather incendiary in the minds of a right-wing white community that felt they signified sit-ins, Freedom Riders, demonstrations, and the horribly misguided liberal pieties of *To Kill a Mockingbird*, the latter of which would now be spread from coast to coast on neighborhood movie screens.

Adding to the uncertainty that Pakula and Mulligan shared about the film's success was the fact that both the very nature of moviegoing and the specific films playing in theaters were undergoing a seismic change. With television now dominating the leisure hours of Americans, free, comfortable entertainment was available seven days a week in one's own living room. If you ventured out of the house now, it was no longer a case of just going to the movies and accepting what was playing because it was available and on the neighborhood screen; instead, you now went to the movies expressly to see one particular film.

Given the options abounding on-screen, could *Mockingbird* strike a chord with moviegoers, or would it seem hopelessly passé? Italian neorealism and French New Wave cinema were acquiring heretofore unheard-of American distribution. *La Dolce Vita, Through a Glass Darkly, Two Women, Shoot the Piano Player,* and *Divorce Italian Style* were competing for viewers with the outstanding but more standard Hollywood fare of *Lawrence of Arabia, Dr. No, The Man Who Shot Liberty Valance*, and Gregory Peck's own *Cape Fear*. Whatever the stylistic differences between these disparate films, all of them seemed a long way from Maycomb, Alabama, in the year 1933.

How, then, would *Mockingbird* be received by the critics? The answer came back quickly: with raves. Said the industry standard-bearer *Variety*, "A major film achievement, a significant, captivating and memorable picture that ranks with the best of recent years." Peck's performance was singled out, garnering him the best industry reviews of his career: "Peck . . . not only succeeds but makes it appear effortless, etching a portrayal of strength, dignity and intelligence."

When the film was accorded its general release in February, the praise continued, led by the often-prickly Bosley Crowther in *The New York Times*: "There is so much feeling for children in the film that has been made from Harper Lee's best selling novel, 'To Kill a Mockingbird' . . . so much delightful observation of their spirit, energy and charm as depicted by two superb discoveries, Mary Badham and Phillip Alford . . ." He did add a caveat that "it comes as a bit of a letdown at the end to realize that, for all the picture's feeling for children, it doesn't tell us very much of how they feel," but by then it didn't matter, for the widely read review ended by simply calling *Mockingbird* "the fine film that Alan J. Pakula and Universal delivered to the Music Hall yesterday."

Additional raves rolled in from other major newspapers, with Leo Mishkin in the *New York Morning Telegraph* enthusing about Peck's "remarkable figure of innate strength and nobility." The performances of the three children were almost universally praised, and the hard-to-please Judith Crist observed in the *New York Herald Tribune* that even given some inherent sentimentality, the film's "stature and lasting substance stem from the beautifully observed relationship between father and children and from the youngsters' perceptions of the enduring human values in the world around them." The overseas critics added to the chorus of praise; this was not just a southern American story, or even an American story, but a universal tale of childhood. The headline in London's *Daily Express* summed up the prevailing reaction: "A Tale of Three Tots Delivers Real Childhood to the Screen."

To be sure, there were naysayers, with the leading members of that fraternity found in the New York–centric trio of Andrew Sarris, Brendan Gill, and Pauline Kael, all three writing in a tone of "we best understand what's at stake here" while slashing away at what they took to be the simplified liberal pieties at the center of the film. While the entire southern portion of the United States seemed to be struggling with the very idea of integration and the right to vote, Sarris, Gill, and Kael, it seemed, simply took it upon themselves to instruct their reading audience in the correct way to analyze the situation.

Sarris, in particular, objected to what he termed the movie's relation of the "Cult of Childhood" to "the Negro Problem," prior to positing that "[b]efore the intellectual confusion of the project is considered, it should be noted that this is not much of a movie even by purely formal standards." A walking encyclopedia of film history, Sarris had already proven himself knowledgeable, indeed erudite, and did, in fact, adroitly analyze the faults he found with the adaptation in purely cinematic terms. The problem with his criticism, however, lay in how he undercut his own argument by referring to Foote's script as a "fuzzy digest" of Lee's book. Whatever else the script was, a fuzzy digest it was not.

Sarris certainly raised interesting points along the way: "The Negro is less a rounded character than Liberal construct, a projection of the moral superiority Negroes supposedly attain through their suffering and degradation. . . . It is too late for the Negro to act as a moral litmus paper for the white conscience." Valid points indeed, yet Sarris once again indulged in overkill: In writing "When the Negro is convicted on evidence of a flimsiness sufficient to acquit Trotsky in a Stalinist court," he conveniently forgot that trials in the rural South in the 1920s and 1930s oftentimes were conducted in just such a manner, that Italian-Americans were lynched in New Orleans on just such flimsy evidence, and that the teenaged Emmett Till had lost his life for the mere act of supposedly whistling at a white woman.

Writing after Peck won the Academy Award for Best Actor, Pauline Kael reported that after the actor's win "there was a fair amount of derision throughout the country: Peck was better than usual, but in that same virtuously dull way." In the process, the brainy Kael leaves one wondering, as always, about the underpinnings of her bold assertions. How exactly did she measure such "derision throughout the country"? By conducting a scientifically sound poll across all fifty states? By traveling cross-country herself in order to gauge the exact amount of that derision? Or, perchance, was she in fact referring to her own small circle of white, educated, New York–centric friends?

Brilliant as she was, Kael never did respond favorably to anything she considered remotely "square"—her animus toward *The Sound of Music* three years later fairly dripped off the page. The sheer sentiment of a *Sound of Music* or *Mockingbird*—or more likely, what she perceived to be the sheer middle-class sentimentality of the piece—is what appeared to horrify her. But, as one commentator answered by placing *Mockingbird* in rather heady company, sentiment was precisely the point: "Neither *Great Expectations*, *King Lear*, nor *To Kill a Mockingbird* could be accused of hiding their sentiments." It is in the deliberate choice of the word *sentiment* that the key lies: Yes, *Mockingbird* deals with sentiment, but almost never with sentimentality. There is, in fact, little that is sentimental about a novel dealing with race, rape, and the death of three major characters, but in her zealous rush to judgment, Kael seemingly lost the forest for the trees.

The final member of the New York City trio dismissing *Mockingbird*, Brendan Gill of *The New Yorker,* seemed never to have met a racial issue he didn't want to address from his lofty perch of white liberalism. Discussing Sidney Poitier, he actually wrote, "It must be irritating for the American Negro," making it sound as if he had a direct pipeline to the thought processes of the entire African-American community. (Gill wasn't alone among cultural commentators in his wildly misguided assumptions; in August 1967, at the height of the controversy over William Styron's *The Confessions of Nat Turner*, the *New York Times* described the white, patrician Styron as "an expert in the Negro condition.") Snorting about Bob Ewell's death, Gill wrote, "The moral of this can only be that while ignorant rednecks mustn't take the law into their own hands, it's all right for nice people to do so."

It's not that these criticisms lack validity, because like any film, *To Kill a Mockingbird* contains a number of flaws. But in the rush to appear made of finer intellect than those who would embrace such middlebrow fare, these commentators indulged in rhetorical overkill, afraid to let their interesting ideas speak for themselves.

Such critical carping was in the minority, however, and in any event, it did not matter greatly; the box office soared at both Radio City Music Hall and theaters across the country, ultimately registering a gross of $13,128,846, or roughly $100 million in today's money. It was a more than stellar box-office return for a very small black-and-white period piece containing virtually no romance, sex, or violence.

As the film's release spread across the nation in February 1963, the news grew even better. The movie netted Golden Globe nominations for Best Picture and Director, and wins for Peck as Best Actor and Bernstein for Best Original Music Score; there was even a special award as the Best Film Promoting International Understanding, recognition that allowed *Mockingbird* to follow in the footsteps of the visitor from outer space film *The Day the Earth Stood Still*. Two prestigious British Academy of Film and Television Arts (BAFTA) nominations for Best Film and Best Foreign Actor soon followed, but even these were topped by the biggest prize of all—eight Academy Award nominations.

In a year filled with extraordinary films—*Lawrence of Arabia, The Miracle Worker, Days of Wine and Roses, The Man Who Shot Liberty Valance, What Ever Happened to Baby Jane?* and *The Manchurian Candidate*—*To Kill a Mockingbird* stood out by virtue of its multiple prestigious nominations: Best Picture, Best Actor (Gregory Peck), Best Supporting Actress (Mary Badham), Best Cinematography, Black and White (Russell Harlan), Best Original Music Score (Elmer Bernstein), Best Art Direction/Set Decoration, Black and White (Alexander Golitzen, Henry Bumstead, and Oliver Emert), Best Director (Robert

Mulligan), and Best Adapted Screenplay (Horton Foote). How much of the ballyhoo did Badham comprehend? Very little, and it didn't matter. "I don't think there was any clue that I had as to what it all meant. Later I had a better understanding of it," she said. At the time of the nominations, it was Peck who came up with the cleverest reaction to the good news, quickly firing off a witty telegram to a delighted Harper Lee: "Dear Harper, Congratulations on your eight nominations for the Academy Awards."

When the big night of April 8, 1963, arrived, the ceremony began with the technical awards. Best Art Direction/Set Decoration was awarded early on, and provided a big win for Bumstead, Golitzen, and Emert over the mammoth *The Longest Day* and the searing *Days of Wine and Roses*. It was in some ways an unexpected prize, and left the *Mockingbird* team wondering if there might just be a chance that their film could win the biggest prize of all, Best Picture?

Any such thoughts were dashed when Russell Harlan's balanced, muted cinematography lost the prize to the thundering *Longest Day*, and Mary Badham lost the Best Supporting Actress award to the sixteen-year-old Patty Duke, who won for her performance in *The Miracle Worker*. In many ways, Badham's category proved the toughest of the entire night, with the youngster competing not just against Duke but also the veterans Shirley Knight (*Sweet Bird of Youth*) and Angela Lansbury (*The Manchurian Candidate*). Badham's reaction to losing? "An enormous amount of relief." She had no speech prepared, and years later she stated, "Patty Duke was absolutely brilliant in *The Miracle Worker*."

Bernstein lost the award for Best Original Music Score to Maurice Jarre's sweeping work on *Lawrence of Arabia,* but a cheer went up among the *Mockingbird* team when Horton Foote's screenplay won out over an extraordinary group of fellow nominees, including the estimable Vladimir Nabokov for *Lolita,* as well as the favored duo of Robert Bolt and Michael Wilson for *Lawrence of Arabia*. What made Foote's win particularly memorable was not just that he was three thousand miles away from the ceremony, at his home in Nyack, New York, but that when presenter Bette Davis announced "Horton Foote for *To Kill a Mockingbird*," the pajama-clad Foote was not even watching the telecast. "We were sitting in my son's room who had the only television in the house, and my oldest son had gotten disgusted and said, 'Well, *Lawrence of Arabia* is getting everything,'" Foote recalled. With the set turned off, in those pre-Internet days Foote only found out about his win when the phone began ringing and neighbors stopped by to convey congratulations. The quiet Horton Foote now found himself the first Academy Award–winning screenwriter to be based in Nyack, New York.

Mulligan, not unexpectedly, lost the Best Director award to David Lean for his brilliant work on *Lawrence of Arabia*, the British auteur recognized for his seamless melding of personal story and epic canvas. But there were whoops of delight when Peck was announced as the very popular winner of Best Actor, and his win went a long way toward cushioning the sting of *Mockingbird*'s somewhat expected loss of the Best Picture award to the panoramic *Lawrence of Arabia*.

Upon hearing his name called by Sophia Loren, a delighted Peck leapt up from his seat, bounded to the stage, and instantly thanked Harper Lee. His was a popular win; respected within the Hollywood community, Peck had won for a film embraced by all of filmland. *Mockingbird*'s trio of wins had, in fact, allowed Hollywood to do what it has always done best—pat itself on the back, in this case for its enlightened views on race relations. The win had also proved that a small, delicate story, filmed on a spartan budget and only grudgingly supported by its releasing studio, could still reach an audience clear across the country. Indeed, such was the tensile strength of Lee's basic material that the film's Academy Awards, handed out in front of a viewing audience of tens of millions on the year's highest-rated television program, once again substantially boosted sales of Lee's monumentally popular bestseller.

Peck, Mulligan, Pakula, and Harper Lee were thrilled by *Mocking-*

bird's prizes. Their baby—and the film did feel that personal to the foursome—had won three prestigious Academy Awards, and cemented both the success of the film's worldwide release, and its place in the public eye as a first-class and "worthy" piece of filmmaking.

The question was, Did the film really deserve such respect?

A STRAIGHT SHOT TO THE HEART

As far as I'm concerned, that part is Greg's for life. I've had many offers to turn it into musicals, TV, or stage plays, but I've always refused.
That film was a work of art, and there isn't anyone else who can play
the part. I was one of the luckiest people in the world. . . . I know what
Gregory Peck, the gifted and consummate professional, brought to
the part—he included himself.

—Harper Lee

We weren't setting out to change the world, to put an end to racial
bigotry. . . . Our objective was to tell the story the way Harper wrote
it. And hope that it would entertain people, move people, and that
they'd leave the theater with something to think about.

—Gregory Peck

Very few great American novels have ever been turned into similarly
great films; no extraordinary film adaptations of Fitzgerald, Heming-
way, Melville, Wharton, or Faulkner have ever seen the light of day.
Exceptions to this rule do occasionally turn up, most notably in John
Ford's 1939 adaptation of *The Grapes of Wrath,* a movie that proved

not only the inherent strength of the underlying source material but also that John Ford was every bit as gifted a director as John Steinbeck was a novelist.

There is also the unique example of Margaret Mitchell's *Gone with the Wind,* which, whatever one thinks of its merits as a book, won the Pulitzer Prize, still sells thousands of copies per year a full eight decades after publication, and in 1939 became an extraordinary landmark motion picture, winning numerous Academy Awards in 1940. Its antediluvian racial politics aside, it remains one of the very few old films—*Citizen Kane* is another—that general audiences today do not treat in a condescending "Oh, isn't this charming" fashion. It remains a technically accomplished, visually stunning adaptation that does, in fact, succeed on its own purely cinematic terms. (In fact, the similarities between Harper Lee and Margaret Mitchell remain striking, most notably in the fact that both women wrote Pulitzer Prize–winning novels of the South, before experiencing such overwhelming and unceasing public attention that the success of the novels turned into albatross as much as triumph.)

To this very short list of triumphant film adaptations, however, can be added *To Kill a Mockingbird,* a Pulitzer Prize–winning novel that, thanks to the skills of Horton Foote and Robert Mulligan, had been turned into a film that remained faithful to the spirit of the book while succeeding on its own purely cinematic terms. In the words of film historian Jeanine Basinger, "It's very hard for film adaptations of popular books to fully come to life, in part because audiences already have a preconceived notion of how the story should look in their heads. On top of that, *Mockingbird* was a book which wasn't just popular—it was already beloved. And yet, in quite a few ways, this adaptation really does measure up. Great credit must be given to Horton Foote and Robert Mulligan."

Mulligan's sensitivity and attention to detail is apparent from the very start, with an opening sequence that immediately draws the viewer into the idiosyncratic world of childhood. A piano is heard before any imagery appears on-screen, a child hums, and her hands find a treasure trove of random objects secreted away in an old cigar box—a skillful foreshadowing of the soon-to-be-intermingled worlds of Boo, Scout, and Jem. The sound of a ticking clock is laid in, softly augmented by flute and harp as a child's black-and-white marbles strike each other (a viewer paying strict attention can see the reflection of a crew member in one of the marbles). Small groups of solo instruments are then added, the sound of a music box succeeded by that of a solo clarinet. The excitement and curiosity, as well as the sense of longing inherent in a child's view of the world, are all captured here—what will become the major musical theme for the children has been introduced.

It actually strikes the viewer as natural that the film is unfolding in black and white, not because of any budgetary constraints, but because the entire story plays out as a memory piece in which Scout's journey toward adulthood begins in black-and-white certainty, before ending in appropriately gray ambiguity. The dust from the unpaved streets, the perspiration dripping down faces, the creaky porches of the faded houses—thanks to Bumstead, Golitzen, and Emert, viewers have landed smack in the middle of Depression-era Alabama. As Mulligan would remark in later years, so realistic were the settings that for decades after, people would insistently tell him they knew exactly where the film had been shot, because they knew that very town intimately. The film's extraordinary production design unquestionably played a significant role in the popularity of the film; just as children want to hear the same story over and over with every single phrase intact, so, too, did this familiar-looking setting reassure.

Unafraid to take its time, the movie opens with the camera panning over trees, the sound of birds coming to the forefront as Kim Stanley's beautifully judged narration begins. Few films in the twenty-first century utilize voice-over—it's as if we're all too cynical to accept such direct storytelling. But here the narrator is telling us a story that has already happened, and in its backward glance the narration works beautifully—simultaneously wistful and knowing, the marriage of the visual and narrative striking the elegiac tone key to the film's affect: a sense memory of the way we were. Stanley murmurs the first line of the film—"Maycomb was a tired old town, even in 1932 . . . when I first knew it"—and the viewer begins drifting back in time.

Foote's opening smartly utilized Lee's own words, a choice that immediately reassured the millions who had already read and loved the book as to both the film's authenticity and the fact that no wholesale liberties were going to be taken with an already-beloved story. Moviegoers remembered these deceptively low-key but intricately developed phrases, and in effect released a collective sigh of contentment upon hearing them: Audiences instinctively felt that they were in good hands. The opening works not just because of Stanley's perfectly modulated voice (most critics and audiences loved Stanley's narration, although a minority opinion is struck by Lee's good friend Diane McWhorter, who notes, "Stanley's voice doesn't sound like Harper Lee's—like the grown-up Scout. She's too much the gracious lady and not a firebrand"). It also works because the novel's narration, from which these opening words were adapted, itself reads like a voice-over, one addressed directly to the reader. Jean Louise is casting a backward glance at Scout, the young girl trying to puzzle out the ways of the adult world—a youngster both like and unlike any other. As soon as moviegoers hear the wonder and weariness held in Kim Stanley's voice, they know that this adult version of Scout has experienced both great elation and sadness in her life—it's all present in the inflection. Said director Mulligan, "From that very voice I believe that Scout has grown up to be a writer." In fact, so perfectly judged is Stanley's narration that audience members often find themselves wishing there were more of it, not only because of the actress's soothing voice but also because further narration would have reinforced the movie from Scout's perspective, rather than the Atticus-centric version that ultimately plays out in the second half of the film.

Mary Badham then swings into view on a rope, an overall-wearing girl who runs like a boy and is hell-bent on a direct line into the action. No prissy southern belle, she's the Scout of every reader's imagination, and through Mulligan's adroit use of low camera angles, the viewer is drawn into a world that unfolds from her six-year-old point of view. The children remain the chief protagonists throughout the first half of the movie, but so skillful is the camerawork and Aaron Stell's editing, that when the transition to their role as observers occurs at the trial, the switch in perspective remains nearly seamless.

From the start, it is apparent that Horton Foote has successfully captured the mood and tone of the novel. When Jem announces that he won't come down from the tree until Atticus says he'll play football for the Methodists, Atticus's two-word response is a matter-of-fact and not unkind "Suit yourself"; this low-key response, uttered as he rather laconically moves on to his other activities, tells the viewer acres of information about both his personality and his relationship with his son. Atticus Finch is at home in his own skin, and for all the seriousness of his work, he does not take himself too seriously. He is simply not interested in throwing a football, and won't do so just to please his son. He treats Jem with a respect akin to that exhibited by one adult for another.

Expecting the same courtesy from his son in return, Atticus operates from the belief that every human being, no matter his or her age, is worthy of respect and consideration—the actual cornerstone of a true social network. It's why characters from Horton Foote's nine-play *The Orphans' Home Cycle* could wander over to this Maycomb County, sit down for a spell, and fit right in, because they speak the very same language: considerate, polite, and with oceans of nonverbalized emotions lying right beneath the surface. Both Foote and Lee are interested in digging beneath that veneer of social politeness in order to expose the darkness beneath. In Lee's case, that darkness is wrapped around the gaping wound of racism and the pernicious self-deception that allows the "ladies and gentlemen" of society to countenance the ultimately murderous injustice that swallows Tom Robinson.

For Horton Foote, the darkness is revealed in a pervasive small-town sadness, a loneliness that can quickly tumble into despair when societal and self-inflicted lies alike are actually believed. For both authors, there is a concern that the small-town southern world in which they live is disappearing before their very eyes; at the same time, their shared appreciation of small-town charm and idiosyncratic behavior is bookended with a refusal to accept the lies we tell ourselves, no matter how seemingly attractive their surface. The truth, both authors insist, must be acknowledged and will, in fact, set you free—but always at a price.

As the movie begins to introduce all of the major characters, scenes unfold in sure-footed, near leisurely fashion, framed by long takes that echo the unhurried rhythms of the time. There is no jump-cutting, no MTV-style editing in which one frenzied image leapfrogs over another. Would *Mockingbird* be allowed to unwind in such deliberate fashion today? Would a quiet first-time novel by an unknown author even be granted a major studio release? In a twenty-first century where film executives are more interested in the art of the deal than in the film itself, *Mockingbird,* one suspects, might prove a nonstarter. With studio eyes now trained on the all-important overseas grosses, and when the most successful films are propelled not by incisive dialogue, but, instead, by a frenetic succession of increasingly explosive and nonverbal images, it seems unlikely that the film would find a place in the neighborhood multiplex. Script notes would likely demand a speeded-up pace as well as a romance between Atticus and Miss Maudie, and yet, given half a chance, when today's overstimulated, short-attention-span children are exposed to the film at home, they are emotionally seduced by the slow, steady rhythms of the story. It may take a while, but by the time of the trial, they are hooked.

When a mad dog—a portent of the coming evil of Bob Ewell—arrives on the scene, the movie begins to turn darker. As the tension builds, and Calpurnia calls for Atticus to come home and take care of the mad dog, the sequence ends in a dissolve, a rare misstep, one that forever after haunted director Mulligan. "Why did I dissolve to that?

I should have recut that. I hate dissolves," he later said. It is, in the end, of relatively no import. Atticus fells the dog with a single shot because the man who refuses to hunt turns out to be the best shot in the county. There is amazement on the faces of Scout and Jem and the point has been made: Atticus—any father—maintains layers of mystery even to his own children.

For all of his moral heroism, Atticus remains an everyday man, a single father forging a path while trying to guide his children through the messy affair of growing up. Adults understand Atticus, while children want him to be their father. He is not just identifiable but also attainable; in Hollywood terms, we all may love watching Fred Astaire dance, Frank Sinatra sing, or Cary Grant charm, but we know that we can't even remotely approach their otherworldly skills. Gregory Peck's Atticus, however, embodies a status we think we can attain. In point of fact, we can't—he is nearly flawless, his character unimpeachable, but his import lies in the fact of the audience thinking he is just like us, a slightly better version of our own best selves.

The reason why Atticus's near perfection never grates lies in the on-screen rapport between Peck and Badham. Under Mulligan's gentle guidance, Badham delivers a performance of such ease and spontaneity that she actually helps nudge Peck into a more relaxed than usual performance. Said Jeanine Basinger, "Mary Badham is the antithesis of the cutesy child star. She is fresh and natural. Here you have a child with no experience, sharing the screen with a major Hollywood movie star, but Peck takes his star power and his nobility—his Lincolnesque quality—and fits it right into the milieu. Peck's stiffness—the almost detached quality he could display at times—was softened here, and their rapport is evident. It's clear he knew how to be a father."

The freewheeling nine-year-old and the occasionally constrained, even shy, Peck have combined to create a very touching and believable father-daughter relationship. When Atticus and Scout sit together on the porch, the courtly father telling his tomboy daughter not to get into fights, he holds her oh so tenderly, the camera angle perfectly conveying the contrast between his big hands and her small frame. It is, in fact, when Atticus wraps his all-embracing arm around her shoulder that the audience is not just touched but jolted into a deeper level of identification: In one fatherly gesture, he here conveys all the protection in the world that anyone could ever want. It is this certainty that caused viewers to so embrace the look, sound, and feel of this on-screen world that they yearned to be a part of the scene, to live inside the movie and become Finches themselves. Even as they knew the impossibility of that desire, the wish nonetheless persisted.

If, as seems true, most people remember scattered moments from films they saw as adolescents more than they do the arc of the entire film, this scene represented that singular moment in *Mockingbird,* the instant that took adult viewers back to their own childhoods—both the one longed for and the one actually experienced. Such was the power of the scene that memory and reality now met up in a particularly dizzying spin through time, resulting in a new question: Was the older viewer experiencing the film through a new adult perspective, or willfully falling into a rose-colored remembrance of who he or she was when first watching the film?

This sequence is matched in power by the scene in which Atticus explains to Scout that some day her mother's pearls, a totemic item associated with the parent she barely knew, will be passed along to her. Peck's playing is here so tender and understated that the look of sheer delight on Badham's face is instantly recognizable as that of any child receiving an unexpected piece of wonderful news. Stretching, eyes widening, and about to fall asleep, she is a universal vision of childhood security and contentment.

When Atticus listens from the porch as his children discuss their barely remembered mother, the scene resonates precisely because this most primal of relationships is discussed in the lightest-possible fashion. A young brother and sister are here trying to puzzle out their own places in the world, and while Foote has supplied the words, and Badham and Alford the acting, it is Mulligan who makes the sequence come fully alive; beginning the scene with the camera peering into Scout's bedroom through an open window, he goes on to reverse the perspective when Atticus walks out onto the porch, the better to listen in on his children. Parent–child, protector–eavesdropper—the roles change in the blink of an eye and the reverse of a camera angle as all three Finches attempt to decipher the loving but complex bonds and boundaries of what it means to be a family. In the view of Jeanine Basinger, "Robert Mulligan is a very underrated director. He doesn't have a large body of work, but it is of a very high quality. He has such a strong feeling for place in all of his films that he makes the audience understand the milieu. He really has a poetic feeling of place, and as a result is able to mine the emotional truth at the core of the story."

When Jem looks through his collection of treasures—marbles, pennies, and a broken watch—he is examining a child's entire hidden world. In fact, it is this scene that lodged in the memory of Pakula's Yale friend Stephen Frankfurt when it came time to design the film's title sequence. Frankfurt, who shot that sequence on his own kitchen table with a neighborhood girl whose face we never see, did not actually want to utilize any music during these first two minutes of the film; Pakula, however, insisted that music would prove essential in capturing viewers' interest, and composer Bernstein acquiesced. Taking a minimalist approach through a sparing use of instruments, he elevated the entire sequence into a case study of less is more. Although title songs had just started to increase rapidly in popularity, there was not, fortunately, a theme song heard over the credits, no folksy Burl Ives warbling, "You caint know a man till you walk in his shoes—and it's a sin to kill a mockingbird . . ."

Equaling the stellar work of Bernstein is that of Russell Harlan. So finely wrought is his camerawork that when Atticus is shown facing down a potential lynch mob at the jail, the entire emotional through line of the children's literal and metaphorical search for their father is conveyed through the cinematography alone: The action is photographed from a child's point of view, with the camera held waist-high in order to convey the sense of youngsters moving through a sea of men's legs, their small figures visually overwhelmed by the shadow-filled nighttime street.

Like all children, Scout and Jem want to see what is hidden, and in the process they discover that Atticus is guarding the jail by himself. Without yet fully realizing it, they now comprehend that alone with his book, their father is more of a man than the entire mob of racist townsmen put together. (On-screen, the scene is immediately reminiscent of John Ford's *Young Mr. Lincoln,* in which Henry Fonda's Abraham Lincoln defends men accused of murder by defiantly facing down a lynch mob at the courthouse doors.) When Scout turns the entire (unscored) confrontation upside down by innocently asking, "Don't you remember me, Mr. Cunningham?" a straightforward question that makes Mr. Cunningham and all the other men ashamed of their actions, she has triumphed in a way her father never could have. The camera angle shifts accordingly, and it is Scout, holding the moral high ground, who now seems taller than the men. What took paragraphs to explain on the printed page has been conveyed through a single camera angle.

Interestingly enough, although this climactic jailhouse scene of a lone righteous American quietly defending an innocent man lands with great impact, Peck did not like his own performance in the scene: "I know, if nobody else does, that I played that scene without understanding it and I can see the flaws in the acting. Once you understand a part, then everything falls together without any effort— voice, expression, gestures. When you don't understand it, you bluff through." Did he bluff here? It doesn't look it, but ever the self-critical professional, Peck remained unsatisfied.

Throughout this scene, Atticus, Scout, and Jem have literally been surrounded by near-total darkness, and when Atticus reassures Tom, "They're gone. They won't bother you anymore," the camera is placed at a distance, thereby reinforcing just how alone Atticus and

Tom have been. The screen fades to black—no mistaken dissolve here, as there was at the end of the rabid dog sequence—because Mulligan is deliberately and emphatically punctuating the end of a crucial sequence. Atticus (with the inadvertent help of his children) has bravely faced down a lynch mob, and in his principled stand he has delivered true justice. The scene must end in a blackout because of its contrast with the very next sequence; as the blackout ends, the viewer is jolted into a new awareness as—*bam*—wagons and horses are seen crowding the daytime streets of Maycomb while carrying men and women toward the big social event of the year—Tom Robinson's trial.

That trial contains the highest of stakes, yet Foote and Mulligan have ensured that there is no melodrama on hand. In fact, the sequence succeeds precisely because of what is left out. There is no clichéd snapping of a lawyer's suspenders as he addresses the jury, no "aw shucks" peering over eyeglasses—just one small-town attorney trying to do his best while dealing with a deck stacked against him. The only theatrics come from Mayella Ewell, purveyor of the biggest and most pointed lies of all. In a film with few close-ups, her climactic outburst is shot entirely in close-up, the better to convey her pathetic circumstances. She is scared of testifying, afraid of Atticus, and terrified by her own father, the latter situation not just a result of Wilcox's immersing herself in character, but also a direct outcome of her stealing a single glance at her on-screen father, Bob Anderson: "He scared me to pieces," she said.

Tom, of course, is doomed the minute he says of Mayella, "I felt sorry for her." A black man daring to feel sorry for a white woman? As soon as the words are uttered, Peck's expression changes—a slight but definite movement that conveys his knowledge that the case is now lost. It is one of many small touches from director and actor alike that add to the texture of the trial sequence, which ultimately plays out as a movie within the movie.

Until the courtroom testimony actually starts, the children try to find out what is happening by either peering through windows or scrunching down to view the proceedings through balcony railings. It is only when the actual testimony starts that Mulligan's deliberately child's-eye camera angle changes, with the children now photographed as observers; it is Atticus who has taken over center stage. (Given the subject matter of the trial, Alford, Badham, and Megna were not present during most of that filming, called to the set only for their necessary reaction shots.)

The perspective has changed, and with that decision comes a series of finely detailed moments that successfully enhance the audience's visceral reaction to the film, most notably the camera's revelation that Dill, Scout, and Jem are the only white faces in the segregated balcony of the courtroom. The camera pans and the entire racial stratification found in Maycomb is silently revealed in a matter of seconds. When Dill falls asleep in the arms of the African-American Reverend Sykes, the gentle yet strong performance of Bill Walker as the minister makes the image all the more poignant. Treated as a second-class citizen and relegated to the balcony, the Reverend Sykes still remains concerned for Dill's welfare, a man of the highest morality worth the entire white population seated downstairs.

In another equally effective piece of staging devised by Mulligan and cameraman Russell Harlan, Atticus seems to talk directly to the audience, rather than constantly referring to the jury. It's a calculated risk that pays off in emotional impact, because with Peck shot in the foreground throughout, he remains the very image of what Pakula called "a morally towering" figure in the community.

Mulligan is here carefully building the trial to the moment when the verdict is announced, the audience by now fully outraged that Tom has even been charged for a crime he clearly did not commit. When the verdict is announced, however, Mulligan has Peck underplay the moment, and therefore heightens its effectiveness; Atticus displays absolutely no surprise at hearing the word *guilty*. Screenwriter Foote was following Lee's lead in his depiction of Atticus's reaction, but Mulligan smartly does not succumb to the temptation of having a beloved Hollywood star curry audience sympathy with a calculated display of outrage. Atticus Finch understands his community and knew this verdict was coming. Is he upset? Yes. Surprised? No.

The entire trial, in fact, has been staged with such power that by the sequence's end, a viewer might be forgiven for thinking that Atticus's job is that of a criminal lawyer habitually defending the oppressed, rather than his actual work as an office-bound trusts and estates lawyer.

It is, however, only after the verdict is announced that Mulligan stages the pièce de résistance: As Atticus prepares to leave the courtroom, he does not glance up to the balcony, remaining oblivious to the fact that all of the African-American spectators are standing up in a show of respect for him. He has not defended Tom Robinson for the approval of his black neighbors; he did it because it was the right thing to do, and they know it. In effect trying to shoulder the burdens of the broken world of the South, Atticus has, of course, failed, but his greatness lies in the very act of trying.

Those who criticize the moment as sentimental miss the point that Atticus knew he was going to lose; he understood from the outset that all of his efforts would prove futile in the racist judicial system of the time, but he also had to persist in trying to do the right thing. Atticus's reaction, and Mulligan's staging, guarantee that by film's end, we think of Atticus not so much in terms of what he has accomplished, but, rather, in the light of what his moral code tells us about him. Mulligan and Foote here present Lee's key point in straightforward fashion: Moral courage is usually inconvenient, and any recognition of the courageous nature of the actions most often comes years later, if at all. It all plays out on-screen as if one of John F. Kennedy's eight biographies in *Profiles in Courage* (1957) had been translated to the Alabama of 1933, in the person of Atticus Finch.

As Atticus gathers his papers, the Reverend Sykes states with gentle but unmistakable moral authority, "Miss Jean Louise, stand up. Your father's passin'," and the barest hint of music comes in. Soft strings and a hint of woodwinds provide a variation of the children's theme, but this time with the addition of new harmonies. It is a beautifully judged moment by Bernstein, the music proving all the more startling by coming at the end of a twelve-minute scene free of any background score. (In fact, the entire thirty-five-minute trial sequence is nearly devoid of music, with the exception of a forlorn-sounding solo flute played briefly as the jury leaves to deliberate.) The new harmonies underscore the harsh lesson Jem, Scout, and Dill have just learned firsthand: The world is not a clear-cut universe of black-and-white morality, but, rather, one in which endless shades of gray overwhelm daily life in a mist of memories, half-truths, and deception.

The three children do not comprehend the verdict, and Mulligan's care with the youngsters is here on full display: Dill, attempting to appear worldly but in reality the most fragile of the three, has his arms crossed over his knees, hugging himself in consolation. Jem is not yet able to fathom either the guilty verdict or the irony that at Atticus's "weakest" moment—losing the trial—he has, thanks to his efforts and unimpeachable moral code, become the strongest of men. Instead, Jem buries his face in his arms while trying to listen to Miss Maudie (Rosemary Murphy) state: "There's some men in this world who are born to do our unpleasant jobs for us. Your father's one of them." (Said Rosemary Murphy of filming *Mockingbird,* "You knew you were in something special. It was a fascinating experience. I was very respectful of where I was and thrilled to be there. Gregory Peck was accessible and a real gent.") It's a nicely played scene, illustrative of the fact that it's actually Jem, not Scout, who has the moral conversion in the story; he is older and can comprehend more of what has happened than can Scout. Scout, several years younger than Jem, here fulfills the role of observer, conveying Jem's state of mind to readers and viewers alike. In Jem's inability to accept the outcome, repeating the words "It ain't right" over and over, he appears, in fact, to be speaking for Harper Lee. There is no sermonizing and no overt theatricalization, but the message is clear: Life is unfair. Always has been, always will be.

With the trial concluded, the movie deliberately speeds up. In quick succession, Tom Robinson is killed while trying to escape from jail, and Bob Ewell, full of venom, confronts Atticus at the Robinson home, spitting directly in his face. The camera placement alone conveys Jem's fear of Bob Ewell during this encounter, but Mulligan holds a surprise in reserve: The confrontation between Atticus and Ewell is shot from a respectful distance until the exact moment when Ewell spits in Atticus's face, whereupon—*whoosh*—the camera moves in, underscoring the power of the moment by the surprise of the decision. The interplay of shadow and light, the movement of the camera— Harlan's work here tells the story without a single word being spoken. In Mulligan's words, "Russ Harlan was a joy to work with. He really served the picture. His work was just wonderful."

Harlan's technical expertise certainly heightened the moment, but Peck himself is superb here, revealing his gift for making pacifism read as an act of great courage, in fact as the very essence of heroism. Atticus "wins" the confrontation by simply refusing to fight back and sink to Ewell's level. (It's an action that provides a very interesting parallel to Peck's then recently released *Cape Fear,* in which his character—another attorney—refuses to shoot the killer played by Robert Mitchum. He refuses to react with violence, knowing that the far greater punishment for the killer lies in his having to spend all his remaining days in jail, an unending confinement from which there is no hope of escape.)

With a jump cut immediately following Atticus's confrontation with Ewell, the viewer is propelled forward in time, observing Scout and Jem as they walk to school for a nighttime Halloween pageant, a somewhat disinterested Scout carrying the giant papier-mâché ham she will have to wear in order to help celebrate the agricultural virtues of Maycomb County. Their arrival at school dissolves into a shot of an increasingly impatient Jem waiting for Scout after the pageant, a gently humorous sequence that serves nicely to set up the near-murderous events that follow; Scout, the last person to stumble out of the school's back door, has managed to lose her shoes while inside of her costume, and when the viewer receives their first chuckle-inducing image of Scout trapped inside of the giant ham, the only parts of her that remain visible are her eyes. As Jem tries to guide his encumbered-in-ham sister home, they seem to represent Maycomb's own version of Hansel and Gretel, forging ahead as the path through the woods turns increasingly dark. As they move amid the nighttime shadows and windswept trees, the children's theme first heard during the opening credits is here recapitulated, turning increasingly ominous in tone, until the world turns upside down as Bob Ewell tries to kill both of them. Boo, the supposed monster, saves the children and carries Jem home through the leaf-strewn nighttime streets (Mulligan proudly noted that the superimposed leaves constituted the film's only special effect); it is Boo's presence that melds Scout's fantasy world with that of the harsh adult world, and his childlike sense of what is right and wrong has now positioned him as the true antithesis of the ugly racism permeating Maycomb.

As the light hits Boo square in the face while he hides behind the bedroom door, Scout murmurs an interested, tender greeting of "Hey, Boo." Comprehension has dawned on her: Monsters can be good, and "good" citizens can prove evil. With this two-word greeting, the piano and flute music, which had originally represented Boo and the fear of the unknown, turns into a violin solo, one that, the CD liner notes accurately state, sounds "lyrical." The beauty and fragility of life has been exposed in two words—"Hey, Boo." It's not just Scout who has learned something; the movie includes the entire audience in its steady gaze, because the adult Jean Louise is remembering events from her childhood twenty years earlier. Are there "others" in our own lives? How do we treat them—with Scout's understanding, or as nuisances to be stepped over?

In a lifetime of measured remarks, Atticus has never put more meaning into a sentence than when, after shaking Boo's hand and thanking him for saving the lives of his children, he introduces Scout and Boo to each other, stating with great respect, "Miss Jean Louise, Mr. Arthur Radley." In a nearly perfect blend of actor and character, what the actor Gregory Peck and the character of Atticus Finch both show here is a sense that nothing in life matters more than giving one's word, that a good name is of more import than all the money in the world. What is actually conveyed by calling Boo "Mr. Arthur Radley"? Everything—because at our most vulnerable, when we feel hopelessly adrift, we all want to be treated with the respect Atticus accords Boo. Three words, six syllables. No explanation necessary—and a curtain of difference and noncomprehension falls away.

Duvall, all ghostly pallor and dyed blond hair, had prepared for his scenes by staying out of the sun for six weeks, the better to achieve his albinolike appearance (one termed "angelic" by Pakula). In this, his very first substantive film role, Duvall manages to convey every one of Boo's conflicting emotions—caution, excitement, gratitude, and wonder—without a single word being spoken. It's an early sign of why famed acting teacher Sanford Meisner later stated, "There are only two actors in America. One is Brando, who's done his best work, and the other is Robert Duvall."

Scout's amazement at actually meeting Boo is made all the more powerful by the close-ups Mulligan here accords both Badham and Duvall. Used sparingly until the trial, such close-ups remain all the more powerful in their rarity: Mayella's breakdown in court, Ewell's spitting in Atticus's face, and now Scout's climactic meeting with Boo. All three sequences are filmed in close-up, every one of them successfully heightening the drama.

Sitting side by side on the porch, Scout and Boo look at each other with trust and fondness, until Scout takes his hand and leads her new friend back to his house. Standing on the front porch of the Radleys' house, Scout sees the world, her world, anew—this time from Boo's perspective. For perhaps the first time in his life, Boo feels accepted. There is a profound sweetness to the scene, yet one that does not distort the sadness underlying its reality: Scout and Boo will never see each other again. Boo's acceptance is momentary, but for now that is enough.

As the movie speeds to a close, Mulligan's courage lies in his determination that the film remain quiet; he expects the audience to listen. While those who favor the auteur theory decry Mulligan's lack of a personal signature, his supposedly impersonal style is precisely why *Mockingbird* remains such a rewarding film. Uninterested in drawing attention to himself, he simply wants to tell the story, his work registering as the very embodiment of director Sidney Lumet's assertion that style is simply "the way you tell a particular story." Drawing a distinction between true stylists and what he calls "decorators," Lumet stated, "Critics talk about style as something apart from the movie because they need the style to be obvious. The reason they need it to be obvious is that they don't really *see. . . .* The decorators are easy to recognize. That's why the critics love them so."

As Sheriff Tate and Atticus discuss Boo's actions, the two men remain stationary on the porch, a means of staging that once again forces the audience to listen carefully. The sheriff admonishes Atticus that a black man has been killed for no reason, and that since the man responsible for that tragedy is now also dead, it is time to "let the dead bury the dead." Only at the conclusion of this dialogue do the two men once again move, the power of such stillness underscoring Mulligan's faith in the audience.

In what could be construed as a Christ-like gesture, Atticus has seemingly sacrificed his strict adherence to the law for the good of Boo Radley and the entire town, but looked at in another light, perhaps the near-perfect Atticus has feet of clay after all; he is letting Boo walk home a free man, for the emotionally charged but oh so human reason that Boo has just saved the lives of his children. Just like Scout,

Atticus himself has learned that sometimes you gain and lose at the very same time.

Whatever the life lessons involved, so strongly did *Mockingbird*'s exploration of the notion of heroism land with audiences that Atticus Finch, in the very winning person of Gregory Peck, now became America's favorite father: an idealized and, not coincidentally, completely nonsexual paternal figure. (A few short years later, Sidney Poitier would inherit this same mantle with movies like *To Sir, with Love*.) No sexual tension pervaded the screen—just comfort, wisdom, and an all-embracing sense of protection and paternal wisdom.

Americans actually seemed to feel better about themselves after watching (or reading) *Mockingbird,* believing that they could glimpse themselves as well as their fellow Americans in the figure of Atticus, that they, too, possessed a righteous morality capable of standing up to an entire community. It was largely a fantasy, but such wish fulfillment had, of course, underpinned the Hollywood dream factory since its inception.

If the vast majority of Americans did, in fact, embrace the very notion of *Mockingbird,* with the release of the motion picture a new and troubling undercurrent nonetheless bubbled to the surface; small but insistent, this school of thought asked if *Mockingbird* simply represented another manifestation of white people patting themselves on the back while feeling that they were blessed with a nobility capable of leading African-Americans into the battle against racism.

There was more than a bit of truth in this query, because even in 1963, at the height of the most pitched battles for civil rights, it was clear that it was the Reverend Dr. Martin Luther King, Jr., and generations of black people acting on their own behalf who led the battle for equality, not well-meaning white liberals. Some now asked if Harper Lee even had the right to tell this story: a privileged white woman telling the story of segregation in the South? How could she possibly understand what it felt like to live the life of a second-class citizen? Was *To Kill a Mockingbird* no more than a white fantasia, a feel-good topical solution that in the end never addressed the underlying root causes of the systemic problem? In its well-meaning but, they argued, ineffectual approach, was *Mockingbird*'s soothing "walk a mile in the other man's shoes" solution just making the situation worse?

The question had to be asked: Was *To Kill a Mockingbird* actually racist?

IS *TO KILL A MOCKINGBIRD* RACIST?

To Kill a Mockingbird's publication made invisible the very people it claimed to care about.

—Colin Dayan of Al Jazeera America at the time
of *Go Set a Watchman*'s 2015 publication

Although a small but persistent core of criticism questioning whether *To Kill a Mockingbird* was racist began to raise its head as the popularity of the book and film grew, the novel had powerful and influential fans within the African-American community, chief among them the Reverend Dr. Martin Luther King, Jr. Said Dr. King, "To the Negro in 1963, as to Atticus Finch, it had become obvious that nonviolence could symbolize the gold badge of heroism rather than the white feather of cowardice." In Atticus Finch, Dr. King had recognized a kindred spirit, another man who believed in "the strength of moral force." Dr. King's viewpoint was echoed by Andrew Young, a leader of the civil rights movement and future ambassador to the United Nations, who similarly explained, "*To Kill a Mockingbird* is a book that inspires hope in the midst of chaos and confusion. And those kinds of books last for a long time."

But, as pointed out by Mary Tucker, who taught school in Monroeville, both before and after desegregation, many black people, even in Nelle's hometown, professed no interest in reading the book, and those who did oftentimes disliked it, their list of reasons beginning with their fervent objection to the use of the "N word." Further critics of *Mockingbird* called the lessons of the book simplistic, arguing that by setting the book in a past three decades removed from the civil rights turmoil of the 1960s, Harper Lee had let American readers off the hook, allowing them to tell themselves with smug certainty, "I would never say or do such horrible things."

Did the book display a "great white father" attitude in which, out of a misguided sense of noblesse oblige, the material soothed rather than challenged? Was the book popular because it presented a fairy tale–like leading man who reassured white readers? Indeed, was Atticus Finch yet another iteration of a white man riding into town to save the poor black man who can't help himself? Where, critics asked, were any of the black men and women who consistently put their lives on the line in order to combat segregation? In truth, they were nowhere in sight, a fact that lends the book a sense of imbalance—but then again, that was not the story Harper Lee chose to tell.

Was Atticus just another example of worn-out liberal pieties and excuses? Particularly in the movie, if one looks closely at the town of Maycomb, aside from Bob Ewell there doesn't appear to be another individual racist in town. A mob at the jail, yes, but a fully differentiated individual? No. Just as *The Sound of Music*, set at the time of the Anschluss, barely showed any Nazis (and those depicted never seemed to carry guns), it can be argued that in the entire town of Maycomb, Bob Ewell seems to be the one and only racially insensitive individual on hand. The novel, of course, has more room for character sketches of casual bigots like Mrs. Merriweather and Aunt Alexandra's circle of church friends; as always proves the case with translating a book to film, favorite characters and scenes have to be sacrificed in the interests of narrative drive and dramatic momentum. The result of such excisions, however, is that, well played as the lynch mob scene is, the angry group of men confronting Atticus outside of the jail seems not so much hateful as misguided, and only Mr. Cunningham is presented as a distinct individual, one who quickly drops his racist ways thanks to a bit of talk with Scout. This potentially murderous mob appears to simply be a collection of good-hearted men who possessed, in Atticus's words, "blind spots along with the rest of us." Is Atticus soft-pedaling the racism that could lead a man to join a lynch mob? And could a hardscrabble, weathered farmer like Mr. Cunningham really be guided to the path of righteous action by virtue of a few sentences from a six-year-old girl? In what universe do such men actually exist? In fact, does the core material constitute what critic Thomas Mallon termed "a kind of moral Ritalin, an ungainsayable endorser of the obvious?" In the end, is *Mockingbird* nothing more than what *Time* magazine, in its review of the film, referred to as "fatuous side porch sociology"?

Oddly, part of the criticism that Atticus Finch seems too good to be true could be extended to Tom Robinson as well; both men are hardworking, possessed of infinite patience, and devoted to their families. Tom, in fact, appears to be such a paragon of virtue that he is even willing to help the bedraggled and clearly unstable Mayella Ewell. Faced with such near perfection, viewers and readers alike can certainly be forgiven for wondering if either Atticus or Tom actually possessed a single recognizable flaw.

Indeed, in the depiction of Atticus as a Christ-like figure, he seems to be preaching in the courtroom. Do the black people in the courtroom, segregated in the balcony, represent his disciples? If Atticus is the Christ figure, why does he never make eye contact with his disciples sitting upstairs?

In reality, the most troubling aspect to Atticus's personality is that he is never heard raising an objection to the fact that the black population of Maycomb must sit in that segregated balcony. (In a similar fashion, the adult Mary Badham mused that only as the decades passed did she realize how few white citizens in her hometown of Birmingham, Alabama, actually challenged the laws of segregation during her childhood.) Is he really a moral and just man, standing up for racial equality, or, rather, a state legislator and pillar of Maycomb who, in the words of one commentator, operates in a segregated town "living his own life as the passive participant in that pervasive injustice"? In some ways, that is an unnervingly accurate take on the character of Atticus; he is not looking to change laws, but, rather, hearts and minds, and changes in the laws are what constitute the first and most necessary step in dismantling the corrupt system. An appeal for a change in hearts and minds is to be applauded, but it also never represents a threat in any way to the existing power structure.

Has Atticus made peace, albeit uneasily, with the social and legal structure? It is certainly possible to argue that Atticus is simply asking the all-white, all-male jury to exchange one prejudice, against African-Americans, for another, against "white trash." Troubling questions all, but the problem with just such arguments is that it involves judging a character in 1930s Alabama against the social standards of early twenty-first-century America. Depression-era Maycomb simply existed light-years away from a twenty-first century so politically correct that Columbia University students asked for a "trigger warning" regarding the inclusion of Ovid's classic *Metamorphoses* as part of the introductory humanities course because they declared themselves offended by its sexual violence. More to the point, for Lee to portray Atticus as an avenging angel taking on the entire race and class system of 1930s Alabama would have been false; even the most outspoken liberals in the Alabama of the mid-1930s were not raising a cry for the abolition of segregation, but, instead, simply insisting upon a less onerous version.

What does remain true, however, is that it is decidedly more difficult in the twenty-first century to accept Atticus's telling Scout that Mr. Cunningham is basically a good man with blind spots when those blind spots lead him to become part of a mob ready to lynch Tom Robinson. In similar fashion, *Gone with the Wind* remains a staggering cinematic achievement, but it is patently ridiculous, even harmful, to believe, as the film's opening credits would have it, that slave-owning men and women of the pre–Civil War South lived in "a land of Cavaliers and Cotton Fields called the Old South . . . Here in this pretty world, Gallantry took its last bow." Those words won't find much favor within the African-American community, just as Atticus's words to Scout about Mr. Cunningham strike many as unnecessarily apologetic on behalf of an overt racist.

And yet the fact remains that Atticus is a man of integrity who forthrightly takes on a case that no one else in the town will touch, and does so without apologizing or signaling his discomfort; he desires justice and wants the letter of the law upheld. He is a lawyer, and his words in a 1930s Deep South courtroom when defending a black man charged in an incendiary case of supposed interracial rape remain measured and full of reason.

Atticus's message—Harper Lee's message—that you can never fully know another person until you step inside his skin, is, in fact, another iteration of universality as the premise of all art, the idea that "another's mind, another's creation, can be entered and absorbed, that we are not atomized individuals incapable of connection." In this variation of E. M. Forster's dictum "Only connect" lies an adjunct to the melting-pot myth of America. Is such connection—that is, stepping into another's shoes—ever truly possible in art? Are the emotions and actions of others who are markedly different still universally recognizable and understandable? Certainly it seems a possibility in live theater, where a slow but sure movement toward color-blind casting has resulted in all-black versions of *Cat on a Hot Tin Roof* and *A Streetcar Named Desire,* as well as the casting of James Earl Jones as the patriarch of an otherwise-white family in the Pulitzer Prize–winning *You Can't Take It with You.* (The reverse, of course, seems unthinkable at this point, with there being no talk whatsoever of white actors playing leading roles in any of the ten plays comprising August Wilson's extraordinary cycle depicting African-American life in the twentieth century.)

All of which leads to the looming question of cultural appropriation; here defined as the objections by minority groups to the use of their culture, or even characters of their ethnicity, by artists not belonging to those groups, *cultural appropriation* was not a term in common use at the time of *Mockingbird*'s publication. In the nicely turned phrase of Sam Tanenhaus, artists of the time were "intellectual free agents, who could steal whatever they found." Nonetheless, through the years a small but persistent pocket of criticism has accused Harper Lee of just such cultural poaching. Did Nelle, a relatively privileged white woman, have the right to write about the black experience or even utilize black characters? If members of traditionally marginalized groups have historically experienced great difficulty in publicly defining their own place in an often adversarial culture, why should someone representative of that oppressive culture have the right? Or, as the question is posed in the concluding number of *Hamilton*, Lin-Manuel Miranda's multicultural, distinctly twenty-first-century take on American history, "Who Lives, Who Dies, Who Tells Your Story?" Was it permissible for Harper Lee to provide an interpretation of the black experience to white America? Or are all of these questions examples of political correctness run amok, what the British historian E. P. Thompson termed "the enormous condescension of posterity."

Ta-Nehisi Coates, whose bestselling *Between the World and Me* considers the state of twenty-first-century race relations in America, seems to have no time for *Mockingbird,* which he has flatly stated he has never read, with no intention of doing so. It may just be that he thinks of something like *Mockingbird* as constituting a case of mere "good intentions," motives that he considers nothing more than "a hall pass through history, a sleeping pill that ensures the dream."

Revering Malcolm X because "he would not turn the other cheek for you. . . . He would not be your morality," Coates presents a dark vision of America that finds meaning in the struggle itself, and is more attuned to the dark world of German émigré film director Fritz Lang than that of Robert Mulligan. His bleak rendering of the present-day United States, in which he views victims of police shootings not as the victims of a single officer, but, rather, as victims of fear and the perversion of justice underlying the country's economic and political structure, echoes the precise social conditions that led to Tom Robinson's death: the retention of the white power structure at the expense of justice. That perverted sense of values was Harper Lee's target, but to her small-in-number-but-vocal critics, she did nothing more than set up straw figures, suitable for a self-satisfied white liberal bayonetting.

Perhaps both sides of the cultural dilemma were best summed up by esteemed African-American writer James Baldwin, who moderated a 1968 debate between William Styron and actor Ossie Davis, at the height of the national discussion about both Styron's novel *The Confessions of Nat Turner* and its proposed film version. Styron, a good friend of Baldwin's, had already bitterly cataloged the accusations hurled against him for appropriating the story of Nat Turner, the slave turned rebel leader, and a key figure in African-American history: "I'm a racist, a distorter of history, a defamer of black people, a traducer of the heroic image of 'our' Nat Turner." Baldwin understood exactly why the protests about the film proved to be so fervent. He said, "Bill's novel is a private act, but what happens when it's onscreen and disseminated at this time in our history? There's a possibility that thousands of black people will die." For all that it sounds like rhetorical overkill to speak of thousands of deaths, at the time of the debate racial protests had already roiled inner-city streets for three consecutive summers, and as pointed out by Sam Tanenhaus, who wrote about the *Turner* controversy in 2016, Martin Luther King, Jr., had been murdered only two months before the Styron-Davis debate (Robert F. Kennedy's assassination occurred just one week after it). The potential for further damage remained enormous. And yet, as Baldwin further opined, Styron had the right to publish his novel "because no one can tell a writer what he can write." In a statement startlingly reminiscent of Atticus Finch's philosophy, Baldwin later explained, "It's a book I admire very much. He had to try to put himself in the skin of Nat Turner. . . . It was a white Southern writer's attempt to deal with something that was tormenting him and frightening him. I respect him very much for that."

Did the criticisms of *Mockingbird*—dismissed by the Left, cursed by the Right—deter Harper Lee from writing another novel? Did she grow tired of being called both a racist and a n——— lover? Or did the pressure of following up a Pulitzer Prize–winning novel with another book simply become too much to bear? Whatever the reason, after the publication of *Mockingbird* in July 1960, Harper Lee pulled one of the most famous disappearing acts in the history of American letters. In a country increasingly concerned with the headlong pursuit of fame, Harper Lee virtually disappeared, and, in literary terms, purposefully fell silent.

Fifty-five years silent.

13

THE LEGEND GROWS: HARPER LEE'S FIFTY-FIVE YEARS OF SILENCE

Reporter: "Do you find your second novel coming slow?"
Harper Lee: "Well, I hope to live to see it published."

Harper Lee to good friend Tom Butts: "Have you ever wondered why I never wrote anything else?"
Tom Butts: "Well, along with about a million other people, yes."

When *To Kill a Mockingbird* turned into a national literary sensation shortly after initial publication, it proved inevitable that the press would beat a path to Harper Lee's door and pester her with questions that centered around one all-consuming topic: Was she writing a second novel and when would it be published?

As far back as 1958, Lee had actually planned an entire series of books, and in a letter of that year written to Joy and Michael Brown, she forthrightly stated, "I have my work cut out for me for the next fifteen years." She then went on to list the subjects of all six novels:

1. *A race novel*
2. *A Victorian novel*
3. *What Mr. Graham Greene calls an entertainment*

4. *I'm going to tear Monroeville to pieces*

5. *A U.N. novel*

6. *A novel set in India in 1910*

Of this novel set in India, Nelle further wrote that agent Annie Laurie Williams would "sell this to the movies. . . . The heroine will be named Portulaca Brown, an Anglo-Indian. She will have all her teeth, and they will gleam beautifully in Technicolor on a Stethoscopic Screen. There will be a Plot."

Lee concluded the letter by humorously asking, "Can you feed and lodge me for so long? Much love, Nelle."

There were even fascinating hints of a new book contained in a December 1962 letter written by Truman Capote to friends, in which he stated, "I can't tell you much about Nelle's new book. It's a novel and quite short. But she is so secretive." A mere two months later, in a Chicago press interview at the time of the movie's release, she was asked, "How do you feel about your second novel?" Lee's response was a succinct "I'm scared," an answer that leaves open the issue of whether or not she had actually yet put pen to paper.

As speculation mounted about Lee's next novel, she penned two magazine articles. The first was a piece for *McCall's* magazine entitled "Christmas to Me," a sweet-natured recounting of the unexpected Christmastime check she had received from Joy and Michael Brown. The second was an article for *Vogue* entitled "Love—In Other Words." (There was also, at this time, a short *Esquire*-commissioned nonfiction article on life in the South, which the magazine rejected because Lee turned in a piece completely different in tone and outlook from what had been requested.)

Nelle may not have liked giving interviews, but in a quintessential Lee performance—self-deprecating and sharply observed at the same time—a 1964 radio interview found her dropping hints of novels planned for future publication. Speaking about her desire to write a series of novels about the fast-disappearing small-town world in which she grew up, Nelle stated, "My objectives are very limited. I want to do the best I can with the talent God gave me. . . . I believe there is something universal in this little world, something decent to be said for it, and something to lament in its passing. In other words all I want to be is the Jane Austen of South Alabama."

During this radio interview, which proved to be her last official in-depth talk with the press, Lee did actually state, "I'm working on another novel. I'm a slow worker, a steady worker. So many writers don't like to write. They don't enjoy turning a thought into a reasonable sentence. I do like to write. Sometimes I think I like it too much because when I get into work I don't want to leave it. I'll go days and days and days without leaving the house." What's most interesting about this final interview is the manner in which Nelle goes on to define herself as a true writer, driven in her need to express herself: "You see, more than a simple matter of putting down words, writing is a form of self-discipline you must learn before you can call yourself a writer. I think writers today are too easily pleased with their work . . . [there's a] lack of sitting down and working a good idea into a gem of an idea. There are people who write but I think they're quite different from people who must write. Writing is simply something you must do. . . . You must not write 'for' something; you must not write with definite hopes of reward. Any writer worth his salt writes to please himself . . . to communicate with himself."

In George Orwell's famous essay "Why I Write," he outlined his four reasons for writing, all of which Harper Lee actually seemed to possess: sheer egoism, aesthetic enthusiasm, historical impulse, and political purpose. It all seemed promising enough at the time, but Nelle's literary silence deepened, and Alice Lee seemed to contradict the very possibility of a second novel when she eventually told a BBC interviewer that the manuscript for the novel had been stolen from the house and the book abandoned. In a conversation with neighbor Marja Mills years later, Alice admitted that the second novel had simply never progressed beyond the outline stage.

In August 1965 Nelle did, in fact, write a short piece for *McCall's* entitled "When Children Discover America," but there was still no further sign of a second book. The interviews for which the press continued to clamor, and which would have kept her in the thick of the publishing world, frustrated her, the distortions and liberties that the press took with her life and those of her loved ones proving to be a source of increasing irritation. It wasn't that she had nothing to say; in fact, far from it. She remained a charming interviewee, sketching in her assessment of southern society ("Any time we work is time wasted but we have to do it in order to have time to hunt and fish"), and winning in her self-deprecation: "I was exposed to seventeen years of formal education in Monroeville schools, Huntingdon College, and the University of Alabama. If I ever learned anything, I've forgotten it." But by now, the interviews hardly seemed worth the aggravation and invasion of privacy, and by the mid-1960s she had stopped talking to the press altogether. Throughout the ensuing years, other factors appear to have played a role in her literary silence, as well. Her closest allies in the publishing world, those who made her feel protected and whose advice she respected, had died—her agent Maurice Crain in April 1970 and editor Tay Hohoff in January 1974—and with their deaths, part of the pleasure she found in writing seemed to have disappeared.

Certainly she didn't need the money. *Mockingbird* had made her financially secure for life, and as a true child of the Depression, no matter how large her royalty checks, she kept her requirements to a bare minimum. She spent absolutely no money on luxuries; if she had a bed, a bathroom, and a typewriter, she could live comfortably, and in fact lived in only three different, rather nondescript apartments throughout a half century spent in Manhattan. In the words of Alice Lee, "Books are the things she cares about." If she spent any money at all it was because, as one biographer reported, "she did value the opportunity to give bountiful sums to charity and to educate people behind the scenes."

In reality, her literary void was not absolute, because very occasionally a piece of nonfiction would appear; in 1983, she reviewed Albert James Pickett's *History of Alabama* for the Alabama Heritage Festival, but other than that, the silence remained deafening.

Finally, in the 1980s, tantalizing hints about a new book began to emerge. She spent a great deal of time in Alexander City, Alabama, researching a true-crime book that centered around W. M. Maxwell, a suspected serial killer from the area who had also been a part-time preacher. Her love of research had remained constant. "Instant information is not for me. I prefer to search library stacks because when I work to learn something, I remember it," she said. The book Nelle had in mind would be akin to *In Cold Blood*, and she did in fact research the story of the killings extensively, spending a great deal of time soaking up the atmosphere of the town. In the end, however, she never wrote the book, possibly scared off by the frightening people at the heart of the story, or perhaps simply losing interest in the process itself.

There was never one single incident that made Nelle decide she would not write another novel, but most of all her silence may have been about her aversion to the press attention that came with publication. Said her sister Alice, "I don't think any first-time author could be prepared for what happened. It all fell on her, and her way of handling it was not to let it get too close to her." Retreat proved to be the order of the day, her ever-growing audience frustrated by its inability to either read any additional novels or witness the creative development of a singular talent and vision. It was a difficult situation to accept, but Nelle's fans began to realize that her entire writing career was likely to remain a single winner-take-all undertaking; she had grabbed the brass ring and succeeded beyond anyone's wildest expectations, but the psychic cost of her success had proved enormous.

In truth, her silence was rare but not unique; neither J. D. Salinger nor Ralph Ellison ever published a second novel after their respective overwhelming successes with *The Catcher in the Rye* and *Invisible Man*, although Salinger's two novellas, *Raise High the Roof Beam, Carpenters* and *Seymour: An Introduction* were published together in one volume and Ellison's *Juneteenth* was published after his death. In terms of interactions with the public, Salinger's reclusiveness was of a depth and conviction to make Lee appear a social butterfly.

The success of *Mockingbird* certainly had not sent Nelle off the rails, because her feet were planted much too firmly on the ground. It was inconceivable that she would ever travel down the same road as Ross Lockridge, who had scored a massive success with his southern-themed *Raintree County* (1948) and seen it turned into an Academy Award–nominated film starring Elizabeth Taylor, only to become depressed and ultimately commit suicide without ever writing another book.

Instead, all speculation about Harper Lee finally seemed to center around one rueful question: How could she ever top a Pulitzer Prize–winning, Academy Award–winning global hit? She couldn't. The longer her silence, the greater the interest in what she might write, yet at the same time, her burden of living up to *Mockingbird* grew ever more impossible. Nelle, it seemed, was living out the lament of Cole Porter, who had once remarked, "No matter what I write or how good I think it is, the critics state, 'Definitely not up to his usual standards.'" Nelle even addressed the issue herself, intrafamily, telling one of her cousins, "There is nowhere else to go but down."

She bluntly told Tom Butts that there were "[t]wo reasons [for not writing]. First I wouldn't go through all the pressure and publicity I went through with *Mockingbird* for any amount of money. Second, I have said what I wanted to say and I'll not say it again." Both reasons make sense, but Butts, who knew Lee well, remained puzzled by her second reason; given the very definite opinions he had heard her express on everything connected with modern-day life and politics, he felt she had plenty more to say—especially on the larger-than-life topics of race, community, and family.

If, as Andy Warhol once prophesized, in the future everyone will be famous for fifteen minutes (although even Warhol could not have foreseen that in the twenty-first century people would begin to demand their fifteen minutes), Nelle remained completely uninterested in such notoriety, and actively shunned the attention. As novelist Mark Childress noted about her modus operandi, "Turning away from the church of fame takes courage." (It was an attitude echoed forty years later by Lee's fellow southerner, playwright Margaret Edson, who in 1999 won the Pulitzer Prize for her play *Wit,* then returned to teaching social studies in Atlanta without ever writing a second play.) The ethos of *People* magazine, let alone reality television, remained repugnant to Nelle's core values. In the words of the Reverend Thomas Butts, "She grows frustrated with a country and a culture grown coarse and obscene."

In Harper Lee's reluctance to lead any sort of public life, one can spot the autobiographical elements she planted within the character of Scout, who forthrightly states, "I could stand anything but a bunch of people looking at me." In reality, while Lee may have opted out of the public eye, she certainly did not cut out contact with her friends in either Monroeville or New York City. The paradox lay in the fact that her reclusiveness only served to make her legend grow, turning her into a southern literary version of Greta Garbo, a woman who did not want to be alone so much as she wanted to be left alone. Just as happened with Garbo, Lee's disappearance turned her into a figure upon whom the public could write its fondest hopes—tabula rasa. Who, in fact, was the real Harper Lee? Since only a handful of close friends possessed any firsthand knowledge, the public now felt free to create their own versions of her persona.

In a final irony, which Lee herself seemed to appreciate, Monroeville, whose small-town character had made her want to escape to New York, increasingly turned into her sanctuary, one far away from the media spotlight. Once she was back in Monroeville, neighbors long used to her ways protected her from prying outsiders, allowing Nelle to go about her daily routine with no hint of interference. Even better, never once did they ask her if she was writing another book.

14

LIFE AFTER *TO KILL A MOCKINGBIRD*

To Kill a Mockingbird will be the first line in my obituary, and that's all right with me.

—Gregory Peck

Mockingbird changed, created, and shaped my life.

—Mary Badham

GREGORY PECK

To Kill a Mockingbird did more than make Gregory Peck an Academy Award–winning star; it made him beloved—at the very young age of forty-six. Says Jeanine Basinger of Peck's near canonization, "That ramrod-straight quality of his is good for the film—his sort of masculine beauty fit the audience's conception of Atticus Finch—but more than anything else, he and the character of Atticus came to represent hope, the belief that good can triumph over evil. Those are very strong, elemental beliefs and wishes on the part of the audience."

If he ever grew tired of the incessant *Mockingbird* questions—no matter what film he was promoting, *Mockingbird* was the one movie he was sure to be asked about—he never let on. The public's comingling of actor and character, overlaid with Peck's awareness that audiences wanted, indeed needed, to believe that someone just like Atticus really did exist in everyday life, led to an extraordinary and occasionally dizzying hall of mirrors.

Peck reacted by embracing both his identity as Gregory/Atticus, as well as the attendant rapturous gaze of the public that followed him for the rest of his life. In fact, it wasn't just the public who conflated Peck with Atticus but the press as well, and soon after *Mockingbird* was released, the star began having to answer nonsensical questions like that posed on his trip to the Cannes Film Festival with *Mockingbird* in May 1963. Asked "Do you like Negroes as you did in the film?" Peck replied with a response straight out of *Mockingbird*: "For one reason or another I have never felt intolerance. I judge Negroes on personality, intelligence and quality as I would anyone else."

In the wake of *Mockingbird*, Peck quickly found himself back in Atticus mode as a psychiatrist trying to heal three soldiers in *Captain Newman, M.D.* (1963). He did follow through on Sophia Loren's Academy Award–night request to work together—only a churl could have refused La Loren—but *Arabesque* (1966) was okay, nothing more, with Peck lacking the requisite light touch of Cary Grant or even Jack Lemmon.

A fascinating projected reunion with Mulligan and Pakula on an adaptation of Ray Bradbury's *The Martian Chronicles* unfortunately never materialized, although he worked once again with both men when cast as a rancher in *The Stalking Moon* (1968). His character played out as a tougher, less amiable variation on Atticus, but one with striking similarities: a less-than-eager hero who could not ignore a cry for help. It's a solid, underrated Western character study, Peck's dignity still intact even in the far West, with the film making audiences who were willing to accept the lack of gunfighting sit up and pay attention. For all its effective atmosphere, however, it was not a box-office hit; audiences, it seemed, wanted "their" Gregory Peck to remain overtly heroic.

While continuing to work at a steady pace, he also undertook a list of civic duties that would have made Atticus himself proud: After donating fifty thousand dollars to the Inner City Cultural Center in 1966, he also served as the president of the Academy of Motion Picture Arts and Sciences in 1967, and was appointed the first chairman of the American Film Institute (AFI). Awards began piling up one right after the other: the Academy's Jean Hersholt Humanitarian Award, the Screen Actors Guild Life Achievement Award, and the 1969 Presidential Medal of Freedom all came his way, and on a nationwide tour of twenty-four cities, he raised five million dollars for the American Cancer Society. It all played out as exactly the sort of offscreen life Atticus Finch would have created if he had ever decided to settle in the film industry.

The public's knowledge of Peck's own happy marriage cemented the perception of his Atticus-like personality. He never registered as tabloid fodder, singularly lacking as he was in the tumultuous personal life that would have colored audience perception in a movie theater. Instead, he firmly and unequivocally morphed into the quintessential American male movie star for the post–World War II era: upright, solid, occasionally stolid, a moral man of unimpeachable character—Spencer Tracy for a new generation. In the words of *Variety,* "equal parts Grant Wood and the Arrow Collar man."

By now, he had acquired such gravitas that he seemed the flesh-and-blood personification of a Lincolnesque presidential figure, but a run for office never interested him. In the words of Orson Welles, "There's only going to be one actor to be President, and the right one—as I keep telling him if he would ever listen to me—is Gregory Peck. Bad actor, but he'd be a helluva President, you know." (Welles's simultaneous compliment and dig placed Peck in the good company of Joseph Cotten, whom Welles told, "You'll never be a good actor, but with your curly hair you'll have to get by as a star.") In fact, if President Johnson, to whom Peck remained close, had run for reelection in 1968, he planned to nominate Peck as U.S. ambassador to Ireland.

Even in the midst of his nonstop offscreen activities, Peck continued to keep up a grueling schedule of filmmaking. *I Walk the Line* (1970) was not particularly successful—no one really wanted to see

Peck playing a lovesick sheriff pining away for Tuesday Weld—but the film demonstrated his willingness to try out new types of characters, and he continued to search for material deemed suitable for a leading man now past the age of fifty.

There was pain, the greatest of all developing in the mid-1970s, when his son Jonathan committed suicide. Depression set in and a clear-eyed devastating self-analysis: "Jonathan's greatest problem was that he set goals which were too high. Part of the reason he set such high goals was that he was the son of a famous man." Others analyzed in words that stung, with Jonathan's girlfriend, Nancy Stesin, saying of Peck and Veronique, "They did their dance. Greg could be cold to Jonathan and his other children. His loyalty was to Veronique. She rules the roost." Softening the blow, Stesin went on to analyze that Peck's mistakes were those of "benign neglect," but Peck felt that his all-encompassing focus on career had contributed to Jonathan's death. He did not cast around for others to blame, but looked fiercely within: "Whatever the causes were, whatever the mistakes his mother and I have made . . . I don't know. But my regret that I will live with for the rest of my life was that I was in France instead of here." Atticus might have been nearly perfect, but Peck himself, a loving father to all five of his children, remained vulnerable.

He drew closer to his four remaining children, and they recipro-cated his devotion. Daughter Cecilia spoke of her father's willingness to "show up for everything we did. He would be in our rooms doing homework with us. . . . He would write us/me long directives about how the choices I was making then would affect the rest of my life. . . . Now I recognize he was reaching out to me in the only way he could. Nobody else in my life was receiving letters like that." Peck's youngest son, Tony, who successfully battled alcoholism, talked of squandered opportunities, of having been given much without having to work for it himself: "My father never let me down. I let myself down. With Dad what you see is what you get. He is totally like the lawyer he plays in *To Kill a Mockingbird*. Gregory Peck is Atticus Finch." It was a heartfelt tribute from son to father, unintentionally revealing by virtue of the fact that by now, even Peck's own son framed the portrait of his father in terms of Atticus Finch.

If the pain of losing Jonathan lasted forever, the depression did lift, and he scored the biggest box-office hit of his career opposite Lee Remick in *The Omen*. If playing the father of a devil child seemed less than dignified, it brought Peck back to the forefront of the public's consciousness; in 1976, only *One Flew Over the Cuckoo's Nest* and *All the President's Men* (the latter directed and produced by Alan Pakula) grossed more. He played further against type as an aging Nazi in *The Boys from Brazil* (1978); the film received bad reviews, but he nonetheless received a Golden Globe nomination as Best Actor in a Drama.

He entered a new and final phase of his career playing real-life figures, beginning with the titular role in *MacArthur* (1977). The film itself proved a hit-and-miss affair, but Peck turned in a solid performance, with Vincent Canby in *The New York Times* noting that like MacArthur, Peck himself possessed a kind of "lofty manner—even when he's being humble." Traces of MacArthur's endless sense of grandeur and attendant noblesse oblige logically enough found their way into Peck's interpretation of Abraham Lincoln in television's 1982 miniseries *The Blue and the Gray*; in some ways, by now it felt as if Peck had been training for the role of Lincoln his entire life, bearing out *Time* magazine's twenty-years-earlier assertion in its review of *Mockingbird* that "Peck, though he is generally excellent, lays it on a bit thick at times— he seems to imagine himself the Abe Lincoln of Alabama."

The Scarlet and the Black, a well-received 1983 television movie, found him relaxed and in his element playing Hugh O'Flaherty, a Vatican monsignor who helped thousands of Allied prisoners escape the Gestapo. "When I read the script, I felt a little the way I felt when I got my hands on *To Kill a Mockingbird*. I felt that I knew this fellow O'Flaherty just reading the script, just as I knew Atticus Finch and had known him always," Peck said. Atticus, Monsignor O'Flaherty, MacArthur—at times it seemed as if Mount Rushmore immortalization was next on the agenda, and by now no one really would have objected.

Growing more relaxed both on-screen and off, the ever-sober Peck now began to display his wry sense of humor more frequently in public, and in accepting the 1989 AFI Lifetime Achievement Award at a ceremony hosted by his *Roman Holiday* costar Audrey Hepburn, the seventy-three-year-old Peck smilingly admitted, "I was genuinely surprised. I always saw this as an award for older people.... Along the way the associations have been so rewarding. The directors—Willy Wyler, Vincente Minnelli—I owe them so much. Not everything... But—a lot." As he made his way to the dais to accept the award, music from *To Kill a Mockingbird* played, and among the heartfelt tributes that poured in were those from Pakula, Mulligan, and Mary Badham. It wasn't all humor, however, and given his stature as Saint Atticus of Hollywood, the by now iconic Peck felt no compunction in politely dressing down a roomful of industry heavyweights in his acceptance speech: "Making millions is not the whole ball game, fellas. Pride of workmanship is more. Artistry is worth more."

As he settled comfortably into the role of elder statesman, there were still surprises along the way, most notably when he revealed that he and Michael Jackson had gone horseback riding together at Jackson's Neverland ranch, and that Jackson had actually memorized all of the dialogue of *To Kill a Mockingbird* "and he was full of questions about it." It proved quite a combination—Jackson, the perpetual man-child, looking for his own sense of home after his tumultuous stunted childhood, and Peck/Atticus who represented a father figure for all—not just his own five children but also for Jackson, Mary Badham, Phillip Alford, and millions of filmgoers. If Julie Andrews's Maria von Trapp in *The Sound of Music* represented the personification of the ultimate happy ending, a loving mother for lost souls and children of all ages, then Peck represented the equivalent idealized father, his soothing voice, tall, lean body, and gracefully aging visage the perfect embodiment of a fantasy father at once both real and just out of reach, a figure onto whom audiences could project their ever-fading yearning for belief.

His career finally came full circle when he once again played a southern lawyer, albeit one without Atticus's moral compass, in a cameo role for the Martin Scorsese–directed 1991 remake of *Cape Fear.* It proved to be his last feature-film performance, and if it turned out that he had never established himself as an electrifying actor of unlimited range like Olivier, he had certainly crafted a solid, conscientious, and sometimes powerful body of work, reigning as a true movie star in an era when very few still existed. The roles dwindled, but he kept himself in the public eye, and it now seemed like he had a new full-time job accepting the highest honors in the land, most notably the 1991 Kennedy Center Honors, the 1992 Film Society of Lincoln Center Career Achievement Award, and the 1998 National Medal of Arts.

Returning to the stage, he toured the country in *A Conversation with Gregory Peck,* a one-man show that allowed audiences the chance to bask in the actual presence of Atticus Finch and in which, to the surprise of no one, he proved to be both charming and courtly. Like Atticus with his pocket watch, Peck was always amiable and on time; he had, in the words of his daughter, Cecilia, "too much respect for other people to keep anyone waiting." The show mixed anecdotes, film clips, and an audience question-and-answer period, and Phillip Alford and Mary Badham each joined their on-screen father for several of those appearances. In Badham's own words, anytime Peck called to ask if she could help him out, she would "just cancel everything" and appear. The most popular audience questions always centered around *Mockingbird,* and audiences delighted in hearing Peck recount how he would teasingly ask his good friend Harper Lee, "What have you done for me lately?" In their own conversations, Lee would ask him what he talked about in *A Conversation with Gregory Peck,* and when Peck replied that he spoke "quite a bit about you," Lee issued a humorously blunt "Oh my God!"

Given his own liberal political philosophy, it seemed entirely natural that Peck was tapped to narrate *Super Chief: The Life and*

Legacy of Earl Warren, a 1989 documentary about the liberal chief justice of the United States Supreme Court. By now, so ingrained was the sense of Peck as Atticus that it even seemed entirely natural to the public that after attorney Harry Lee Coe III of Hillsborough, Florida, successfully prosecuted the horrific case of two white men setting a black man on fire, one of the first commendations Coe received was a letter of congratulations from Peck: "When I saw this photo in the *NY Times*, I could not help identifying with you, and thinking that in this case, you have played the role of Atticus Finch in real life, taken on the challenge, and won an important victory for all of us." Let others feel straitjacketed by the public's insistence on mixing up actor and role—Peck held no such qualms: "The movie is my little pipeline to an entirely other generation.... Having won [the Academy Award] makes you feel at home with yourself."

Having reached the stage of lion in winter, and secure both in his talent and place in screen history, he by now had no problem criticizing some of his lesser work: "I hated myself in *Days of Glory.* I thought I was completely artificial, stagy. I thought about *Keys of the Kingdom,* well, he's sincere, but that's about all." He could be charmingly self-deprecating about his lesser efforts, noting, "One good thing about the bad movies is that people don't remember them. Nobody ever comes up to me and says 'I hated you in *I Walk the Line!*'" He summed up his career with a clear-eyed practicality: "I have made a handful of pictures that still play pretty well and are worth keeping. I have a lot of pictures that were commercially successful and, you might say, artistically spotty. And then I have a handful of turkeys."

The friendship with Harper Lee endured and Peck disclosed that he continued to speak to the author a half dozen times per year: "When Veronique and I are in New York and she's there we see her and have lunch with her." In a Hollywood awash in blockbuster action movies and increasingly bereft of original dramatic roles, the idea of a *Mockingbird* remake or sequel was continually floated, but Lee and Peck not only controlled the rights but also remained firmly united in their opposition to the mere idea. Said Peck, "Oh God no! We are all resolved not to allow it to be colorized and not to allow a sequel. Harper, Bob, Alan and I actually own the film. Universal only distributes it."

He never did write a memoir about his film career or personal life; with his reserve and sense of propriety, he would not have wanted to present his mistakes in print, or, perhaps more to the point, those of his friends, family, and acquaintances. When he died on June 12, 2003, just days after an AFI poll had named Atticus Finch the greatest movie hero of all time, he was hailed in countless newspaper write-ups as America's quintessential leading man, with the subtitle in the *Time* magazine obituary simply stating, "When he died Gregory Peck took movie idealism with him."

Through the cumulative weight of his entire body of work, but particularly thanks to the role of Atticus Finch, in the public's eye Peck had become not just a movie hero but also the personification of the quintessential American: the man his fellow citizens liked to think reflected not just their country but their own very best selves—a champion of the underdog. Wish projection it may have been, but it proved no less potent for the strength of the desire.

When Peck died, his family telephoned Harper Lee to tell her the news, and she traveled to Los Angeles for the funeral, pronouncing, "When he played Atticus Finch he had played himself, and time has told all of us something more: when he played himself he touched the world." Brock Peters, whom Mary Badham by now considered a father figure, just as she had Peck, was chosen to deliver the eulogy, one great actor saluting another. By the time of Peck's death, the two men had been friends for forty years, and Peters's graceful eulogy emphasized not Gregory Peck the actor, but Gregory Peck the humanitarian: "In art there is compassion, in compassion there is humanity, with humanity there is generosity and love. Gregory Peck gave us these attributes in full measure. . . . Atticus Finch gave him an opportunity to play himself." After singing Duke Ellington's "They Say," Peters closed with a heartfelt "To my friend Gregory Peck, to my friend Atticus Finch, vaya con Dios."

MARY BADHAM

At the conclusion of filming on *Mockingbird,* Mary Badham returned to her private girls school in Birmingham, Alabama, and spent time rekindling her love of horses. Said her mother, "Mary's an actress, but she's also our daughter. She's been offered television series and other movie roles, but we don't want her to work that much. She has plenty of time ahead of her." Mary herself was interviewed in January 1963, right before *Mockingbird*'s general release, and did not evince much interest in a Hollywood career: "I wouldn't want to live in Hollywood because I couldn't afford to keep a horse here. But someday I'd love to make a western so I could show how I can ride. . . . But the real reason I don't want to live here is that when I'm in Hollywood I miss Birmingham very much. When I'm in Birmingham I don't miss Hollywood at all."

In fact, reentry into Birmingham did not prove easy, and she found herself treated differently by the other students. "It was a tough transition and I felt like a yo-yo," she recalled. "You're treated like an adult one day and like a little child the next. You have so much expected of you and then it's like nothing." But it was more than the adult/child dichotomy—Mary herself had changed during filming. She had lived for six months in a racially integrated complex in Southern California, and the racial attitudes she found back home in the deeply segregated Birmingham of 1962 were disorienting—she now seemed an outsider in her own hometown. "The attitude was 'Lord knows what she might've learned out there!' . . . Some families, I'd been welcome in their homes, and after the film, I was no longer welcome. . . . I was ostracized and it was painful."

She made two more movies after *Mockingbird*; the first found her playing Natalie Wood's younger sister in another southern-themed drama, 1966's *This Property Is Condemned,* but the thrill was gone. "I learned it was real work. It definitely became business and not a very pleasant business at that. . . . Before it was all kind of like a dream and we were just playing, but then it became real work.... By the time the picture was finished I was on the verge of a nervous breakdown. I was that bad."

There was to be one more movie, a role in the William Castle–directed 1966 thriller *Let's Kill Uncle* (the casting director was her brother, John, who went on to fame as the director of *Saturday Night Fever*). *Let's Kill Uncle* proved a much better experience than *This Property Is Condemned*, as Castle, a genial presence on the set, was sympatico with children and proved to be, in Badham's words, "an angel of mercy."

The experience of *Let's Kill Uncle* had brought a sense of fun back into acting, but after one *Twilight Zone* episode ("The Bewitchin' Pool") and one episode of *Dr. Kildare*, she retired. Finishing high school in Arizona, she met her husband, eventually returned to Alabama, married, and raised children.

Although far removed from the Hollywood scene, Badham still kept in close touch with Peck throughout the years. With her mother having died three weeks after her high school graduation, and her father two years after she got married, Badham, in her own words, "felt cut off. So after they were gone, Atticus would call and check on me. If he was going to be on the East Coast, he'd say, 'I'll take you out to lunch.' Whenever I'd be in California I'd always go up to the house and visit. I always wanted him to be proud of me.... [He] really guided me and encouraged me not only during the filming of the movie but also throughout my life." She commented, "He remained a big, big influence in my life until he died in 2003," and recalled, "That same gentle guidance you see on film he shared with me growing up." In another interview, she said, "I've always tried to live up to his expectations."

Long retired from the film business, Badham has nonetheless remained in the *Mockingbird* business, speaking at schools, libraries, and literary festivals throughout the country and overseas; one such trip took her to Russia, where she found herself surprised and moved by the fervent response to material that seemed to surmount all differences in language and culture. Whether it was giving a speech or, as proved the case in a 1999 appearance with a symphony in Kansas, providing voice-over narration while the orchestra played Elmer Bernstein's score, she never tired of talking about the film, earnestly declaring, "The film has so much to give to its audiences and it's such a great teaching tool for our future generations."

Her two children now grown, Badham works as an art and furniture restorer and lives in rural Virginia with her professor husband, Richard Wilt. Surprisingly, she never read *To Kill a Mockingbird* until she gave birth to her own daughter in 1983 (and when her daughter grew old enough to watch the film, she succinctly commented, "Mommy, you were so cute!"). Although she briefly came out of retirement to film a cameo in the independent film *Our Very Own* (2005), and does not rule out another acting job should she like the script, the film business mostly remains in her life as memory, one focused on the happiness found with *Mockingbird* rather than the tough times experienced on *This Property Is Condemned*. Said Badham, "What a wonderful business, to be able to go and be somebody else for the day. Thank God all I basically remember are the good times. I don't remember much of the hard times."

Those happy memories were tested when she returned to Universal Studios in order to visit her brother, John, while he directed *Bird on a Wire* (1990), with Goldie Hawn and Mel Gibson. Twenty-eight years after *Mockingbird*, Scotty, the guard at the studio gate, was still at his old post; telling him that she wanted to visit the backlot, Badham prepared to drive right to the old set, only to be stopped by Scotty's rueful reply: "No, leave your memories where they are." For the time being, she did just that, but in 1996, when she returned to the lot for a *Vanity Fair* reunion photo shoot with Gregory Peck, Brock Peters, and Phillip Alford, her illusions were shattered as soon as the limo driver took her to the Maycomb street set. "How does it feel to be home?" asked the driver, but confronted by a ruined set, Mary was not prepared for the intense emotions that washed over her. Asked the sympathetic driver, "Didn't they tell you? . . . One of the guards became disgruntled and burned half the studio down." In Badham's words, "They had brought in other buildings and created sort of a street, but it certainly wasn't what I had remembered. Everything was gone." Thomas Wolfe, it seems, was right. You can't go home again, even, or perhaps especially, when that home was a fantasy in the first place.

In the words of Brock Peters, the *Vanity Fair* photo shoot allowed the foursome to have a "family reunion," with Peters, Peck, and Badham teasing Phillip Alford for having turned his back on Hollywood. Noted Peters, "Now apparently he has relented a little." The "youngsters," Phillip and Mary, were now in their mid-forties, with their own children the same ages as the duo had been at the time of filming *Mockingbird*. As for that decades-earlier day when an angry Alford tried to roll Badham into an equipment truck, Phillip said, "She and I are very close now and we love each other, but I was thirteen and John was nine and Mary was nine and we despised each other."

Most poignantly of all, as the decades passed, Badham spent a great deal of time trying to locate John Megna and rekindle their youthful friendship. After leaving messages literally all over the country, she finally heard from John and they forged a close-knit long-distance friendship. When Megna talked of planning a cross-country trip in his RV, Badham volunteered to help drive part of the way and serve as his guide through her home state of Virginia. As time passed and she did not hear back from him, she continued to leave messages, until she finally received a call from his sister. "As soon as I heard her voice I knew he was gone," Badham recalled. "It was very sad." Megna had died on September 4, 1995, a casualty of the AIDS epidemic.

Secure in her work and happy in her marriage, Badham nonetheless felt the loss deeply. Another tie to her *Mockingbird* past had been severed, which made her embrace the legacy of her storied film all the more. As she said in one interview, "This is God's picture and a lot of people think that's silly. But if you think about the time period this picture was made, it had a lot of important things to say that still need to be said today and will go on being needed for ever and ever."

PHILLIP ALFORD

Three years after completing work on *To Kill a Mockingbird,* Phillip Alford played one of Jimmy Stewart's sons in the highly popular *Shenandoah.* Other first-class credits followed, including the *Walt Disney's Wonderful World of Color* episode "Bristle Face," with Brian Keith; the 1969 *CBS Playhouse* drama *Appalachian Autumn,* with Arthur Kennedy and Teresa Wright; the television movie *The Intruders*; and an episode of *The Virginian* entitled "A Time of Terror." But even as the work continued, Alford grew increasingly uncomfortable in the changing, drug-saturated Hollywood culture of the late 1960s and early 1970s. "I didn't do drugs," he said, "and I didn't really know how to react to it. So I got uncomfortable and came home after I did *The Virginian* and just never went back."

Upon his return to Birmingham, Alford completely quit acting. Holding a jaundiced view of the "money is king" world of Hollywood, he opined, "That business is not real. The money's not real, how you're treated is not real." Always wary of being a child actor who overstays his welcome, he wanted nothing more than to avoid the fate of Hollywood youngsters who are cosseted one day and completely ignored the next, washed-up at age twenty-five because they are no longer deemed cute. "By then they don't know how to do anything else so they drift into the wrong directions. They get bitter, get into trouble, go into alcohol or drugs, and basically ruin their lives," Alford explained.

He joined his father's construction business in Birmingham, married, and had "the two most wonderful children in the whole world," but even after he severed his connection with the film world, his ties with Gregory Peck remained. Staying in touch with Peck throughout the years, he grew to revere the actor not just as a friend but also as a genuine father figure. "This man had a tremendous influence on my life for thirty-five years," Alford said. "I see him now as just as much of a father figure as my own father was.... I just can't say enough how I feel about him."

Inducted into the Alabama Walk of Fame in 1989, and now a sixty-nine-year-old businessman in Birmingham, Alford has once again begun speaking with pride about his time in Hollywood, equally grateful both for his time on *Mockingbird* and for the fact that he is no longer a part of the show-business scene.

JOHN MEGNA

John Megna continued to act after *Mockingbird*, appearing in the very popular *Hush . . . Hush, Sweet Charlotte* (1964) and amassing a list of television credits, ranging from *The Alfred Hitchcock Hour* and *Star Trek* to the 1976 television film *The Boy in the Plastic Bubble*, with John Travolta.

He acted in one more classic film, appearing (uncredited) as the young Hyman Roth in *The Godfather: Part II* (1974), and his other film credits run the gamut from the serious *Go Tell the Spartans* (1978) to the nonsensical *The Cannonball Run* (1981). After graduating from Cornell, he became a high school English teacher and began directing for the stage. When he died of AIDS-related complications in 1995, he was forty-two.

ALAN PAKULA

It seems the shadows we see on film take a long, long time to fade.

—Alan Pakula

In the immediate post-*Mockingbird* years, Mulligan and Pakula first spoke of collaborating on a film version of John Cheever's acclaimed *The Wapshot Chronicle*, a fascinating prospect that, unfortunately, never came to pass. The duo did, however, collaborate on five more films, a list that began with *Love with the Proper Stranger* (1963) and went on to include another study of parent-child relationships scripted by Horton Foote, the darkly hued *Baby the Rain Must Fall* (1965). Their partnership remained solid, but Pakula's heart lay in directing, and in 1965, as he prepared for a directing career of his own, he and Mulligan amicably dissolved their partnership. They would work together once again on 1967's *Up the Down Staircase,* but after completing that successful film, each pursued independent projects of his own.

No longer afraid of putting himself on the line, Pakula began directing in 1969, scoring a hit with *The Sterile Cuckoo.* "Somehow for me, I find being older freeing. The older I get, the less fear of total exposure I have," he noted. His choice of material ranged from the journalistic thriller *All the President's Men* (1976) to the anguish of *Sophie's Choice* (1982), and the majority of his films proved both critical and box-office hits. An Academy Award nominee and winner of the New York Film Critics Circle Best Director Award for *All the President's Men,* he also wrote and directed the smash hits *Presumed Innocent* (1990) and *The Pelican Brief* (1993), and guided Jane Fonda (*Klute*), Jason Robards (*All the President's Men*), and Meryl Streep (*Sophie's Choice*) to acting Oscars. In an industry noted for directorial egos run amok, he remained a low-key presence, a man described by Horton Foote as being filled with "passion, enthusiasm, and conviction. He has no sense of ego."

Unafraid to reveal his own vulnerabilities, in 1998 he spoke boldly about the then rather taboo subject of (his stepson's) manic-depressive illness: "For a lot of people the idea of mental illness is something that separates you. Rather than making me feel separate, it just made me feel how fragile we all are. . . . We all live on the abyss, all of the time. And some reminder of that is not all bad."

By now, Pakula's agent was his old casting director Boaty Boatwright, who recalled that after the director was killed in a freak car accident in 1998—a seven-foot steel pipe smashed through the windshield of his Volvo station wagon on the highway—one of the very first calls of condolence that she received was from Phillip Alford, whom she had not seen in over twenty years. The *Mockingbird* ties had endured throughout the decades, and although Alford did not attend Pakula's memorial service, Mary Badham did; the *Mockingbird* team of Badham, Boatwright, Gregory Peck, Horton Foote, and Robert Mulligan attended both the memorial and the postservice gathering at the Tavern on the Green restaurant. It all proved a fitting tribute to the gentlemanly Pakula, who was not only memorialized by a Who's Who of film and television, including Diane Sawyer, Mike Nichols, Arthur Miller, and Harrison Ford, but also elegantly eulogized by Peter Jennings as a "spectacular, eccentric, complicated, and extremely modest man who gave a lot of people a lot of happiness and a lot of strength."

HORTON FOOTE

After Horton Foote won the Academy Award for *Mockingbird,* his career moved from strength to strength, his place among America's greatest screenwriters and playwrights growing ever more secure during the next half century. After collaborating again with Pakula and Mulligan on *Baby the Rain Must Fall* (based on his play *The Traveling Lady*), he worked on both stage and film versions of *Tomorrow* (1972), wrote the nine plays that comprise *The Orphans' Home Cycle,* and won both an Oscar nomination for *The Trip to Bountiful* (1985) and a Pulitzer Prize for 1995's *The Young Man from Atlanta.* Even with all of this acclaim, however, Foote himself was quick to point out that it was *To Kill a Mockingbird* that retained a special place in his heart: "I enjoyed working on it a lot, and we made lasting friends, which is the nicest part of all."

Written over the course of several decades, his masterwork, *The Orphans' Home Cycle,* unfolded as a three-part epic based upon the life of his own father. Through the specific lens of his family's history in the town of Wharton, Texas, Foote, accurately dubbed "the theater's great chronicler of existential sadness in small-town America," utilized no fewer than nine one-act plays to address the universal themes of loneliness and life's impermanence.

Deeply impressed by *The Orphans' Home Cycle*, Harper Lee spoke of the artful manner in which it managed to record an American society "disappearing before our eyes," going on to note that in his examination of mores and values, Foote's "steady gaze and wisdom [imparted] something priceless: the truth of what made the [men and women] who they are." In their somewhat different ways, Lee and Foote did, in fact, possess remarkably similar worldviews and artistic concerns: What and where is home? How do we define family? Can home and family last, or are they fated to fade before our very eyes? It was no accident that Foote began *The Orphans' Home Cycle* with a suddenly fatherless twelve-year-old boy being bluntly informed, "You're on your own now"; for all of their down-home folksiness, both Lee and Foote, it turned out, gazed unflinchingly at life's harshest truths.

With the passage of time and a concurrent change in social mores, Foote's fellow Texans had reevaluated their reaction to his Academy Award–winning screenplay for *Mockingbird*. When *To Kill a Mockingbird* came out, "down here people called up my cousins to ask how I could write a 'nigger-loving screenplay.' But now I think the South is proud of the film," Foote said. By the time of 1983's *Tender Mercies*, which starred his close friend Robert Duvall as a country-and-western singer, ironic parallels with *Mockingbird* abounded; once again the studio releasing the film had no interest in undertaking a wide-scale distribution, dismissing the movie as an art film of limited appeal until critical acclaim and highly favorable word of mouth changed their minds. In fact, the film, powered by Foote's beautifully written, subtle, and instantly recognizable character study, proved a small-scale audience pleaser and won Duvall his first Oscar and Foote a second, this time for the only nonadapted screenplay of his career.

Foote died in 2009, right after completing the ninth and final play in *The Orphans' Home Cycle,* just days short of his ninety-third birthday. He had lived long enough to hear his name mentioned in the same breath as Tennessee Williams and Arthur Miller, justifiably acclaimed as one of the premier American dramatists of the twentieth century.

BROCK PETERS

Given the limited opportunities afforded African-American actors in Hollywood, Brock Peters's varied and lengthy list of credits in the post-*Mockingbird* years speaks to the true range and extent of his talent. In his first notable appearance after *Mockingbird,* he starred in a 1963 television program about Harriet Tubman entitled "Go Down, Moses," following up that triumph with two performances of note: onstage as *Othello* (1963), and on-screen in *The Pawnbroker* (1964). Alternating among stage (Tony nomination in 1972 for *Lost in the Stars*), film (*Soylent Green*, 1973), and television (*Mission: Impossible, Cagney & Lacey*), he reached an entirely new generation of fans a full two decades after *Mockingbird,* thanks to *Star Trek,* both on-screen (parts IV and VI) and on television (*Deep Space Nine*).

Peters continued to speak out on racial issues throughout his career, and garnered industry-wide attention for the controversy that arose from his 1970 film *The McMasters.* Peters was portraying a character who seemed the exact opposite of Tom Robinson, a Union soldier who rapes a Native American woman (played inexplicably by the non-Native American Nancy Kwan); post-filming controversy arose because although the screenplay called for Peters's character to express remorse for his actions, the filmmakers deleted those scenes from the final cut, leaving behind a brutal character whose one-dimensional nature so upset Peters that he took the highly unusual step of asking the Screen Actors Guild to remove his name from all credits: "This cut of the film dehumanizes the character I created and moves it close to a brutish unpalatable stereotype. It does not reflect the judgment and taste which I have tried to make the hallmark of my career."

He returned to the stage repeatedly, starring in *The Great White Hope* and the national tour of *Driving Miss Daisy.* He won an Emmy in 1982 for *Voices of Our People,* received the Screen Actors Guild's twenty-seventh annual Achievement Award in 1990, and reached yet another enormous new audience by supplying the voice of Darth Vader for an audio recording of *Return of the Jedi*. He noted the huge strides made for actors of color since the time of *Mockingbird*, yet regretted the lingering racism that still pervaded the industry: "Eddie Murphy, Richard Pryor, Whoopi Goldberg are doing things we all dreamed about ... obviously there's been a change.... [But] we haven't banished the problem of racism in the industry or in the society."

Two years after delivering his touching eulogy for Gregory Peck, Peters died in 2005, at the age of seventy-eight. By the time of his death, he had amassed three Image Awards, two Drama Desk Awards, the NAACP Humanitarian Award, and Life Achievement Honors from the National Film Society.

ROBERT DUVALL

Shortly after *To Kill a Mockingbird*, Robert Duvall worked once again with Gregory Peck on *Captain Newman, M.D.*, after which he began a decades-long climb to major Hollywood stardom, morphing into the ultimate big-screen embodiment of the character actor as leading man. If he never became a screen icon in quite the same manner as Peck, his ability to completely disappear into all of his roles established him as extraordinarily versatile, and for decades he remained one of the most sought-after actors in all of Hollywood.

His own favorite among his roles was that of a mentally handicapped farmer in *Tomorrow* (1972), Horton Foote's adaptation of the Faulkner short story; in many ways, the farmer registered as a logical extension of Boo Radley, albeit this time possessed of a voice. It was to be another eleven years before his Oscar-winning turn as singer Mac Sledge in Horton Foote's *Tender Mercies*, but in between those two films there were beautifully wrought turns in *M*A*S*H* (1970), *The Godfather* (1972) and *The Godfather: Part II* (1974), and *Apocalypse Now* (1979); along the way, he garnered no fewer than six Oscar nominations for *The Godfather, Apocalypse Now, The Great Santini* (1979), *The Apostle* (1997), *A Civil Action* (1998), and *The Judge* (2014).

Throughout the course of his career, he won two Emmys, four Golden Globes, and a BAFTA Best Supporting Actor citation, but it was in his trio of Foote-scripted performances, *Mockingbird, Tomorrow,* and *Tender Mercies,* that he gave indelible life to proud and inarticulate southern men, men to whom, in the words of one commentator, the "redeeming power of love" is ultimately revealed. He happily worked again with Foote on 1991's *Convicts,* and the two men retained their very close friendship until Foote's death. Although the role of Boo Radley had been a small one, Duvall retained a special fondness for *To Kill a Mockingbird,* always referring to it as his big break; in a special tribute to the experience, throughout the years he made a point of naming a number of his dogs Boo Radley.

ROBERT MULLIGAN

After his Oscar-nominated work on *Mockingbird,* Mulligan reunited with Pakula and Foote on *Baby the Rain Must Fall,* and scored subsequent hits with films ranging from *Inside Daisy Clover* (1965) and *Up the Down Staircase* (1967) to *Summer of '42* (1971), *The Other* (1972), and *Same Time, Next Year* (1978). His last feature film came in 1991 with *The Man in the Moon,* which featured Reese Witherspoon's debut; Mulligan, once again fully at ease with adolescents, coaxed a solid performance from the neophyte, one that featured the flinty toughness she would bring to all of her roles. (One can see her playing Scout in a film adaptation of *Go Set a Watchman,* a southern tough gal leading with her chin, all steely resolve as she strides through life, this generation's steel magnolia. She did, in fact, narrate the audio book of *Go Set a Watchman.*)

If none of his post-*Mockingbird* films quite recaptured the same magic, they all displayed a quiet intelligence engaged in pondering the foibles of everyday life. By turns wistful (*Summer of '42*) and bemused (*Same Time, Next Year*), Mulligan's films remained resolutely life-size.

Explosions and car crashes held no interest for him, and although he found himself drawn repeatedly to southern settings, regardless of the setting what all of his films share is a gentle acknowledgment of just how simultaneously painful and rewarding the human condition can be.

By the time he died, in 2008, at the age of eighty-three, he had received critical praise from the likes of Stanley Kubrick (who featured a clip of *Summer of '42* in 1980's *The Shining*) and François Truffaut, who wrote, "If there were French directors as lucid as Mulligan, as capable of telling something more than anecdotes, the image of our country on the screen would be a bit less oversimplified."

ELMER BERNSTEIN

Throughout the course of his legendary career, Elmer Bernstein wrote a staggering total of over 200 scores, in the process working with a list of the greatest directors in Hollywood history, from Cecil B. DeMille to Martin Scorsese. He received a total of fourteen Academy Award nominations, and if his sole Academy Award came for lesser work on *Thoroughly Modern Millie* (1967), it scarcely mattered—by then he was already assured of a place in the Hall of Fame.

His range proved extraordinary, from subtle dramas like *Birdman of Alcatraz* (1962) and *Hud* (1963) to rollicking Westerns like *True Grit* (1969). Although he professed disappointment that by the late 1960s film scoring had morphed into a desperate search for a two-minute theme that could hit the pop charts, he remained in demand and up-to-the-minute, working on several music videos, most notably that of Michael Jackson's *Thriller*.

With his keen sense of film history, he established a Film Music Collection dedicated to reconstructing classic film scores by the likes of Max Steiner, Bernard Herrmann, and Alfred Newman. His own place in that history emerged in unexpected and touching fashion when he was asked by director Todd Haynes to score Haynes's Douglas Sirk homage *Far from Heaven*; told by Haynes that the film had a temporary score that he'd have to listen to while watching a rough cut, Bernstein balked, telling Haynes that he never worked from a temporary score, whereupon he found out that the score Haynes had chosen for such a purpose was Bernstein's own—for *To Kill a Mockingbird*.

By the time he died, in 2004, he had amassed not just fourteen Oscar nominations but also an Emmy Award, five Grammy nominations, and two Tony nominations.

HENRY BUMSTEAD, ALEXANDER GOLITZEN, OLIVER EMERT, RUSSELL HARLAN, ROSEMARY ODELL, AND AARON STELL

Like Horton Foote and Elmer Bernstein, production designer Henry Bumstead succeeded in building a genuinely legendary career, one that found him working with A-list directors running the gamut from Ernst Lubitsch and Mitchell Leisen to Billy Wilder, Alfred Hitchcock (four times), and Robert Mulligan (four times). Perhaps his crowning career achievement had been his brilliant, eerie, and ultimately iconic design for *Vertigo,* but after *Mockingbird,* he also won a second Oscar for his work on 1973's *The Sting.*

By the time of his retirement, he had worked on over one hundred feature films; the thirteen films he designed for Clint Eastwood included *Letters from Iwo Jima* and *Flags of Our Fathers* (both 2006) and two Oscar-winning Best Pictures: *Unforgiven* (1992), for which he received another Oscar nomination, and *Million Dollar Baby* (2004). Having won the Art Directors Guild Lifetime Achievement Award, Bumstead completed his association with *Mockingbird* by donating his storyboards and original location scouting report to the Old County Courthouse Museum in Monroeville shortly before his death. Ninety-one when he died in 2006, he was eulogized by the tough-to-please Clint Eastwood in words that summed up the true extent of this great designer's achievement: "Bummy was one of a kind. He seamlessly bridged the gap between what I saw on the page and what I saw through the camera lens."

By the time Alexander Golitzen died, in 2005, at age ninety-seven, he had amassed a similarly extraordinary list of credits: over three hundred films, fourteen Academy Award nominations, and three Oscars—for *Phantom of the Opera* (1943), *Spartacus* (1960), and *To Kill a Mockingbird*. Elected to the Art Directors Guild Hall of Fame, he continued working well into the 1970s, designing the box-office blockbusters *Thoroughly Modern Millie* and *Airport* (1970), and scoring a final Oscar nomination in 1974 for what proved to be his last film, *Earthquake*.

Set decorator Oliver Emert followed up *To Kill a Mockingbird* with films ranging from the *The Ugly American* (1963), starring Marlon Brando, to the Doris Day sex farce *Send Me No Flowers* (1964) and the Western *Shenandoah* (1965). His last major film, the World War II adventure *Tobruk,* came in 1967, and his official retirement two years later. He died in 1975, at the age of seventy-two, a year and a half after cinematographer Russell Harlan passed away; Harlan, in fact, shot only seven more features after *Mockingbird,* although 1962 had proved to be a banner year for him, with Oscar nominations for both *Mockingbird* and *Hatari!* He had received a total of six Oscar nominations by the time of his retirement, ending his career as Julie Andrews's cinematographer of choice on both *Hawaii* (1966) and *Darling Lili* (1970).

Continuing her *Mockingbird* connections, the veteran Rosemary Odell worked once again with Peck on *Captain Newman, M.D.*, with Oliver Emert on *The Ugly American,* and with Phillip Alford on *Shenandoah.* At the time of her retirement, in 1969, she had amassed a list of 114 credits. She lived for another twenty-three years, dying in 1992, at age sixty-seven.

Editor Aaron Stell reunited with Pakula, Mulligan, and Foote on such films as *Baby the Rain Must Fall, Inside Daisy Clover,* and *The Stalking Moon.* He retired in 1982 after working on a total of 137 films. In 1996, the year he died, at age eighty-four, he was the recipient of the American Cinema Editors Career Achievement Award, and in 2012, Orson Welles's *Touch of Evil,* on which he had worked, was voted one of the seventy-five best-edited films of all time.

HARPER LEE

Are you old enough to remember when people were less ignorant? I am.

—Harper Lee, letter to Wayne Flynt, February 18, 2005

Having weathered a second major onslaught of press interest after the Academy Award–winning success of *Mockingbird,* Harper Lee soon emphatically turned her back on any further publicity, her last formal interview coming in 1964. She did, however, still make occasional public appearances in the 1960s, and in March 1965, she gave a rather prescient speech to West Point cadets, one that rings all the more true in the radically divided United States of the twenty-first century. Said Lee, "The irony is, if we divide ourselves for our own comfort, no one will have comfort. It means we must bury our pasts by seeing them, and destroy our differences through learning another way."

While it may be true that most writers harbor a desire to be heard in person as well as on the page, welcoming the chance to publicly pontificate after spending so many solitary years writing, Nelle continued to turn in the opposite direction, coming to resemble no author so much as B. Traven, the reclusive writer of the classic *The Treasure of the Sierra Madre*, who simply disappeared from public view. She continued to spend the majority of the year living anonymously in New York City, and in an odd way, she came to resemble a strange version of Truman Capote's Holly Golightly in *Breakfast at Tiffany's*—both women said and did exactly as they pleased and refused to marry or "settle down." *Independence* remained their byword.

As the years went by, Lee developed macular degeneration and began using hearing aids, but she still kept up a full schedule of exploring the city she loved so much, riding buses throughout Manhattan while clad in an all-purpose tracksuit. A die-hard Mets baseball fan, she suffered through season after season of the New York team's poor results, but she enjoyed attending games at Shea Stadium. She kept up with the times, acquiring a cell phone, but admitted, " I . . . do not know how to answer it—just use it to call people."

As the new millennium approached, the request for interviews persisted, but Nelle's disinterest only hardened. Appear on Oprah Winfrey's wildly popular television show and be praised by the powerful Oprah herself? No thanks. Knowing of Oprah's love for *Mockingbird,* she did agree to a friendly lunch with the television host, but after twenty minutes, Winfrey realized Nelle would never consent to appear on the show. Said Lee to Oprah, "If you know Boo you'd understand why I'd never do another interview because I'm really Boo." (In fact, Oprah did land Nelle's last published piece of writing prior to *Go Set a Watchman,* when in July 2006, Lee wrote a letter to *O, The Oprah Magazine,* detailing her love of books and the importance of reading.) At times, it seemed as if the queen of England, Greta Garbo, and Harper Lee were the only public figures who wouldn't agree to appear on Oprah's show, but Oprah understood both Nelle's reluctance as well as the scope of her achievement, saying of *Mockingbird,* "It took inner wisdom and compassion for her to understand what it was like to be in someone else's skin. It was clear she had sat in that courtroom inside of his skin. That's pretty damn brave."

Spending the winter months back in Monroeville, she continued to live simply with her sister Alice in their one-story brick ranch home. Alice, who continued to practice law well into her nineties, oversaw Nelle's business affairs and served as gatekeeper for those wishing to interview her sister (when told she should have a form letter for saying no to interview requests, Nelle joked that her form letter would state "hell no!"). Although middle sister Louise appeared to be a more cautious observer of Nelle's success, having told her son's teacher decades earlier that *To Kill a Mockingbird* was "ridiculous," all three sisters remained close throughout their lives, the shared familial bonds forming the bedrock of their adult lives. With Alice and Nelle sharing the same house for several months of the year, the youngest and eldest Lee sisters remained remarkably close, with Nelle writing to a friend, "Alice is truly and without a doubt the most remarkable person I ever knew." While Alice went to the office, Nelle would read or visit with friends; there never had been evidence of a serious love interest, male or female, although as far back as 1961, Truman had written to the Deweys of Kansas that he was worried about Nelle because, he thought, she was "unhappily in love with a man impossible to marry."

After spending the day seeing friends or reading one of the hundreds of books scattered throughout the house, Nelle would join Alice for a leisurely dinner and discussion of the day's events in Monroeville. With both sisters still able to drive, they often took leisurely trips into the surrounding countryside they both loved, leading Nelle to observe, "One thing about us, we can appreciate beauty without needing to possess it." Love of countryside and all, Nelle remained as gimlet-eyed as ever about her surroundings, tartly noting how developers seemed to name new subdivisions for the very elements they had just destroyed; after bulldozing stately old oak trees, what, she asked, would the developers name that area? Oak Groves.

By now, Nelle's dislike of the spotlight had grown to such extremes that when it came time for her to renew her driver's license, she waited with a friend until the courthouse closed; only then would she walk in to renew her license, the town offices happy to service Monroeville's most famous resident as she wished. Exactly who was going to bother her at the end of a workday in her small hometown was anyone's guess, but for Lee, privacy now rated as a near obsession.

Mockingbird continued to shadow Nelle as both point of pride and occasional albatross, and in a particular moment of frustration over dinner at the Excel Main Street Diner, she told her young friend Marja Mills, "I wish I'd never written the damn thing." When Mills asked if she really still felt that way, Lee replied simply, "Sometimes. But then it passes."

While interviews remained out of the question, she did appear at a very few select public events. Never having graduated from the

University of Alabama (where a street on campus had been named for her), she agreed to accept an honorary degree in 1990, her total speech at the ceremony consisting of two words: "Thank you." After she was inducted into the Alabama Academy of Honor in 2001, the Academy, in conjunction with the University of Alabama, conceived a yearly essay contest in her honor, for which she agreed to serve as one of the judges. The contest was open to high school students writing about *Mockingbird,* and culminated in an annual luncheon, which Nelle attended. Even then, in the most congenial and protected of settings, she remained uneasy about such a public appearance, and, as her friend Marja Mills wrote, "as the event drew closer, a swirl of apprehension, resentment and irritation gained momentum." (Lee herself revealed a more humorous take on her reluctant public appearances in a 2006 letter to Wayne Flynt: "Nowadays I follow a mantra of great egotism: I'm older than anybody here. I know more than anybody here, so why should I be so afraid of anybody here? It works for about 15 minutes.") Nonetheless, dutifully appear she would, even agreeing to speak to a *New York Times* reporter, if only about the students: "They always see new things in it. And the way they relate it to their lives now is really quite incredible."

In her very rare public appearances, she could be amusingly blunt; addressing the Alabama Academy of Honor in 2007, she told those assembled, "It's better to be silent than to be a fool." She could also turn crotchety, refusing to be in touch with Mary Badham because "Mary acts like that book is the Bible." Hers proved to be a highly ironic comment, given the 2006 UK World Book Day poll, which rated *Mockingbird* as the one book every adult should read, relegating the Bible to second place.

Cantankerous or not, she kept watch on her legacy, and when not one but two movies on Truman Capote appeared, *Capote* (2005) and *Infamous* (2006), she made a point of watching both. By the time of the two films, Capote had been dead for over twenty years, but long before his death, the friendship between the two literary legends had fallen victim to his jealousy and substance abuse. Theirs had been a relationship unlike any other—two world-famous writers from the same small town whose relationship stretched from childhood into adult life; even with the decades of friendship between them, however, Capote had never acknowledged Lee's rather herculean efforts spent researching the background material for *In Cold Blood,* instead merely crediting her as "assistant researchist" and dedicating the book to her.

Throughout the years, rumors had floated that Capote had helped write *Mockingbird,* and while the rumors were completely without merit, Truman seemed reluctant to publicly refute them. As a close friend of Nelle's, he had, in fact, read the manuscript and suggested some edits, but Nelle had written all of *Mockingbird* by herself; with Truman's ego, if he really had helped her write the novel, he would have been the first to let others know of his contribution. The book was not his and couldn't be. The two friends shared a gift of appreciation for the rural, off-kilter, all-out southerness of their environment, but he did not possess the gentle sense of humor that suffused *Mockingbird*; his was a brittle, wounding humor, not one of bewildered and bemused recognition of life's oddities and contradictions.

Truman's downward spiral had accelerated greatly after his beloved high-society female "swans" cut him out of their lives upon publication of his gossipy, barely fictionalized story "La Côte Basque, 1965." (In fact, Lee herself had noted that after Truman's betrayal of Babe Paley in this story, on the rare occasions when she and Paley ran into each other, the glacially composed Paley would be reminded of her former best friend, Truman, and begin to cry.) Capote's decline continued to gather force, until it eventually grew completely out of control; the emptiness dating from his difficult childhood, which he had once filled with work, gossip, and measured amounts of booze and drugs, had now been turned upside down, the drinking and drugs no longer measured, the gossip, even about his friends, blindingly mean-spirited. The work dwindled away to an intermittent trickle, until finally only silence remained.

It's not that Nelle herself couldn't drink to excess; author Marja

Mills reflected on how drink could turn Harper vitriolic in phone calls: "It struck me as the flip side of her lust for life. With great passion comes temptation. With extraordinary gifts come demons." Great success and all, Nelle was not exempt from the 3:00 A.M.-of-the-soul loneliness that afflicts every member of the human race at one time or another, but, unlike Truman's, Nelle's bouts of drinking were sporadic and proved to be the exception rather than the rule.

The decades-long intimacy between Nelle and Truman completely disappeared, and by the time he died, in 1984, no one was very surprised; saddened, yes, but stunned, no. By then, it seemed to everyone as if Truman had been dying in public, particularly in his increasingly addled television appearances, for a very long time. Although the two childhood friends had been estranged for years, Nelle attended his funeral in Los Angeles. She was blunt on the subject of her former friend: "Truman was a psychopath, honey.... If I understand the meaning of the term ... he thought the rules that apply to everybody else didn't apply to him."

In watching the two films based on Capote's life, Nelle was not just reexperiencing her once-close friendship with Capote; she was also faced with the unsettling feeling of watching herself portrayed on-screen by not one but two actresses: Catherine Keener (*Capote*) and Sandra Bullock (*Infamous*). As for the performances and screenplays, Lee was of two minds: Watching a scene of Catherine Keener attending a reception after *Mockingbird*'s opening night, she drily remarked, "If there was a premiere and a party in New York, they didn't invite me." As far as verisimilitude, she bluntly noted, "*Capote* had my name but that was the end of any likeness."

Her reaction to Academy Award winner Sandra Bullock's depiction of her in *Infamous* was a succinct "I never wore socks" (with black pumps), but she was generous in her praise of Philip Seymour Hoffman's portrayal of Capote, presciently noting, "That was uncanny. He'll get an Oscar for this." As relayed by Marja Mills in her memoir *The Mockingbird Next Door*, Nelle's viewing of *Infamous* proved more than a bit surreal because of her ever-increasing deafness;

having first warned Mills, "You don't know how Hollywood works. They do stuff and then they tell you about it later," Lee then had Mills play the movie one scene at a time on the DVD player. At the conclusion of each scene, Mills would pause the movie and then loudly repeat the dialogue directly to Lee. They eventually made their way through the entire movie, until, at film's end, Mills commented to her friend upon the screenplay's liberties: "Well, it was an interesting experience telling you what you didn't say." Lee's amused response: "You see?" In the end, Nelle did rather approve of *Infamous,* telling Mills that she had written a letter to director Douglas McGrath, admitting, "You have a creature of such sweetness and light and called her Harper Lee that I forgive the socks."

As she headed into her ninth decade, she retained her sense of humor, musing aloud that as her friend Horton Foote grew older, he began looking "like God, but clean-shaven." She remained not just a voracious reader but also a surprisingly savvy consumer of current pop culture, growing into a big fan of the Pulitzer Prize–winning comic strip "Bloom County," by Berkeley Breathed. Inspired by Lee's depiction of Maycomb, Alabama, "Bloom County" eventually featured at least a dozen strips that referenced *Mockingbird,* much to Lee's delight.

Her bonds with the Peck family continued even after the passing of Gregory in 2003, and Peck's daughter, Cecilia, named her son Harper in honor of Nelle. It was Veronique Peck who persuaded Nelle to accept the Los Angeles Public Library Literary Award in 2005, even though her lifelong aversion to flying meant she would be traveling nearly three thousand miles cross-country by train. The award, fittingly, was presented by Brock Peters, and predictably, her entire acceptance speech consisted of precisely two sentences: "I'll say it again. Thank you all from the bottom of my heart." By this time, so rare were Lee's public utterances that those two sentences alone merited an article in *The New York Times.*

Just as Katharine Hepburn turned from fiercely private to surprisingly public in her later years, Nelle, with the passage of time, actually began to increase her public profile by small degrees. In 2002, she accepted an award from the Alabama Humanities Foundation, even appearing in person at the annual fund-raising event. Four years later, she traveled to Notre Dame University, where she received an honorary degree, and that same year she accepted the Birmingham Pledge Foundation's Lifetime Achievement Award for helping the cause of racial understanding, and also attended Horton Foote's ninetieth birthday party.

In 2007, she was inducted into the highly prestigious American Academy of Arts and Letters, but in April of that year, she suffered a stroke, which resulted in a partial paralysis of her left arm and leg, a condition not revealed to the public. She endured months of hospitalization and physical therapy, first in New York City and then at the Lakeshore facility in the Birmingham, Alabama, suburb of Homewood. After six months of rehabilitation (Wayne Flynt reveals that during this time she listened to the books-on-tape version of *Mockingbird* read by Sissy Spacek), she moved to an assisted living facility called The Meadows of Monroeville. Monroeville was, now and for all time, her home.

She faced her slow and painful recovery with characteristic grit, and by November 5 of that year had recovered sufficiently to travel to the White House, where, with Veronique Peck alongside her, she received the Presidential Medal of Freedom from President George W. Bush. (So ingrained is public perception of Lee's genuinely liberal outlook that it comes as something of a shock to read close friend Wayne Flynt's assertion that "Alice and Nelle became more conservative politically with the passing years, until they preferred George W. Bush to Barack Obama.") Members of the extended Lee family as well as friends from both New York and Alabama attended the ceremony; she looked happy and alert, but ever the iconoclast, she gave her medal to her agent, Samuel Pinkus, reasoning that he had lost family members in the Holocaust and that as a result he deserved it more than she.

Shortly thereafter, however, she sued Pinkus, the son-in-law of her longtime agent Eugene Winick, for maneuvering her into signing over the *Mockingbird* copyright without any payment. Claiming that Pinkus's machinations occurred in 2007, after she had suffered her stroke, she alleged that she had no memory of agreeing to relinquish her rights to the book. She fired Pinkus and replaced him with the London-based firm of Andrew Nurnberg Associates (although, oddly, for a time Pinkus remained as coexecutor of her literary estate). Eventually, the novel's copyright was reassigned to Lee in 2012.

The awards kept proliferating, and in May 2008, she agreed to accept an honorary law degree from the Alabama Bar Association for the creation of Atticus Finch; Finch was, the citation read, "the personification of the exemplary lawyer in serving the legal needs of the poor." Three years later, she agreed to be inducted into the Fellowship of Southern Writers, although she had refused the honor until Wayne Flynt deliberately mentioned that Horton Foote very much wanted his good friend Nelle to be included as another member. As it was, she accepted her induction only upon the conditions that she need not attend and that Flynt could speak in her stead.

Sister Louise died in October 2009, aged ninety-three, and by now neither Nelle nor Alice was well enough to be present at the graveside service. The three sisters had remained extraordinarily close their entire lives, and both Nelle and Alice felt the blow deeply. One month after the funeral, in a letter to Wayne and Dartie Flynt, Alice wrote a loving, gently humorous tribute to both of her sisters: "We three sisters really enjoyed our own company. Once we heard that a friend described us as follows: 'They laugh a lot; they enjoy their own company; they can't agree on a single thing, not even the temperature.'" Characteristically, even after this loss, Nelle rallied, and in the fall of that year she did make it to the annual awards ceremony of the Alabama Academy of Honor, an event she had enjoyed since her own induction in 2001.

Now nearly deaf and with severely limited eyesight, she was still able to move about in her wheelchair, although her physical world had shrunk to the confines of the Meadows. She remained aware of the fresh wave of publicity in 2010 that was tied in with the fiftieth anniversary of *Mockingbird*'s publication, and her room at the Meadows did, in fact, feature a framed caricature from two-time Pulitzer Prize–winning cartoonist Steve Breen, which celebrated that golden anniversary by depicting an American eagle reading *Mockingbird*.

By this time, Nelle's short-term memory had faded, leading Alice to remark to Marja Mills, "[Nelle's] surprised at anything that she hears because she doesn't remember anything that's ever been said about it." The one-hundred-year-old Alice had by now given up her legal practice of nearly seventy years and handed over control of her sister's business affairs to Tonja Carter, who had started as Alice's secretary and then attended the University of Alabama Law School before joining Alice's firm upon graduation. Alice had now moved to an assisted living facility herself (although not the Meadows), where she died in November 2014, at age 103, eight months before the publication of *Go Set a Watchman*. (Would Alice, Nelle's strongest and most trusted protector, have countenanced the publication of *Watchman*? The answer will never be known.)

Nelle was not strong enough for a 2010 trip to Washington, D.C., where she was to receive the National Medal of Arts from President Obama, and she remained as fiercely private as ever while living at the Meadows (said good friend Thomas Butts, "The good Lord himself couldn't get to her"). Tonja Carter proved herself a devoted watchdog, vigorously defending Lee not just from the ever-nosy press but from any person she felt threatened her client's masterpiece, no matter how slight the perceived infraction. When a collection of recipes was published in book form as *Calpurnia's Cookbook*, Carter, feeling that the book infringed upon Lee's novel, threatened legal action against the Mockingbird Museum, where it was being sold, demanding that the entire print run be destroyed (in the end, some copies were eventually saved).

Under Carter's legal guidance, Lee sued the museum in 2013 for selling unlicensed items associated with *Mockingbird*, further deeming the T-shirts, totes, key chains, soap, and coffee mugs an excessive appropriation of her creation, and therefore an impediment to trademarking the novel's title. As lawyer, spokeswoman, and estate trustee, Carter had formidable power; said Sallie Randolph, a lawyer who represents many authors, "This level of involvement is highly unusual." (Even Nelle's next-door neighbor, Marja Mills, felt the sting of Carter's displeasure after writing *The Mockingbird Next Door,* a gentle, flattering portrait of the sisters; when her publisher, Penguin, issued a press release stating that the Lee sisters had cooperated with the book, Nelle, through Carter, released a statement in 2014 denying that she had approved the memoir.) In 2014, lawyers for both the museum and Harper Lee agreed to a settlement, whose terms remained confidential. As reported by Lee's biographer Charles Shields, the museum's attorney did, however, agree to publicly apologize in the name of the museum for any implication "that Miss Lee is not in control of her own business affairs."

All of these events were duly reported in the media, because the reclusive Harper Lee remained print-worthy no matter what she did. The biggest news of all, however, was yet to come, because in February 2015, HarperCollins released a statement that was splashed across front pages around the world: After fifty-five years of silence, Harper Lee was publishing a second novel.

15

GO SET A WATCHMAN

Mary Murphy: "Did you ever think you'd see this published?"
Lee: "Of course I did. Don't be silly."

—Conversation between documentary filmmaker Mary Murphy
and Harper Lee

When the news broke in February 2015 that Harper Lee's lawyer, Tonja Carter, had discovered a heretofore-unknown manuscript of Lee's entitled *Go Set a Watchman* and that HarperCollins would be publishing this "new" novel by Lee, readers around the world were thrilled; at the same time, the outcry over whether Lee actually understood what was happening grew so severe that five months later Carter was moved to write a fifteen-hundred-word explanation of the events in *The Wall Street Journal* (which shares a parent company with HarperCollins).

According to Carter, she had met in October 2011 with both Nelle's former agent Samuel Pinkus (who had set up the meeting) and Sotheby's appraiser Justin Caldwell in order to undertake a full accounting of Lee's assets. In Carter's recounting, "Nelle's safe-deposit box contained several items, including an old cardboard box from Lord & Taylor and a heavy, partially opened but tightly wrapped mailing envelope sent from Lippincott, the original publishers of *To Kill a Mockingbird,* to Alice Lee and postmarked Jan. 3, 1961." Carter further explained that the Lord & Taylor box contained "several hundred pages of typed original manuscript." Carter did see a reference in the pages of manuscript to a character named Hank, a childhood friend of Jean Louise Finch's brother, Jem, with whom Jean Louise is "almost" in love. Carter reasoned, however, that Hank was simply a character cut from *Mockingbird*: "I thought, That's another short story that didn't make it into *Mockingbird*." It was assumed that the manuscript was simply a "later chapter" of *Mockingbird,* and, related Carter, after being asked by the two men to find a copy of *Mockingbird* for the sake of comparison, she found one and then left the meeting. (Joe Nocera, in *The New York Times,* labeled Carter's assertion that she left the meeting early a "preposterous claim.")

According to Carter's account, there the matter rested until the summer of 2014, when she heard at a Lee family gathering that Nelle had actually once written another complete novel. "I went back to the safety-deposit box another day—I started to go through the marked up manuscript of *Mockingbird* and I saw a blank page that said *Go Set a Watchman*." Added Carter: "I immediately went to Nelle. . . . I said, 'Nelle, when I was in the safe-deposit box, I found something.' She said, 'What?' I said, 'It's a manuscript of a novel called *Go Set the Watchman*.' She said, 'It's *Go Set a Watchman.* . . .' I asked, 'Is it finished?' Nelle replied, 'I guess it's finished, it's the parent of *Mockingbird*.'"

Nelle then granted her lawyer permission to read the manuscript; thrilled by the discovery, Carter told Lee's literary agent, Andrew Nurnberg, about the manuscript. He was equally excited but was, in his own words, "very wary because nobody knew about the manuscript's existence. What if it were second-rate Harper Lee? What if it shouldn't be published? . . . I approached it with some excitement—considerable excitement—but [wanted to] also have my feet on the ground."

At this point, Carter had a few others read the manuscript but cautioned against expectations, calling it a complete book but a "first submission . . . not edited. . . . It is exactly as she submitted it." Those Carter allowed to read the manuscript were "a couple of other people . . . outside of Harper's circle. People that Harper knew, independent of any deal, and they said 'It's good.' "

The manuscript was taken to HarperCollins (Lippincott, Lee's original publisher, had been acquired by Harper & Row, which later became HarperCollins) and the New York–based publishers proved, understandably enough, ecstatic at the idea of publishing a "new" novel by Harper Lee. Said HarperCollins publisher Michael Morrison, "I was blown away. I was shocked. I felt like I was being handed the most sacred thing I would ever hold in my hands." A statement from Harper Lee was released by the publisher in February 2015: *Go Set a Watchman* had been discovered by "my dear friend and lawyer Tonja Carter." Lee said, "I thought it a pretty decent effort. . . . I am humbled and amazed that this will now be published after all these years." The discovery of the manuscript rated as worldwide news, with readers, publishers, and even Hollywood stars weighing in. Said Robert Duvall, "I am looking forward to reading the book. The film was a pivotal point in my career. We all have been waiting for the second book."

As soon as the news was made public, the drumbeat of questions about Lee's mental capacity began. Did she really understand what was happening? After all, the reasoning of outsiders ran, she was nearly ninety, deaf, and almost completely blind. Did she even want the book published?

Given that the *Watchman* manuscript was not edited, one wonders what Tay Hohoff might have said about this turn of events. Would she have helped edit the book for publication? Advised Lee that it would hurt the *Mockingbird* legacy? Or, perhaps, feel that it would cast *Mockingbird* in a deeper light? Twenty-five years earlier, in a 1990 letter Lee had bluntly stated of Hohoff, "I was a first-time writer, so I did as I was told." This statement, on one level, could be read as casting doubt on just how willingly Lee had changed her original story line in the transition from *Watchman* to *Mockingbird*. Added Lee: "I couldn't argue with her—nobody ever dared." (At the time of *Watchman*'s publication, Therese Nunn, Hohoff's granddaughter, weighed in on the controversy, stating that it was an affront to her grandmother's legacy that *Watchman* was published after the most minimal of edits—a far cry from Hohoff's intensive work in editing *Mockingbird*.)

Tonja Carter, Andrew Nurnberg, and close friend Joy Brown all jumped into the controversy regarding *Watchman*'s publication and spoke of how, even with all of her physical difficulties, Lee's mental capacity had not been affected. Nelle Harper Lee, they said, understood exactly what was going on. Said Carter, "[Nelle] will take suggestions but in the end she does what she wants to do. She's Harper Lee," a view echoed by Joy Brown, who publicly stated that she had "visited her several times since *Go Set a Watchman* was discovered. She has all her marbles. Her first reaction—absolute surprise. And now she's just delighted with the whole idea of publication."

As testimony, Nelle's friend Wayne Flynt spoke of holding discussions with her about personalities ranging from Truman Capote and Gregory Peck to Thomas Wolfe and even Groucho Marx. According to Flynt, Nelle may have been almost completely deaf, but her mental agility remained intact, and he recounted a bit of their banter:

> Flynt: *"You could be King Lear."*
> Lee: *"And you could be my fool."*

HarperCollins president Jonathan Burnham stressed that the book was going to be published almost exactly as Lee had written it, the only changes coming in the form of minor copyedits: "It is completely finished. It needs virtually no editing. The only editing I think it needs is perhaps a light copy edit. It looks to me like a book that's been worked on and polished, and is very much a finished thing. So it's not going to go through any extensive editorial process." Perhaps more to the point was Joy Brown's comment: "If an editor had come in now and made suggestions, it would not have reflected the Harper Lee who was the writer in the 1950s."

To celebrate publication, on June 30, 2015 the wheelchair-bound Lee went out to lunch with Carter, Nurnberg, publishing executives, and Joy Brown. Given her near-total deafness and severe macular degeneration, questions for Lee were written down in large letters, and while communication proved slow, she happily accepted the first copy of *Go Set a Watchman* from HarperCollins publisher Michael Morrison.

In February of that year controversy over the book had exploded nationwide, with *The New York Times* publishing a front-page above-the-fold story entitled "After Harper Lee Novel Surfaces, Plots Arise." So persistent did the questions regarding Lee's mental status prove to be that Carter was now moved to publicly defend her actions, writing her own explanation of events for *The Wall Street Journal*. State investigators actually came in to review whether Carter had pressured Lee into publishing *Watchman*; they ultimately determined that Lee had not been forced in any way. Through attorney Carter, Nelle herself weighed in on the controversy, pronouncing herself " 'hurt and humiliated' by accusations that she was tricked or coerced into publishing *Watchman*." In Wayne Flynt's telling, she "became angry at [Marja] Mills and some Monroeville residents who claimed she suffered from dementia and was exploited by her attorney."

Lee's friend the Reverend Thomas Butts took a cautious approach to the controversial discovery, saying, "It is sort of strange it had not been found before," but another friend, Cynthia McMillan, a resident assistant at the Meadows facility, described Lee as "sharp as a tack" and "excited about the publication," and added, "It has given her something to focus on since her sister died."

Perhaps the two sharpest summaries of the controversy came from Diane McWhorter, journalist and friend of Nelle's, and Nelle's nephew Hank Conner. Said McWhorter, "I have no doubt that Harper Lee was competent to okay *Watchman*'s publication. . . . I can say with confidence that Tonja would not do anything that Nelle would not want her to do." Wayne Flynt underscores this analysis with his recall of Nelle's nephew Hank Conner's two-day visit to his aunt some weeks before the announcement of publication: "He asked her multiple times if she was certain she wanted the novel to be published. Each time she replied that she did, finally satisfying the single person who understood the situation best and initially had been most skeptical."

When published on July 14, 2015—complete with a rather nostalgic cover of a single train framed by a tree reminiscent of that found on the *Mockingbird* cover—the novel was presented exactly as it had been written fifty-eight years previously, a fact that caused a further bone of contention: Why had a book written over a half century earlier not been edited? Was this really what the meticulous Harper Lee would have wanted? Said publisher Michael Morrison, "We asked Nelle if she wanted to edit the book and she declined. We don't think it needed to be edited." Diane McWhorter weighed in with her belief that it was actually "a gift that she didn't reread the manuscript or edit it. *Watchman* saw the light of day as pure artifact."

Even in the face of such testimony, however, the naysayers were not content, repeatedly asking, "Did Harper Lee decline to edit the book, or was she physically and mentally incapable of any such editing, simply acquiescing to any publication?"

Which leads to the ultimate question: If Nelle had spent the fifty-plus years since *Mockingbird*'s publication without ever writing another book, why was she now allowing a first-draft novel to be published to what would prove to be certain worldwide attention? NPR's Maureen Corrigan bluntly stated, "Allegedly, it's a recently discovered first draft of *To Kill a Mockingbird,* but I'm suspicious: It reads much more like a failed sequel." The absolute answer to Lee's intentions will likely never be fully known, but with the end of her life drawing close, it may just be that Lee looked upon the publication of *Watchman* as one last chance to have her say, a final nod to glory.

The controversy over publication, however, paled in comparison to the furor that erupted over the book's actual content. Set twenty years after *Mockingbird*, *Watchman* finds Scout, age twenty-six and now referred to as Jean Louise, living and working in New York City but returning home for a visit. She has remained a maverick, refusing both to marry her boyfriend, Hank, and to accept the segregation that still rules Maycomb. Along the way, there are disquisitions on politics, religion, and race that collectively paint a much darker picture of Maycomb than that found in *Mockingbird*, and in the process complicating reaction to a book readers thought they understood in full.

The Jean Louise found in *Watchman* has evolved into a woman who "was easy to look at and easy to be with most of the time, but she was in no sense of the word an easy person." By now, Jem has dropped dead of a heart attack, and Scout's relationship with Calpurnia, who left the Finch household when Jem died, has been fractured; the old easygoing parent-child-like rapport with Calpurnia has disappeared and the housekeeper, hurt by the loss of Jem, remains distant from Scout: "[She] sat there in front of me and she didn't see me, she saw white folks." For her part, Jean Louise also remains uneasily cordial with her other maternal figure, Aunt Alexandra, insistently declaring her independence: "Aunty . . . truly, the only way I can do my duty to Atticus is by doing what I'm doing—making my own living and my own life."

It's not just Scout who has changed. It's the town itself, the old traditions and reassuring markers of polite society starting to unravel in the face of a rapidly changing world. Atticus, now seventy-two, is living in a new house in a different part of town, and an ice-cream parlor stands on the grounds of the old Finch house. Scout has returned to Maycomb and found that what she thought of as home no longer exists. In some ways, it plays out as Harper Lee's miniature version of Thomas Wolfe's *You Can't Go Home Again*, an exploration of returning to a hometown and seeing community and family in an entirely new light; the events in *Watchman* are oftentimes even strikingly reminiscent of Wolfe's own denouement, in which the main character, novelist George Webber, realizes you can't ever fully go home again: "You can't go back home to your family, back home to your childhood ... back home to a young man's dreams of glory and of fame ... back home to places in the country ... back home to the father you have been looking for, back home to someone who can help you, save you, ease the burden for you, back home to the old forms and systems of things which once seemed everlasting but which are changing all the time—back home to the escapes of Time and Memory."

The autobiographical elements that surface throughout *Mockingbird* are already present in *Watchman*. Jean Louise does, in fact, immerse herself in Victorian poetry, just as Harper Lee did, but of more import, she experiences the push-pull of Alabama and New York City in a manner strikingly similar to Harper Lee's own. The pressure to conform, which seemed to increase rather than decrease in the immediate postwar years, marks *Watchman* as a true reflection of the times in which it was written, but neither Harper Lee nor Jean Louise Finch were inclined to capitulate. Both seemed to view the ossified social code of Monroeville/Maycomb with a jaundiced eye, yet both still uneasily straddled the two strikingly different worlds of Alabama and New York City. Explains Jean Louise, "Every time I come home I feel like I'm coming back to the world, and when I leave Maycomb it's like leaving the world. It's silly. I can't explain it, and what makes it sillier is that I'd go stark raving living in Maycomb."

Jean Louise has overcome her small-town destiny through ambition and drive, but, it becomes clear, she exists rather uneasily as both a southerner in New York City and as an expat in her own hometown. When home in Maycomb, she's an insider who is also alienated; her southern roots call out to her and yet she recognizes that in Maycomb she'd be "churched to death, bridge-partied to death, called upon to give book reviews. . . . It takes a lot of what I don't have to be a member of this wedding." By contrast, in New York, Jean Louise (and by extension, one presumes, Harper Lee) could be her own person: "You may reach out and embrace all of Manhattan in sweet aloneness, or you can go to hell if you want to." In other words, as E. B. White writes in his affecting tribute *Here Is New York,* the city offers "the gift of loneliness and the gift of privacy"—a statement with which Nelle and Jean Louise both seemed happily to agree. There is no place for Jean Louise in Maycomb, yet she'll never be completely at home anywhere else.

Scout's childhood air rifle has been traded in for a set of golf clubs, the sport itself remaining a lifelong love of Harper Lee's. "Playing golf is the best way I know to be alone and still be doing something. You hit a ball, think, and take a walk," Lee said. The adult Jean Louise, in fact, strides through her life like the tomboy Harper Lee always remained: "It had never fully occurred to Jean Louise that she was a girl: her life had been one of reckless, pummeling activity . . ."

Watchman hinges, however, on Jean Louise's discovery that Atticus, her idol, is not just dead set against integration but actually espouses racist views. There is certainly no talk of trying to walk around in another person's skin in order to understand that person; Atticus, the one man whom she felt possessed the same character in private as in public, had "failed her . . . had betrayed her, publicly, grossly, and shamelessly." The near-perfect rapport between the all-wise, understanding Atticus and his feisty, smart young daughter has been revealed in a different light. He is here nearly unrecognizable both to the reader and Jean Louise; *Mockingbird*'s Atticus answered only to his own conscience, but *Watchman*'s Atticus seems to espouse the attitude of "you have to go along to get along," and while it seems excessive for Lee to have made him a leading member of the Citizens' Council's board of directors (surely she could have laid out the idea of his attitudes more subtly), Jean Louise nonetheless internally lashes out at him for daring to call her Scout in an attempt to rekindle their old intimacy: "Don't you ever call me that again. You who called me Scout are dead and in your grave."

Scout is hurting greatly, but it just may be that, in David Brooks's apt phrase, there is a bit of pleasure in her suffering: "The pleasure in suffering is that you feel you are getting beneath the superficial and approaching the fundamental. It creates what modern psychologists call 'depressive realism,' an ability to see things exactly the way they are. It shatters the comforting rationalizations and pat narratives we tell about ourselves as part of our way of simplifying ourselves for the world." In Scout's case, how, then, can she maintain affection and love for the one man who unconditionally loved and supported her throughout her life when he subscribes to a social philosophy she abhors?

Given that Harper Lee's father is acknowledged as the model for Atticus, one wonders if Harper Lee at some point harbored any form of resentment toward her own father. It is entirely possible that the Atticus found in *Watchman* was actually reflecting A.C.'s own attitudes, which represented the typical white southern male viewpoint in the 1950s; in 1952, attorney Lee had spoken of church as a venue for promoting salvation, but not, as someone like Dr. Martin Luther King, Jr., would have it, as a means by which to promote social justice. Said Lee to the Reverend Ray Whatley, "Get off the 'social justice' and get back on the Gospel." In the words of Nelle's biographer Charles Shields, "Like most of his generation he [A. C. Lee] believed that the current social order, segregation, was natural and created harmony between the races."

At the same time, Shields takes pains to point out that A. C. Lee's views on race moderated over the years, and the lawyer spoke out against the Ku Klux Klan, bluntly telling a reporter interviewing Nelle that the reapportionment of voting districts to help black voters was important: "It's got to be done." In the view of Wayne Flynt, "His Methodist upbringing had persuaded him that the Kingdom of God was as much concerned with justice in Alabama as with heaven in the hereafter." Said Charles Shields, "By the time *To Kill a Mockingbird* was published, A.C. counted himself an activist in defending the civil rights of Negroes."

What even a loose reading of *Watchman* reveals is that the sections recalling childhood—the Scout years—flow with an ease and love of language simply not present in the (adult) Jean Louise sections, which form the bulk of the book. It is, however, only when the book attempts to explain Atticus's politics that it becomes downright clunky, philosophical debates heavy on moralizing not making for a compelling read.

Readers can be forgiven for experiencing difficulty in trying to fully understand Atticus's racism, because in place of a backstory carefully and subtly explaining his former heroism, one is simply presented with didactic moralizing. Granted, this cumbersome philosophizing is mostly delivered not by Atticus, but, rather, by his brother, Dr. Jack Finch; it is Uncle Jack who tells Scout that the have-nots of the South have now up and demanded their due, tenant farmers and field hands are no longer willing to plow fields, choosing instead to work in factories for much better wages. In resisting the demand for total equality between black and white, Atticus and his ilk, says Uncle Jack, are fighting a rearguard action. But, whether from Uncle Jack or Atticus himself, such heavy-handed editorializing violates a basic literary principle of show, don't tell. If *Mockingbird* flows smoothly, indeed ofttimes thrillingly, from start to finish, *Watchman* more often lurches from set piece to set piece, only partially redeemed by passages worthy of *Mockingbird*'s lyricism. Then again, as pointed out by Diane McWhorter, Nelle was writing about the 1950s in the 1950s, and "it's very difficult to accurately capture a social revolution while it's going on."

Amid the heavy-handedness, Uncle Jack does provide some moments of interesting clearheaded talk, most of which usually circles back to the origin of *Watchman*'s title, Isaiah 21:6: "For thus the Lord said to me: Go, set a watchman; let him announce what he sees." Or, as Jean Louise explains it, "I need a watchman to tell me this is what a man says but this is what he means." In some ways, Uncle Jack's philosophizing as he addresses his niece does deepen our understanding of *Mockingbird,* playing as a logical extension of Scout's journey: "Jean Louise, every man's watchman is his conscience. . . . As you grew up, even when you were grown, totally unknown to yourself, you confused your father with God . . . assuming that your answers would always be his answers. . . . You had to kill yourself, or he had to kill you to get you functioning as a separate entity." But when Uncle Jack goes on to state, "He was letting you reduce him to the status of a human being," readers object precisely because they do not want Atticus reduced to the status of a flawed human being. Just like Jean Louise, they want to retain their illusion of the idealized father figure, the watchman who never wavers.

If, as Uncle Jack admonishes Jean Louise, "[P]rejudice, a dirty word, and faith, a clean one, have something in common: They both begin where reason ends," then Jean Louise's faith in Atticus, her belief in his perfection of moral rectitude, lacked reason. He has turned out to be a flawed man, a product of the times in his response to segregation. This feet-of-clay motif ultimately leads to the one exchange of dialogue that seemed to most shock readers hoping for another visit with their beloved, saintly Atticus; how, they wondered, could such a paragon of goodness actually say to his daughter, "Do you want Negroes by the carload in our schools and churches and theaters? . . . Honey, you do not seem to understand that the Negroes down here are still in their childhood as a people." (The racially charged trial around which *Mockingbird* pivots has already occurred by the time of *Watchman,* is briefly mentioned, and has ended in acquittal for the nameless defendant.)

When Jean Louise lashes back by accusing Atticus of a perverted sense of noblesse oblige as regards Negroes—"If you're good and mind us, you can get a lot out of life, but if you don't mind us, we will give you nothing and take away what we've already given you"—readers realize that they are light-years removed from the gentle philosophizing that informed *Mockingbird.* Instead, what readers of *Watchman* comprehend in rather stark terms is that the segregated world of the Deep South compromises every last white person who lives in it.

At the novel's conclusion, Jean Louise finally realizes she can't rush Atticus, that she can neither beat him nor join him, and that just as Uncle Jack has admonished her, if she doesn't make time for those with different and disagreeable opinions, she will never grow as a person. She stands her ground on the issue of segregation, leading Atticus to ultimately declare, "You may be sorry, but I'm proud of you. . . ." She is affected by his response, quietly telling him, "I think I love you very much," before Lee adds: "As she welcomed him silently to the human race, the stab of discovery made her tremble a little." Reconciliation has been achieved, but it all feels more than a bit uneasy—and labored.

The world had waited over fifty years for another novel from Harper Lee, which is precisely why *Watchman* rocketed to the top of bestseller lists, with sales at the end of the first week having exceeded 1.1 million. The national controversy upon publication seemed even further fueled by the book's timing: Just as *Mockingbird* had been published as the civil rights movement gained momentum, so, too, did *Watchman*'s publication in the summer of 2015 fit the new century's zeitgeist, touching as it did upon America's open wound of racial injustice. Atticus the racist made headlines during a time of police violence in Ferguson, Missouri; renewed national debate over whether the Confederate flag should fly over the South Carolina state capitol; and the announcement of a $5.9 million settlement reached between New York City and the family of Eric Garner, an unarmed black man killed by police on Staten Island in 2014. For both *Mockingbird/Watchman* and the country as a whole, the more things changed, the more they seemed to stay the same. Americans, it appeared, still needed to be reminded that black lives matter.

In analyzing these issues, Hillary Clinton actually seemed to invoke the very world of *Mockingbird*, writing of "the importance of trying harder to walk in one another's shoes. That means police officers and all of us doing everything we can to understand the effects of systemic racism that young black and Latino men and women face every day, and how they are made to feel like their lives are disposable. It also means imagining what it's like to be a police officer, kissing his or her kids and spouse good-bye every day and heading off to do a dangerous necessary job."

In his twenty-year journey from defender of black men to defender of segregation, Atticus had proven himself a contradictory man, equal parts bigotry and kindness—one who, in the words of Pulitzer Prize–winning author Isabel Wilkerson, "might even be described as a gentleman bigot." As pointed out by Joseph Crespino in a

New York Times article written at the time of *Watchman*'s publication, Atticus, in fact, seems to resemble no one so much as Strom Thurmond; Thurmond, a 1930s New Deal Democrat, had, by the 1950s, become the leader of the pro-segregation movement and an outspoken opponent of the 1954 *Brown v. Board of Education* Supreme Court ruling, which declared segregated schools unconstitutional (this, even though, in a move of staggering hypocrisy, he had fathered children by a black woman). Like Thurmond, the Atticus of *Watchman* seems an exemplar of the white southern male who, after the era of the New Deal, shifted his allegiance from the Democratic party to the Republican and remade the national electoral map in the process.

Like Thurmond, Atticus here seems to believe that the worst of all possible worlds lies in any involvement on the part of the federal government, an evil topped in his mind only by the participation of the NAACP ("standing around like buzzards," in Atticus's words). Calling himself a "Jeffersonian Democrat," Atticus explains that he wants to "manage my own affairs in a live and let live economy" free of government interference. (In one of the novel's more surprising passages, even Jean Louise, when asked for her thoughts on the Supreme Court decision—presumably *Brown v. Board of Education*—actually says, "Well sir, there they were, tellin' us what to do again.") As pointed out by Joseph Crespino, Atticus remains uncomfortably representative of a 1957 *National Review* editorial that asked and answered its own question on racial equality. Could and should white southerners maintain political control over black communities? "The sobering answer is yes—the white community is so entitled because, for the time being, it is the advanced race."

In short, if, as Wilkerson posits, *To Kill a Mockingbird* and the Atticus contained therein represent the national conscience, then in *Watchman* he seems to represent the real United States of the 1950s, rather than the country Americans preferred to believe existed.

Diane McWhorter asks, "Does *Watchman* cast doubt on whether *Mockingbird* was trustworthy after all, or has it propelled us toward a higher truth?" McWhorter answers her own question by admitting, "The answer is both. Harper Lee arrived at a certain truth in *Mockingbird*, but with the addition of *Watchman* we realize that *Mockingbird*'s portrayal of Atticus is not the story of the whole man. He is recognizably Atticus Finch in both books—the stakes were so different by the time of *Watchman.* . . . It's a mistake to ignore *Watchman*; the South will break your heart, and this is another example of that very truth.

"Harper Lee broke our hearts with this, as did Atticus. On the one hand, for all its glaring flaws, I think *Watchman* does help make the story richer. . . . And yet, while the fifty-plus years since *Mockingbird*'s publication have treated that novel very well, it may just be that *Watchman* will ultimately be shunted aside. *Watchman* doesn't fit our redemption narrative; Atticus becomes worse over the ensuing decades, and that cuts across the grain of our national impulse. The desire to go back to a false narrative is very strong, which is something I saw firsthand with how people marked the fiftieth anniversary of the 1963 civil rights marches. Overt racists from the sixties, on the record at the time with wild statements in favor of segregation—people I wrote about in my book *Carry Me Home: Birmingham, Alabama*—presented themselves fifty years later as always having been in favor of integration."

It's interesting to note that the controversy over *Watchman* rarely concerned Jean Louise herself, with readers and critics alike seemingly reassured that they recognized her as a familiar, grown-up version of Scout; NPR's Maureen Corrigan, in fact, responded quite personally, stating that she wanted to "transport Scout to our own time" and take her to a performance of *Fun Home,* the Tony Award–winning Best Musical, in order to show her the new possibilities for "nonconforming tomboys." It's an interesting leap, the show featuring, as it does, a lesbian cartoonist whose father, a closeted gay man, commits suicide, and such daydreaming would, of course, raise a host of new questions regarding the Finch family dynamic.

No, it is ultimately the sea change in Atticus, not Scout, that compels, and it may be that in the end the controversy over *Watchman* really centered on a never fully articulated element inherent in the collective response: The near saintly Atticus of *Mockingbird* is no more, but in his warts-and-all personality and worldview on display in *Watchman,* he may just possess a more recognizably human moral complexity missing from the near-perfect character found in *Mockingbird.*

16

THEME AND VARIATIONS:
EVERYTHING OLD IS NEW AGAIN

In the 1990s, *Library Journal* termed *To Kill a Mockingbird* the best novel of the twentieth century.

—William Grimes in *The New York Times*

A 2009 poll by the *London Telegraph* voted *To Kill a Mockingbird* the most influential book of all time.

—dailybeast.com

THE TWENTY-FIRST-CENTURY APPEAL
OF *MOCKINGBIRD*

Published in 1960, while JFK was running for president and promising a "New Frontier," and released as a movie on Christmas Day 1962, only two months after a nuclear missile crisis in Cuba had been successfully averted, *Mockingbird* had found its initial audiences in an America that, for all of its problems, remained certain of its place in the midst of "the American Century." Eleven months later, however, in the aftermath of President Kennedy's assassination, Americans began growing ever more fearful and suspicious, newly uncertain of their own place in the world. A new national reality took root, one compounded through the years by political cynicism in the aftermath of Watergate, an increased propensity toward violence, and the collapse of the traditional nuclear family. It all amounted to a collective loss of innocence, and yet far from losing its luster, *Mockingbird*'s appeal endured and even grew, a potent reminder of the way we were—and still often hope to be.

Fifty-seven years after the initial publication of *Mockingbird,* it is the bottom-line sales statistics that still startle: Translated into forty languages, the novel sells approximately 750,000 copies every year, a figure that far outstrips annual sales of *The Great Gatsby, The Catcher in the Rye,* or *The Sun Also Rises.* The sheer ubiquity of *Mockingbird* may, in fact, be one reason why the cultural and academic elite often disdain it—the more popular the book grew, the less intellectually respectable it became. In total, some forty million copies have been sold worldwide since 1960, and at the time of Harper Lee's death in 2016, her annual royalties remained in excess of three million dollars, a figure that only increased when *Go Set a Watchman* became the bestselling book of 2015 in the United States.

By some estimates, *To Kill a Mockingbird* remains required reading in over 70 percent of American high schools, the issues of race found in the novel still in the news every day; substitute the attempts of Syrian refugees to enter Europe, the rise of anti-Semitism throughout the West, or the obstacles faced by Mexicans attempting to emigrate to the United States for the prejudice faced by the African-American community in Maycomb, and the understanding hits home for students: These are simply new iterations of the same ancient disdain for "the other."

If, as we continually claim, we want our children to embrace the world in all its diversity, then by enlightening at the same time as entertaining, *Mockingbird* succeeds in a basic task of literature: the expansion of worldviews by means of exposure to differing communities and cultures. Exposure to one culture opens doors to others, and even if, as commentator Tracey O'Shaughnessy has written, they remain doors we do not choose to walk through, a concomitant increase in understanding and respect for others seems almost invariably to ensue.

The appeal of Harper Lee's novel far transcends its use in schools, however, and it came as no surprise when *Mockingbird* was chosen as part of the initial national "Big Read" program, an enterprise started by the National Endowment for the Arts to encourage reading among adults (the program itself was smartly described by Maureen Corrigan as "part literary idealism, part showbiz razzmatazz"). In perhaps an even greater sign of the book's wide-ranging appeal, *Mockingbird* also became a part of the "Big Read in Corrections" program, wherein groups of prisoners collectively read specifically selected novels. The character those prisoners most identified with? Boo Radley.

At the same time that the book's presence remains ubiquitous, the *Mockingbird* film continues to garner substantial interest in the home video market, and by 2016, gross DVD and Blu-ray sales had surpassed ten million dollars. Most notably of all, however, in 1995 the Library of Congress chose *Mockingbird* for preservation in the National Film Registry, citing the film for being "culturally, historically, and aesthetically significant." Once so registered, not a single frame of the film can ever be changed; there can be neither colorization nor editing for time purposes. Scout and Jem will remain as they should, in understated black and white, forever preserved in the shadowy world of childhood.

Thanks to the advent of cable television, *Mockingbird* remains a staple of Turner Classic Movies, turning up on the air repeatedly as part of theme festivals such as "Courage" and "Party Politics and the Movies"; during the latter celebration, famous guests took turns "curating" the series and explaining their selections, and while *Mockingbird* has long been considered an exemplar of liberal thought, its appeal seemed to transcend party politics. Said the conservative Republican senator Orrin Hatch (Utah) by way of explaining his choice of *Mockingbird*: "[It] reverberates with memories of [my] own past as a . . . young lawyer who took on pro bono cases."

Everyone, it seems, wants an Atticus in their life, or, even better, likes to glimpse himself in the Atticus found on page and screen alike. So indelibly did audiences identify with the character that in 2004, Atticus Finch was named the American Film Institute's premier movie hero of the century. The winner of the poll was not a man of action—not one of John Wayne's gunslinging cowboys or James Cagney's tough guys—but, instead, a new kind of hero, a small-town lawyer whose only weapons are words and an unshakable belief in the basic moral integrity of each and every human being. Two years later, a new poll rated *To Kill a Mockingbird* as number two on the list of the all-time greatest American films, topped only by Frank Capra's *It's a Wonderful Life.*

It seemed only fitting, then, that when Gregory Peck was honored with a "Legends of Hollywood" stamp in 2011, the image chosen was that from his performance as Atticus; one year later, the fiftieth anniversary of the film was marked by a special commemorative postage stamp and envelope, which were unveiled at the Monroe County, Alabama, Courthouse. By now, it appeared that everyone, even the United States government, was in the *To Kill a Mockingbird* business, an impression crystallized by the film's fiftieth-anniversary screening at the White House before an audience that included President Barack Obama and the then sixty-year-old Mary Badham.

President Obama has publicly referred to the film as one of his favorites, and he actually filmed his own endorsement, explaining, "A half century later the power of this extraordinary film endures. It still speaks to us. It still tells us something about who we are as a people and the common values that we all share. And if you haven't already had the chance to read the book, I hope you will. It's an American classic and it's one of our family's favorites." It proved a further and very deliberate choice on the part of President Obama to invoke the spirit of Atticus Finch in his farewell address in January 2017: "If our democracy is to work in this increasingly diverse nation, each one of us must try to heed the advice of one of the great characters in American fiction, Atticus Finch: 'You never really understand a person until you consider things from his point of view . . . until you climb into his skin and walk around in it.'"

Obama's affinity for *Mockingbird* makes a great deal of sense, not just in terms of social progress and politics but also in regard to personal philosophy. Atticus, it seems, is, in his interactions with the Bob Ewells of the world, a very real incarnation of the Obamas' oft-repeated mantra: "When they go low, we go high," and in both Atticus and President Obama lies the personification of Dr. Martin Luther King, Jr.'s dictum: "Let no man pull you low enough to hate him."

By some estimates thirty thousand tourists, conservatives and liberals alike, visit the *Mockingbird* museum in Monroeville each year—tens of thousands of visitors traveling to a town of 6,500 far from either the interstate or any major airport. So ingrained is *Mockingbird* in the hearts and minds of these visitors that their trips to Monroeville have begun to resemble pilgrimages; these men and women resemble nothing so much as real-life crusaders hoping to find and hold on to just a little piece of old-time small-town southern hospitality, much like visitors seeking their own Downton Abbey in the English countryside, or the suburban Italian-Americans who undertake their pilgrimages to Manhattan's fast-vanishing Little Italy in a vain search for a sense of old-country authenticity. Monroeville tourists hoping to step back in time to a slower, gentler, and more caring era are inevitably disappointed, confronted as they are with a modern town replete with cell phones, computers, and all possible manner of instant communication; one feature that does remain the same, however, is the area's intractable poverty, which has continued from the Depression to the present day. By one estimate, 20 percent of Monroeville residents still have incomes that fall below the recognized poverty line.

The goal of these pilgrims remains an immersion in worlds granting order, a sense of decorum, and a refuge from lives grown fragmented and increasingly absurd. Wherever the destination, whether the Downton Abbey countryside, Little Italy, or Monroeville, these visitors share a similar desire in their yearning for respect, civility, and manners, for breathing room affording respite from a modern world that values speed over thought, and one in which yesterday is dismissed as utterly devoid of value.

In the present-day demand for instantaneous information, which ironically we never give ourselves time to digest, we all, of course, run the risk of losing our sense of wonder, the wonder the ancient Greeks believed remained the cornerstone of wisdom. As one commentator has it, "Without wonder, we do not dare. Without daring, we do not imagine. Without imagination, we do not move. Without movement, we atrophy. We atrophy socially, but we also atrophy emotionally. Our souls are limitless. Why choke their expansion?"

MOCKINGBIRD TRANSFORMED

The ultimate sign of the basic material's continuing strength, however, may just lie in the numerous works inspired by, adapted from, or transformed by *To Kill a Mockingbird*. From the traditional to the avant-garde, from television to film, no matter how extreme the changes in *Mockingbird*'s basic story, the center always holds.

At the more conventional end of the spectrum, in 1991, the television series *I'll Fly Away* utilized *Mockingbird* as the template for its tale of life in the South of the 1950s. Starring Sam Waterston and Regina Taylor, the series' story line revolved around a white small-town lawyer who takes on racially sensitive cases while trying to raise three children with the help of a black housekeeper.

Two years later, in a radically different, experimental use of the material, filmmaker Martin Arnold directed *Passage à l'acte* (1993); utilizing thirty seconds of the dining room scene from the *Mockingbird* film, he reedited the material into a strange and ofttimes bizarre twelve-minute meditation on tensions within a typical American family. Here was film as a type of performance art, and depending on one's viewpoint, it was either thought-provoking or the visual equivalent of listening to chalk squeaking on a blackboard.

By the time of *Broken,* a 2012 film based upon Daniel Clay's novel of the same name, the basic *Mockingbird* source material had been reimagined in an entirely different country, with Scout and Atticus transformed into characters living in twenty-first-century North London. Scout, now renamed Skunk, is an eleven-year-old diabetic tomboy living with her father, brother, and nanny. Her father, Archie, is a lawyer and single father, and the film features both a Boo Radley figure across the street and a Bob Ewellesque villain living right next door. It is a much darker film than *Mockingbird,* the violence more explicit, but it remains, more than anything else, an homage to *Mockingbird. Broken* is described by its star, Tim Roth, as "an adult children's tale"—a four-word description that also neatly sums up *Mockingbird* itself. Even more powerfully, director Travis Wilkerson's 2018 documentary, *Did You Wonder Who Fired the Gun?*, utilizes clips from the *Mockingbird* film to underscore his movie's searing investigation of his white great-grandfather's shooting of a black man in 1946.

It is in the realm of live theater, however, where *Mockingbird* has made its biggest splash in recent decades. After years of playwrights and producers expressing interest in adapting *Mockingbird* for the stage, in 1969 Harper Lee granted permission for Christopher Sergel to dramatize her novel. The play began performances nationwide shortly thereafter, but the most noteworthy annual production came in Monroeville itself; beginning in 1990, and just in time for the thirtieth anniversary of the book's publication, the play began summer performances at Monroeville's Old Courthouse Museum, which paid sixteen thousand dollars a year for the licensing rights. Lee herself never did attend a performance, but the play proved to be an economic boon for the area; in the six-week "play season," as the locals called it, charter buses brought in audiences from across the South, and local hotels sold out. In Monroeville, the first act of the play was performed outdoors on the lawn of the courthouse, where a row of facsimile gunshot-hall shacks represented the Finch/Radley street; at the conclusion of act one, and in accordance with the mores of the 1930s, the "sheriff" would then call the names of twelve white males to serve as the jury for the act two trial, which took place in the courthouse itself.

This hometown production was not without its own controversy, however, when Harper Lee's lawyer, Tonja Carter, chose not to renew the Monroeville museum's license to present the *Mockingbird* play. Instead, Dramatic Publishing, a company that Carter controlled, licensed the production to the new nonprofit Mockingbird Company, led by its president, Harper Lee, and its vice president, Tonja Carter. Mockingbird Company would now present the play in Monroeville. For the museum, which counted on the play for fully half of its operating revenue, the loss of the license proved a severe blow.

This theatrical adaptation of *To Kill a Mockingbird* has been performed as far afield as England, Israel, and China, and in the United States the role of Atticus has attracted the attentions of the established stage actors Robert Sean Leonard and George Grizzard. A production far closer to Lee's heart, however, came in 2006 when Birmingham, Alabama's white Mountain Brook High School joined forces with the black Fairfield Prep High School to jointly produce a play based upon *Mockingbird,* a production that served as the basis for a documentary entitled *Our Mockingbird.* Harper Lee herself came to see the play, causing Roman Gladney, the student cast as Tom Robinson, to enthuse, "Oh my God, it was like I was meeting the President of the United States."

Using Sergel's stage adaptation of the novel as a springboard, Michael Wilson directed a 2009 production of the play at the Hartford Stage Company, one that also incorporated part of Horton Foote's screenplay into the text. Starring Matthew Modine as Atticus Finch, the play featured performances by Foote's daughter Hallie as the adult Jean Louise, and her husband, Devon Abner, as Boo Radley. In an interesting switch, Modine himself publicly stated, "I found my inspiration for playing the role of Atticus not in Gregory Peck's performance in the film, but in Horton Foote himself . . . strong and stoic, always on high moral ground with his goodness . . . his sense of duty and responsibility to family."

It will be, however, an entirely new theatrical adaptation that is scheduled to open on Broadway in fall of 2018 (the same time that a

Mockingbird graphic novel, adapted by Fred Fordham, arrives in bookstores). The new *Mockingbird* play comes courtesy of Lincoln Center Theater and prolific theater and film producer Scott Rudin, who, in 2016, and after two years of negotiations, acquired rights to stage the play on Broadway and in London (the nonprofessional theatrical rights remain with Dramatic Publishing, which administers the Sergel adaptation). Although Harper Lee had long been hesitant about granting rights for a first-class professional adaptation, according to her agent Andrew Nurnberg, "she finally decided that Scott would be the right person to embrace this."

Rudin had already turned to Oscar (*The Social Network*, 2011) and Emmy (*The West Wing*, 2000–2003) winner Aaron Sorkin to write a new adaptation, a challenge that Sorkin, a lifelong admirer of the novel, readily accepted. In the playwright's own account, he had actually first taught himself the intricacies of dramatic story structure by closely studying the movie of *Mockingbird* and continuously comparing it to Lee's novel. Even while acknowledging the challenge he would now face in adapting *Mockingbird* for the stage, Sorkin never hesitated in saying yes to Rudin's offer: "As daunting a prospect as it is, for so many reasons, this is what you signed up for." Explaining his love for the novel, Sorkin went on to say, "*To Kill a Mockingbird* lives a little bit differently in everybody's imagination in the way a great novel ought to, and then along I come. I'm not the equal of Harper Lee. No one is."

In beginning his work, Sorkin's first instinct had been to simply dramatize specific scenes from Lee's novel, an approach that failed: "I was naïve. I thought, 'Well how hard can this be? Harper Lee has written such a great novel, it stands up pretty easily as a play, just take her scenes and dramatize them.' That doesn't work at all."

Instead, unlike Sergel's adaptation, which clung doggedly to Lee's chronology and dialogue, Sorkin undertook a new approach to the structure, opening the play in different fashion from the novel and movie, and heightening the importance of housekeeper Calpurnia. It is Calpurnia who anchors the Finch household as maternal figure for

Jem and Scout, but in Sorkin's approach, she acts as spur to Atticus, forcing him to realize that he has acquiesced to the systemic racism that pervades Maycomb. Explained the playright, "He is in denial about his neighbors and his friends. . . . He becomes an apologist for these people. . . . He becomes Atticus Finch by the end of the play, and while he's going along, he has a kind of running argument with Calpurnia."

Describing his version as a "memory play," Sorkin, well aware of the pitfalls inherent in Broadway plays that feature children at the center of the action, went on to say, "You won't have to worry that you just spent $125 and watch children romp around the stage for an hour before Atticus comes out." He offered a blunt assessment of writing dialogue for Scout and Jem: "I didn't write their language like they were children."

Sorkin's determination to feature his own take on the material remained plain: "You can't just wrap the original in Bubble Wrap and move it as gently as you can to the stage. It's blasphemous to say it, but at some point, I have to take over." Well aware that he has placed himself at the wrong end of a shooting gallery in trying to satisfy the demands of forty million readers who love the novel, Sorkin humorously acknowledged that his own daughter, who had read the book in school, bluntly told him "not to blow it." In his own assessment, Sorkin wryly conceded that the hurdles he faces are daunting: "There's not much upside. The audience can hate you for ruining their childhood."

17

AT PEACE

The stupid believe that to be truthful is easy. Only the artist, the great artist, knows how difficult it is.

—Willa Cather

The Monroeville of Harper Lee's own childhood has by now long vanished. The Vanity Fair lingerie company is a shadow of its former self, having moved its manufacturing overseas, and the neighboring paper mill shuttered in 2009. The long-vanished dry goods stores of Nelle's youth have been replaced by banks and specialty shops; the Boulware house is now a gas station, the property that held Nelle's childhood home now houses Mel's Dairy Dream, and the next-door lot where the young Truman Capote spent his summers remains empty, save for the last of his aunt's camellia bushes. Visitors on a pilgrimage can glimpse remnants of the stone wall that separated the Lee home from that of Truman's aunt—and nothing more. As pointed out by Adam Gopnik, "The Monroeville Walmart Supercenter has doubtless altered Monroeville more than all the fiendish Yankee conspiracies to undermine the Tenth Amendment."

Nelle herself took a rather practical view of the inevitability of change in her hometown, but her relationship with *Mockingbird*'s presence in Monroeville remained complicated. From the gray mockingbird highlighting the Chamber of Commerce's sign to Radley's Deli and the scenes from *Mockingbird* painted on the side of buildings, there was no escaping the specter of the novel, even if she wanted to; in typically blunt fashion, Lee herself pronounced those twelve-foot-high *Mockingbird* murals "graffiti," and, eschewing even the slightest hint of sentimentality, dismissively wrote to Wayne Flynt in 2004, "There's not a blessed thing historic about the old Monroe County courthouse. . . . A rinky-dink film crew was in town using the old courthouse as a set for the trial scenes in their version of the Scottsboro Case (complete with Redfordlike young actor playing fat and bald Sam Leibowitz)." One can only imagine her reaction to the town's proposed Harper Lee Trail, which is slated to include a museum and copies of houses featured in *Mockingbird*.

The old courthouse-cum-museum features a plaque above the door stating "This room was used as a model for the courtroom scene in *To Kill a Mockingbird*," and even holds a room dedicated to Nelle, but she never did feel the need to visit the museum. Her one visit to any of the six historical sites overseen by the Monroe County Heritage Museum came not on a *Mockingbird*-related matter, but, instead, when Patricia Neal came to town and read Truman Capote's *A Christmas Memory* aloud. Safe to say, participating in the town's proposed "Harper Lee Day" did not feature on Lee's bucket list.

Participate she wouldn't, but Nelle remained proud of her achievement. She never made great claims on her own behalf, and given her disdain for the modern machinery of hype, she stayed more than a tad puzzled by the reverence with which her name was greeted. Even after winning the Pulitzer Prize, she left all claims of greatness to others; with her commonsense approach, she most likely would have agreed with the evenhanded assessment of acclaimed author James McBride (*The Color of Water*): "I think she's a brilliant writer—but Martin Luther King was brave, James Baldwin . . . by calling her brave you kind of absolve yourself of your own racism. . . . She sets the standards in terms of what we need to do today . . . we need one thousand Atticus Finches."

For Nelle, it was the influence her work had upon generations of readers and movie audiences alike that provided a true sense of accomplishment. Throughout the years, both Gregory Peck and Lee herself were told by countless well-wishers that they had chosen to become lawyers because of *To Kill a Mockingbird,* and after her death, *The New York Times* ran interviews with readers whose lives had been changed by the book. Said the sixty-three-year-old James Roth of Minneapolis, "The book was part of my decision to become an activist and go to law school. I've reread the book several times." None of those acolytes proved to be more notable, however, than Morris Dees, the cofounder and director of the remarkable Montgomery, Alabama–based Southern Poverty Law Center. Said Dees, "On a warm night in 1966 I saw *To Kill a Mockingbird.* When Atticus Finch walked from the courtroom and the gallery rose in his honor, tears were streaming down my face. I wanted to be that lawyer." Fifty years later, Dees continues to lead the fight against racial discrimination and hate groups.

Mockingbird's remarkable ability to inspire remains powerfully intact, yet at the same time, one all-enveloping question remains: Does it, like all great art, stand the test of time, or does it retain its appeal only to the still-developing adolescent mind?

The answer: Rereading *Mockingbird* as an adult reveals that its power remains unbroken, as relevant in the post-Obama United States as it was in 1960. If adolescent readers connect viscerally with the book's depiction of bewilderment and injustice, for adults there is a sense of identification with both Jean Louise's wondering, slightly melancholy voice and the clear delineation of the difference between understanding others and imposing one's views upon them. With its insights into the secret hearts of adults as well as children, its concerns with tolerance, forgiveness, and justice, and through its surprisingly clear-eyed view of the inevitable loss of innocence, it remains, as pointed out by Anna Quindlen, rewarding for adult readers in a way J. D. Salinger's *The Catcher in the Rye* never can be.

When rereading the book as adults, readers appreciate anew the fact that for all its charm, the novel actually reflects an adult world of gray moral ambiguity: Tom is wrongly convicted and killed, a murderer (Boo) remains unpunished (albeit for good reason), and racism still reigns. What author Scott Turow refers to as the story's "instructive function, an instructive moral function," remains whole, but when the novel is read through the eyes of an adult, a newly appreciated complexity emerges. Yes, *Mockingbird* is the embodiment of the now tattered mid-century idea that the best writers could explain America to itself and in the process formulate a common history for all readers; at the same time, however, it still speaks both to us and about us, because the racial problems found throughout the past eighty years—from the 1930s setting of the book to the 2014–2015 charges of Ferguson, Missouri, police brutality—represent different sides of the same coin. (In fact, the *Mockingbird* scene in which Jem tries to understand how the unjust verdict in Tom Robinson's case could ever have occurred was much quoted after Darren Wilson did not face charges for killing the unarmed Michael Brown in the Ferguson shooting of August 2014.) In the words of Mary Badham, "This is not a black-and-white 1930's issue. . . . Racism and bigotry haven't gone anywhere. Ignorance hasn't gone anywhere. . . ." As she says, "We're still grappling with these issues. It's just that people changed their clothes, that's all."

In Adam Gopnik's neatly turned phrase, Harper Lee made Maycomb "a permanent amphitheater of American adolescence," and whether reading the novel for the first time or revisiting it with their own children, adult readers often react to *Mockingbird* with a combination of rueful understanding and nostalgia, remembering what it was like to be a child exploring the world in a leisurely fashion far removed from today's world of cyber bullying and helicopter parents. While, as some might have it, nostalgia ain't what it used to be, it does in fact hold enormous sensory appeal; studies have shown that nostalgia offsets feelings of loneliness and boredom, making men and women alike more receptive to strangers, and even, as pointed out in *The New York Times,* helping to make life "seem more meaningful and death less frightening." Said Greek psychologist Dr. Constantine

Sedikides, "Nostalgia makes us a bit more human . . . [it] made me feel that my life had roots and continuity. It made me feel good about myself and my relationships. It provided a texture to my life and gave me strength to move forward." It's a view echoed by American psychologist Clay Routledge, who forthrightly stated, "Nostalgia serves a crucial existential function. It brings to mind cherished experiences that assure us we are valued people who have meaningful lives." Given the fact that no fewer than three major characters in *Mockingbird* die in the course of Scout's decades-later recall of the events, it is all the more interesting to read of Routledge's contention that "[s]ome of our research shows that people who regularly engage in nostalgia are better at coping with concerns about death." All of these reasons, it appears, help to explain how *Mockingbird*'s gentle but very clear-eyed understanding of human nature remains all the more appealing for children and adults alike.

In fact, the continued heartfelt response to *Mockingbird* now seems inextricably tied up in Harper Lee's ability to underscore a sense of community sorely lacking today. In a new millennium where the feeling of community slowly, inexorably continues to fracture, where the oral tradition has been dissipated first by television and now by egocentric social media, socialization seems to take place only in the form of disembodied electronic communication. Writing in 1948, theologian Paul Tillich analyzed his uneasiness that technology "had removed the walls of distance in time and space" but simultaneously strengthened "walls of estrangement between heart and heart." As noted by Hillary Rodham Clinton in her 2017 book, *What Happened*, "if only he could have seen the internet!"

Households lock themselves up, hunched over the electronic devices that splinter even intra-family communication and destroy any sense of neighborhood. (The ultimate irony, of course, is that the more numerous the means of communication we possess—cell phones, Facebook, texts—the worse we actually become at communicating.) It is, needless to say, impossible to picture Atticus tweeting; his seeming formality keeps his public and private lives separate, but today, no such boundaries exist. Shut off unto themselves, watching one thousand channels on a tiny screen, everyone is, in the phrase of the acclaimed 2000 book by Robert Putnam, "bowling alone."

In a twenty-first-century landscape in which the downtown communities where neighbors shopped, gossiped, and drew together have been replaced by sprawling suburbs complete with strip malls and impersonal big-box chain stores, the appeal of *Mockingbird*'s sense of neighborhood and community looms ever larger, an American version of E. M. Forster's dictum "Only connect." It is in Nelle's attempt to outrun the loneliness she sensed within herself and others, in her genuine desire to connect, that part of the novel's genius lies. The writing appears effortless precisely because Harper Lee believed so strongly in what she was writing.

At the same time, *To Kill a Mockingbird* continues to resonate on-screen not just because it is a first-rate film but also because the sort of heroic image exemplified by Gregory Peck has now all but vanished on-screen. Scant evidence of nobility exists in today's entertainment universe, but Peck's Atticus continues to appeal because he represents a reassuringly adult presence, a man who, without many words, simply pursues the right course of action no matter how difficult the journey. In an era where even the perpetual irony of a David Letterman has given way to both the smirking approximations of Seth MacFarlane and the Internet age of snark, Atticus Finch's stature and affect remain powerful precisely because they are presented without irony. When contrasted with a modern era replete with absent, work-obsessed, and often preoccupied fathers, men who continue to approach the foreign shores of adulthood still wearing baseball caps backward as they approach the age of fifty—a generation of Peter Pans writ large—there is a reassuring maturity to Atticus that resonates with parents and children alike. We all want the comfortable and comforting relationship with our parents that Atticus, in the winning person of Gregory Peck, has with his children: Casual enough to let them call him by his first name, comfortable enough to let them explore the world on their own terms, and existing light-years away from the affluent twenty-first-century world wherein parents constantly praise their children and tell them how special they are, Atticus is, in the end, capable of extending an all-embracing sense of protection. He remains a straightforward hero, the ultimate comforting presence who welcomes all of us home.

In the nearly sixty years since *Mockingbird* was originally published, the world has changed more than in the previous three hundred years combined: A sexual revolution stemming from the invention of the Pill rewrote the very nature of relationships, the feminist revolt reshaped both the workplace and home, men landed on the moon, the institution of marriage was opened to members of the LGBTQ community, the first African-American president was elected, and reality television smothered our channels until the very way people behaved and viewed the world was completely transformed; men and women alike now hoped, indeed nearly demanded, that a camera follow them around, the better to record their fifteen minutes of fame.

At the same time, subjected as they are to a daily assault of dark and damaged characters, both in theaters and on home screens, audiences have become immeasurably more sophisticated and cynical, a process that now begins with the violent video games that have forever altered the notion of childhood innocence. In seemingly endless ways, the entire fabric of American life has been distorted beyond recognition, yet people still return time and again to Harper Lee's leisurely evocation of a bygone world that is equal parts comfort and harsh reality. Such a continued heartfelt response to *Mockingbird* plays out as if the entire population wants to grasp the just-out-of-reach and now nearly vanished prize of childhood innocence, the enchanted world of a summertime twilight when all of the elements of the world align into what F. Scott Fitzgerald called "the golden hour."

The United States found in *To Kill a Mockingbird* was unquestionably a more racist, oppressive America, deaf to the desires and hopes of women, homosexuals, minorities, and nearly anyone who did not fit the prevailing definition of "normal"—a reality Harper Lee fully acknowledges in her depictions of Boo Radley and Tom Robinson.

At the same time, what *Mockingbird* offers is a mix of consolation and understanding, granting adolescents a first vivid glimpse that the world is often unjust, indeed downright cruel, but still possessed of moments of great beauty in our collective quest for fulfillment. There is wisdom in its pages about the ache of loneliness, the importance of family, and because everyone mourns their own loss of childhood innocence, a connection to the power of regret, specifically the universal rueful admission "If only I knew then what I know now."

Yes, as dispensed by Atticus, this wisdom is coming from a figure so idealized, so nearly perfect, that he carries more than a whiff of the all-knowing paternalistic Judge Hardy in the whitewashed MGM series of Andy Hardy films. It's why the revelation of Atticus's racism in *Go Set a Watchman* proves so startling. What next? The Pope doesn't bother to go to church? Gregory Peck's impossibly perfect but oh-so-appealing Atticus Finch does, in fact, seem almost too good to be true, but that is precisely the way audiences want him to be, and ultimately a big part of why readers so readily accept the harsher truths contained in the novel.

When asked if any human being could be as noble and idealistic as Atticus, Gregory Peck replied, "I've met two in my lifetime—my own father and Harper Lee's." Given the unsteady nature of Peck's own childhood, this does seem to represent more than a bit of revisionist history, but as the decades passed, even Peck himself fell under the spell of the *Mockingbird* film. It's understandable, because after all those noble parts in *The Keys of the Kingdom, Gentleman's Agreement*, and *The Yearling*, by the time of *Mockingbird*, Peck the man and Peck the screen legend had melded together in the minds of audience and star alike. Atticus may be too perfect for words—who else would tell a daughter that it is not okay to hate even Hitler—but, we realize, he's worth trying to emulate. Ah, the reader or home viewer thinks, if only I could be as good as Atticus. That's the person I'd like to be. He is, in the end, the father figure as avatar of tolerance and justice.

Whatever her critics may say, Lee is never simplistic, because she has clearly pointed out that parental protection has its limits, even when extended by the most devoted of fathers. Part of her great achievement with *Mockingbird* lies in the fact that at the same time the book is providing assurance, she is also making the reader feel uncomfortable. Evil seeps into life, whether in the form of Bob Ewell or our own next-door neighbor; when Atticus tells Jem, "There's a lot of ugly things in this world, son. I wish I could keep 'em all away from you. That's never possible," every parent in the audience can relate.

In many ways, of course, *To Kill a Mockingbird* allows audiences to have their cake and eat it, too. Scout has come face-to-face with the evil of Bob Ewell and survived. She has met the supposedly dangerous Boo and realized, even if temporarily, what it is like to live in another's skin. And, at the end of the night, she has returned to the comforting, all-protective embrace of her own father: "He would be there all night. And he would be there when Jem waked up in the morning." This sense of tranquillity represents a key component in the hold *Mockingbird* maintains over audiences worldwide, presenting as it does a universe in which complete happiness actually seems possible—edges squared off, each piece finding its mate like a completed jigsaw puzzle: brother to sister, parent to child. Family. In the universe of *To Kill a Mockingbird*, love conquers all, and in our collective connection to the innocence displayed on-screen and on the page lies a bridge to both our own lost innocence and to that most elusive quality of all—hope. A hope that may prove faint but that is still beating, a hope that goodness may just win out.

To a surprisingly high degree, *To Kill a Mockingbird* does succeed in capturing what the cover for the paperback edition terms "the human dignity that unites us all." Like the impossibly cheerful *Sound of Music*, it is grounded in autobiographical touches and grants us faith that, just as Anne Frank stated, "In spite of everything I still believe that people are good at heart." When Scout, speaking of Boo, sleepily says to Atticus, "he was real nice," Atticus simply replies, "Most people are, Scout, when you finally see them." It is just this sort of dialogue that may have irritated the intelligentsia for decades, but it continues to strike the deepest of chords with readers and audiences around the world.

Experiencing Maycomb, Alabama, through the eyes of a young girl exploring the world and testing the current of adulthood, audiences somehow feel a bit less alone, a little better able to understand the unending mystery of human existence. In so beautifully explaining that dawning comprehension, Lee's novel and Foote's screenplay succeed because they share the same concerns: a quiet consideration of the human capacity for courage and endurance—the abilities we all possess to either inflict great pain or perform feats that Foote so movingly termed "tender mercies."

At the end of the day, Harper Lee's story did not, of course, end racism—far from it. But in early 1960s America, at the dawn of the civil rights movement, it helped break down racial parochialism in a manner that spoke to Americans of all stripes. In an era before any social media existed, *To Kill a Mockingbird* inspired many a sermon, fostered talk on television and radio, and in the process enhanced a continuing national dialogue. Novel and film ended up reinforcing each other, doubling the story's impact in ways that movie adaptations seldom do. In the words of Oprah Winfrey, "The film made me realize the racial implications of the book." By wrapping a nostalgic look back at childhood around a clear-eyed gaze at how racism diminishes and damages an entire community, Harper Lee did nothing less than help readers and audiences look at America's racial history with a fresh set of eyes.

At a key moment in the film version of *Mockingbird,* Bob Ewell demands of Atticus, "What kind of man are you?" Here, in the query of the novel's villain, is the essential issue at the heart of the human condition because, in the words of Nobel Prize winner Aleksandr Solzhenitsyn, "the line separating good and evil passes not through states, nor between classes, nor between political parties either—but right through every human heart."

For Lee, the determination to live life on her own terms, along with a concurrent refusal to bend her conscience to the racial mores of the times, underscores the very achievement of the novel itself. In the forthright analysis of James McBride, "When it counted, Harper Lee did what was necessary. And how many of us now are doing what's necessary in terms of standing up for the good and for the just?"

It was no surprise, then, that when Lee died in Monroeville on February 19, 2016, at age eighty-nine, leaving a will that transferred her literary properties to a trust created in 2011, there was front-page newspaper coverage around the world. (Wayne Flynt, who delivered Lee's eulogy, reveals in his *Mockingbird Songs* that she had requested her ashes be scattered above Manhattan if she had passed away while still living in New York City. Having died in Monroeville, she is buried in the cemetery next to the Methodist church, resting alongside her parents and siblings.) Far from being a dusty relic from ancient mid-twentieth-century America, she had remained current to Americans of all ages, a name just as familiar to present-day high school students as it was to their parents and grandparents. The obituaries were voluminous, and it seemed fitting that her essence was most fully conveyed in radio commentaries and printed obituaries, in-depth tributes that reflected the slower-paced, thoughtful approach so characteristic of her own writing and way of life.

What, one wonders, would she have made of the events in Charlottesville, Virginia, on August 11 and 12, 2017, when displays of racial vitriol erupted into violence that left three dead and a stunned nation questioning its very identity.

Utilizing the controversy over the proposed removal of a Charlottesville statue honoring Robert E. Lee as a pretext—archconservatives invoked Lee as a symbol of liberty, implementing a "slippery slope" argument of "today Robert E. Lee, tomorrow George Washington," while liberals characterized Lee as a symbol of the Confederacy's defense of slavery—several hundred white supremacists took part in a Unite the Right rally. Carrying flaming torches, which reminded many of nothing so much as Hitler youth rallies, on Friday August 11, 2017, white protestors marched and chanted "White lives matter!" and "Jews will not replace us." Tensions grew, and by the next day, the words of violence had degenerated even further to cries of "Go the f— back to Africa" and, invoking the white supremacist who killed nine African-Americans in a Charleston, South Carolina, church in 2015, "Dylann Roof was a hero!" Violence erupted when rally attendee James Alex Fields, Jr., allegedly drove his car into a crowd of counterprotestors, killing thirty-two-year-old Heather Heyer and injuring nineteen others. When the helicopter carrying two state troopers charged with observing the rally crashed, the death toll rose to three.

For millions who looked to President Trump for leadership, his initial statement that the objectionable behavior in Charlottesville came from "many sides" invoked outrage. A leader who seemed eager to condemn any alleged violence involving illegal immigrants or Muslims, who falsely spoke of "illegal" voters being bused into New Hampshire and of crowds of Muslims cheering the destruction of the World Trade Center, now seemed downright hesitant to condemn those who espoused racial and religious hatred. Shocked by the president's conciliatory tone regarding the white supremacists, critics remained unmoved when, a full two days later and in a hastily assembled news conference, he intoned, "Racism is evil—and those who cause violence in its name are criminals and thugs."

The president's delayed response seemed the very antithesis of Atticus Finch's immediate and deliberate acceptance of the job defending Tom Robinson; if the concepts of liberty and justice were to hold any meaning, then, Atticus believed, the task was necessary, no matter the likelihood of failure. If the main job of any president lies in trying to unite the country, Trump's equivocation and delay in speaking out did more than embolden white supremacists and anti-Semites; he had, in the words of one editorial writer, "torn the national fabric. And the president has torn that fabric deliberately. As he sees it, to inflict wounds is a sign of strength. To heal is a sign of weakness."

As the specter of racism shadowed the nation yet again, the allure of Atticus Finch loomed ever larger, a revered man of compassion who attempted to solve problems by reason and understanding, by stepping into another's skin. Trying to fathom the Charlottesville descent into hatred, it was no surprise that editorial writers and ministers were wont to invoke the figure of Atticus, whose unimpeachable rectitude reminded Americans, indeed citizens worldwide, of their own hoped-for better selves. In the wake of nationwide shock, the cry seemed to be not so much "Where have you gone Joe DiMaggio/A nation turns its lonely eyes to you," but, rather, "Where have you gone, Atticus Finch."

More than ever, he seemed the very personification of the characteristics that, even under the blanket of our collective cynicism, we still yearn for in our leaders. In September 1960, then presidential candidate John F. Kennedy wrote a *Saturday Review* piece analyzing British military historian B. H. Liddell Hart's *Deterrent or Defense,* and in the process stressed a declaration of Hart's that seemed to speak not only to Kennedy's own style of leadership, most notably on display in the Cuban missile crisis two years later, but almost could have been written with Atticus himself in mind: "Keep cool. Have unlimited patience. Never corner an opponent, and always assist him to save face. Put yourself in his shoes—so as to see things through his eyes. Avoid self-righteousness like the devil—nothing is so self-blinding."

Would Lee have spoken out publicly about the events in Charlottesville? Her outrage certainly would seem likely, but her fierce desire for privacy remained to the very end of her life, and public utterances remained anathema to her. At the same time, however, she understood the public hold her very personal Pulitzer Prize–winning novel held on the American imagination, and in writing to friends in Mobile, Alabama, it seems as if she had, perhaps unintentionally, granted insight into both her great achievement and her own life: "People who have made peace with themselves are the people I most admire in the world." In refusing to live anyone else's version of her life, by conducting what Nathaniel Hawthorne termed one's "intercourse with the world" completely on her own terms, and in her determination to record her own particular account of both the madness and the glory of the American story, Nelle Harper Lee had made full peace with herself.

For Horton Foote, the point of *Mockingbird,* indeed the very meaning of life's journey, remained inextricably linked with that notion of peace—but even more so, grace: "I think the journey is what you have to finally be satisfied with, but [you can't] be afraid of the lessons one has to learn. I think that's, in my later years, the thing I've become at peace with, because so often it is grace. It doesn't seem like it at the beginning, but it ends up as grace. And you grow, you find a way to continue."

For Gregory Peck, the answer could be found in the best of his own work, as exemplified by *Mockingbird* itself: "I have a few [movies] like that, that when they're seen, people still enjoy them and get something from them, entertainment, information, a little bit of illumination of the human condition." Exploring this possibility further, he said, "Perhaps they'll carry a thought away with them. Perhaps they'll carry it with them for a while, perhaps they'll discuss it with their friends and it may have some effect eventually in a change of social attitude one way or another. I think that's as much as we can be sure of, but that's ... enough."

Knowing that on film a picture is worth at least one thousand words, when Horton Foote came to the conclusion of his *Mockingbird* screenplay, he ended with the most basic of directions:

We can see Atticus through the window, sitting by his son's bed and holding Scout. Camera slowly pulls back as Atticus looks at the sleeping Jem.
FADE OUT:
THE END.

In Gregory Peck's personal and heavily annotated shooting script, there are, on this same last page, four words scrawled in his distinctive hand:

Fairness
Courage
Stubbornness
Love

Four basic and seemingly ordinary elements of life, out of which, like all great artists, Harper Lee elicited extraordinary reactions.

Straightforward and complex. Comforting and disquieting. Familiar and yet unique.

To Kill a Mockingbird still matters.

NOTES

1. MONROEVILLE, ALABAMA

5   "a patchwork sea": Marja Mills, *The Mockingbird Next Door: Life with Harper Lee* (New York: Penguin, 2014), 9.

6   "[p]eople moved slowly": Harper Lee, *To Kill a Mockingbird* (1960) (New York: Harper Perennial Modern Classics, 2002), 6.

6   "Blood on the leaves": *Strange Fruit*, music and lyrics by Abel Meeropol, 1939.

7   "nervous disorder": *Washington Post*, November 18, 2014.

8   "the most uptight person I've ever met": Gerald Clarke, *Capote* (New York: Carroll & Graf, 1988), 123.

8   "a common anguish": Charles J. Shields, *Mockingbird: A Portrait of Harper Lee* (New York: Henry Holt, 2006), 34.

9   "starched walls of a pink cotton penitentiary": Lee, *To Kill a Mockingbird*, 155.

9   "I think one of the reasons": Mary McDonagh Murphy, ed., *Scout, Atticus, and Boo* (New York: HarperCollins, 2010), 160.

9   "A very nice charming down to earth": George Plimpton, *Truman Capote* (New York: Doubleday, 1997), 243.

9   "That kind of [southern] life produces": Harper Lee, interview

on WQXR, June 1964, as quoted at thebluegrassspecial.com /archive/2010/july10/harper-lee-interview.php.

9   "rambunctious gang feeling": Richard Ford, "Runaway American Dream," *New York Times Book Review*, September 25, 2016.

10   "We lived in our imagination": Alexandra Alter, "A Collaboration in Mischief and More," *New York Times*, July 10, 2015.

12   "Lawyer Lee will spend her future": Shields, *Mockingbird*, 93.

12   "she hated studying law": Ibid., 101.

2. MANHATTAN

15   "Atticus in a skirt": Marja Mills, *The Mockingbird Next Door: Life with Harper Lee* (New York: Penguin, 2014), 33.

16   "We didn't think she was up to much": William Grimes, "'Mockingbird' Author, Elusive Voice of the Small-Town South," *New York Times*, February 20, 2016.

16   "You have one year off from your job": Ibid.

16   "No honey, it's not a risk": Charles J. Shields, *Mockingbird: A Portrait of Harper Lee, from Scout to Go Set A Watchman* (New York: Henry Holt, 2016), 78.

16   "Nelle returned to Crane and Williams with the first fifty pages": Charles J. Shields, *Mockingbird: A Portrait of Harper Lee* (New York: Henry Holt, 2006), 114.

16   "*Go Set a Watchman* will be an eye opener": *From Mockingbird to Watchman*, a film by Mary McDonagh Murphy. First Run Features, 2015.

17   "known to the trade as the Quaker Hitler": Diane McWhorter, "Harper Lee, the National Antidote," *The Slate Book Review*, April 8, 2016.

17   "This reads like anecdotes": William Grimes, *New York Times*, February 20, 2016.

18   "a few thousand dollars": Shields, *Mockingbird*, 116.

17   "It was real": Tay Hohoff, as quoted in *Hey, Boo: Harper Lee & To Kill a Mockingbird,* a film by Mary McDonagh Murphy, First Run Features, 2011.

18   "art of retrospective falsification": Mario Puzo, as quoted in Pete Hamill, *Why Sinatra Matters* (New York: Little, Brown, 1998), 160.

19   "Then and now he has been ahead of his time": John K. Hutchens, "Harper Lee: On Life with Father," *New York Herald Tribune Book Review,* April 15, 1962.

19   "Because the two": letter from Harper Lee to Wayne Flynt, July 31, 2006, in Wayne Flynt, *Mockingbird Songs: My Friendship with Harper Lee* (New York: HarperCollins, 2017), 93.

20   "Don't you ever call me that again": Harper Lee, *Go Set a Watchman* (New York: HarperCollins, 2015), 151.

20   "My father had genuine humility": Harper Lee, as quoted in *Hey, Boo.*

20   "malevolent phantom": Lee, *To Kill a Mockingbird,* 9.

21   "was wading out": George Plimpton, *Truman Capote* (New York: Doubleday, 1997), 21.

21   "Look at what your foolishness has done": Ibid., 22.

22   "I did see him one time later on": *Fearful Symmetry,* produced and directed by Charles Kiselyak, Universal Studios Home Video, 1998.

22   "The Boulware family threatened to sue for defamation": Kerry Madden, *Up Close: Harper Lee* (New York: Viking, 2009), 128.

22   "I just felt that what I had to say": Diane McWhorter, "Harper Lee, the National Antidote."

22   "writing and tearing up, writing and tearing up": Shields, *Mockingbird: A Portrait of Harper Lee, from Scout to Go Set a Watchman* (New York: Henry Holt, 2016), 97.

23   "It's no secret": Ibid.

23   "After a couple of false starts": Jonathan Mahler, "The Invisible Hand Behind Harper Lee's 'To Kill a Mockingbird,'" *New York Times,* July 12, 2015.

23   "Ladies bathed before noon": Lee, *To Kill a Mockingbird,* 6.

24   "It's really a perfect title": Allan Gurganus, as quoted in *Hey, Boo.*

25   "almost like if you have a child who doesn't behave well": Shields, *Mockingbird,* 156.

26   "Absolutely fantastic lady": Plimpton, *Truman Capote,* 170.

26   "Hang on": Gerald Clarke, *Capote* (New York: Carroll & Graf, 1988), 323.

3. PUBLICATION

29   "an act of protest": Mary McDonagh Murphy, ed., *Scout, Atticus, and Boo* (New York: HarperCollins, 2010), 209.

29   "Author Lee, 34, an Alabaman": "About Life & Little Girls," *Time,* August 1, 1960.

29   "novel of strong contemporary national significance": "Engrossing First Novel of Rare Excellence," *Chicago Tribune,* July 17, 1960.

29   "It is pleasing to recommend a book": Herbert Mitgang, "Books of the Times: To Kill a Mockingbird," *New York Times,* July 13, 1960.

30   "sheer numbness": Harper Lee, as quoted at thebluegrassspecial .com/archive/2010/july10/harper-lee-interview.php, July 2010.

30   "A hundred pounds of sermons on tolerance": Glendy Culligan, "Listen to That Mockingbird," *Washington Post and Times-Herald,* July 3, 1960.

30   "For a child's book it does all right": Flannery O'Connor, as quoted in Terry Teachout, "'To Kill a Mockingbird' Review: Changing Its Tune," *Wall Street Journal,* February 27, 2015.

30   "the Evelyn Waugh of our time": Harper Lee, as quoted at the bluegrassspecial.com/archive/2010/july10/harper-lee-inter view.php, July 2010.

30   "intrigued": letter from Wayne Flynt to Harper Lee, March 22, 2006, in Wayne Flynt, *Mockingbird Songs: My Friendship with Harper Lee* (New York: HarperCollins, 2017), 65.

32   "lest it make a martyr of the author": Charles J. Shields, *Mocking-*

bird: A Portrait of Harper Lee (New York: Henry Holt, 2006), 201.

32 "immoral literature": Ibid., 254.

32 "Surely it is plain to the simplest intelligence": Ibid., 255.

32 "I think we are a region of natural storytellers": Harper Lee as quoted at thebluegrassspecial.com/archive/2010/july10/harper -lee-interview.php, July 2010.

33 "*To Kill a Mockingbird* is really the model": Murphy ed., *Scout, Atticus, and Boo*, 182.

33 "What I did present as exactly as I could": John K. Hutchens, "Harper Lee: On Life with Father," *New York Herald Tribune Book Review*, April 15, 1962.

33 "You start with who": Wally Lamb, as quoted in Murphy, ed., *Scout, Atticus, and Boo*, 38.

34 "It's not a matter of pretty writing": "Raymond Chandler Talks About F. Scott Fitzgerald," at https://silverbirchpress.wordpress .com/2012/09/13/raymond-chandlers-view-of-f-scott -fitzgerald/.

36 "I think part of your success": Shields, *Mockingbird,* 184.

36 "Masterpieces are not flawless": Richard Russo, as quoted in *Hey, Boo: Harper Lee & To Kill a Mockingbird*, a film by Mary McDonagh Murphy, First Run Features, 2011.

37 "We're paying the highest tribute we can pay a man": Harper Lee, *To Kill a Mockingbird* (1960) (New York: Harper Perennial Modern Classics, 2002), 269.

37 "may not make you do the right thing": Rick Bragg, as quoted in Murphy, ed., *Scout, Atticus, and Boo*, 60.

37 "There was too much horror around me": Andrew Young as quoted in *Hey, Boo.*

38 "I fell in love with Scout": Oprah Winfrey, as quoted in Murphy, ed., *Scout, Atticus, and Boo*, 200.

38 "kids against the world": Lee Smith, as quoted in Ibid., 179.

39 "induces in the reader": Diane McWhorter, "Harper Lee, the National Antidote," *The Slate Book Review*, April 8, 2016.

39   "This is their home, sister": Lee, *To Kill a Mockingbird*, 243.

40   "It was the first time": Wally Lamb, as quoted in Murphy, ed., *Scout, Atticus, and Boo*, 111.

40   "likened Tom's death": Lee, *To Kill a Mockingbird*, 275.

40   "sort of like shootin' a mockingbird": Ibid., 317.

40   "It's a book": Wally Lamb, as quoted in Murphy, ed., *Scout, Atticus, and Boo*, 112.

41   "I have never seen a greater monster or miracle," Tracey O'Shaughnessy, *Put the Kettle On and Other Cultural Disconnections* (Cheshire, CT: Equa Press, 2016), 149.

41   "Sorry-Grateful," music and lyrics by Stephen Sondheim, from the musical *Company*, 1970.

4. WHAT PRICE HOLLYWOOD?

44   "If she hadn't done that we would not have made the film": Robert Mulligan, "Feature Film Commentary," *To Kill a Mockingbird*, 50th Anniversary Edition, Universal Studios, 2012.

45   "They said 'What story do you plan to tell'": Peter M. Nichols, "Time Can't Kill 'Mockingbird,'": *New York Times*, February 27, 1998.

46   "From the very beginning": Kerry Madden, *Up Close: Harper Lee* (New York: Viking, 2009), 138.

47   "he was willing to pawn his belongings": Margalit Fox, "Robert Mulligan, Director, Is Dead at 83," *New York Times*, December 23, 2008.

47   "The best of this business is the collaboration": Charles Champlin, "For Pakula It's Falling in Love with Love and Being in Love," *Los Angeles Times*, March 5, 1980.

47   "kept wondering what the hell I was doing": "Alan Pakula," *New York Post*, April 15, 1976.

47   "I have known many people who have been so conditioned": John Culhane, "Pakula's Approach," *New York Times Magazine*, November 21, 1982.

47   "closet director": *The Aquarian Weekly*, January 26, 1983.

47 "There's the fear of final exposure": Culhane, "Pakula's Approach."

48 "If I hadn't worked with a director I respected": Ibid.

48 "Coming from Bronx Irish is Hardly Southern": Fox, "Robert Mulligan, Director, Is Dead at 83."

48 "That's what I think is true in life": Terry Curtis Fox, "Interview with Robert Mulligan," *Boston Phoenix,* August 8, 1972.

5. ATTICUS FINCH ON FILM

50 "I can't see anybody but Spencer Tracy": Charles J. Shields, *Mockingbird: A Portrait of Harper Lee* (New York: Henry Holt, 2006), 198.

51 "very much wants to play Atticus": Ibid.

51 "Knowing Rock": Boaty Boatwright, interview with the author, November 1, 2016.

51 "the perfect Atticus": Ibid.

52 "I called them at about eight o'clock in the morning": John Griggs, *The Films of Gregory Peck* (Secaucus, NJ: Citadel Press, 1984), 180.

52 "The right man landed the role": Jeanine Basinger, interview with the author, February 15, 2017.

53 "I saw the burning cross": Lynn Haney, *Gregory Peck: A Charmed Life* (New York: Carroll & Graf, 2005), 305.

53 "I was lonely, withdrawn, full of self-doubt": Gary Fishgall, *Gregory Peck: A Biography* (New York: Scribner, 2002), 30.

53 "I don't care to talk about my childhood": Haney, *Gregory Peck,* 37–38.

54 "I think it had something to do with the fact that my childhood": "Gregory Peck: The Seventeenth Annual American Film Institute Life Achievement Award Program": *American Film,* March 9, 1989, 16.

54 "the story to the audience": Fishgall, *Gregory Peck,* 62.

54 The young actor hurtled down four flights of stairs: Haney, *Gregory Peck,* 85–86.

55   "I was a stagey kind of actor": Bob Campbell, *Sunday Star-Ledger*, October 20, 2001.

56   "He was very patient": Fishgall, *Gregory Peck*, 111.

56   "A man's heart aches seeing his young'uns": *The Yearling*, screenplay by Paul Osborn, Marjorie Kinnan Rawlings, and John Lee Mahin, Metro-Goldwyn-Mayer, 1946.

56   "very closed off and rigid": Fishgall, *Gregory Peck*, 125.

57   "I got the idea that Gregory Peck": Haney, *Gregory Peck*, 152.

57   "I hold no brief for Communists": Ibid., 167.

58   "I felt like my head was going to go off": Fishgall, *Gregory Peck*, 158.

58   "If I don't I'm going to make a fool out of myself": Ibid., 173.

58   "The two keys to Peck's success": Blake Green, "An Evening with the Leading Man," *Newsday*, February 27, 1997.

58   "Overacting is a self-indulgence": William Grimes, "Gregory Peck Is Dead at 87," *New York Times*, June 13, 2002.

59   "They run in rhythm": Haney, *Gregory Peck*, 339.

59   "formidable": Fishgall, *Gregory Peck*, 256.

59   "not completely accepted by his stepmother": Haney, *Gregory Peck*, 316.

59   "simply . . . separate myself from them": Fishgall, *Gregory Peck*, 187.

60   "Greg Peck is never going to be a paranoid killer": Ibid., 186.

60   "I wasn't mad enough, not crazy enough": Haney, *Gregory Peck*, 250.

60   "I've seen them all": Ibid., 318.

60   "That desire to be loved": Fishgall, *Gregory Peck*, 148.

60   "fear of being revealed as the person he was": Ibid., 148–49.

60   "I must say the man and the character": *Life, The Enduring Power of To Kill a Mockingbird*, special issue, 2015, 59.

60   "God was smiling on me": Fishgall, *Gregory Peck*, 232.

6. ENTER HORTON FOOTE

62   "After all I don't write deathless prose": Harper Lee, as quoted at thebluegrassspecial.com/archive/2010/july10/harper-lee-interview.php, July 2010.

62 "very sympathetic towards his ideas": Horton Foote, *Three Screenplays* (New York: Grove Press, 1989), xi.

63 "very low, low, low budget": Gerald C. Wood and Marion Castleberry, *The Voice of an American Playwright: Interviews with Horton Foote* (Macon, GA: Mercer University Press, 2012), 239.

63 "grousing as I usually do": Ibid., 164.

64 "The most extraordinary change is that the town itself": Dan Rather interview with Horton Foote, *CBS News Sunday Morning*, May 1997.

64 "believers in the basic honor and dignity": Marion Castleberry, *Blessed Assurance: The Life and Art of Horton Foote* (Macon, GA: Mercer University Press, 2014), 215.

64 "You better get to that book and read it": Wood and Castleberry, *The Voice of an American Playwright*, 164.

65 "Whatever R. P. Blackmur meant": Ibid., 255.

65 "Scout is sort of an extension": Wally Lamb, as quoted in Mary McDonagh Murphy, ed., *Scout, Atticus, and Boo* (New York: HarperCollins, 2010), 118.

65 "along with and through the eyes of the children": Foote, *Three Screenplays*, xiii.

65 "I must say, she sold me": Wood and Castleberry, *The Voice of an American Playwright*, 43.

65 "You know there's going to come a time": Ibid., 8.

65 "Now listen": Castleberry, *Blessed Assurance*, 213.

65 "Don't talk to me and don't ask me questions": Wood and Castleberry, *The Voice of an American Playwright*, 161.

66 "sprawling": Ibid., 9.

67 "The minute she told me it was based on Truman Capote": Ibid., 70.

68 "Maycomb was a tired old town": Foote, *Three Screenplays*, 5.

68 "That's how I heard all the news I wasn't supposed to hear": Wood and Castleberry, *The Voice of an American Playwright*, 70.

69 "Although some writers are very skillful": Ibid., 10.

69 "Too often you lose the point of view of the children": Robert

Mulligan "Feature Film Commentary," *To Kill a Mockingbird*, 50th Anniversary Edition, Universal Studios, 2012.

69   "Why are writers so unhappy out here?": Foote, *Three Screenplays,* xii.

69   "Come on now, is this really the first draft?": Wood and Castleberry, *The Voice of an American Playwright,* 176.

7. CASTING THE MOVIE

71   "I was at Sardi's": Boaty Boatwright, interview with the author, November 1, 2016.

71   "I grew up in Reidsville": Ibid.

72   "a most remarkable man": Ibid.

72   "I want children": Ibid.

72   "didn't have the rhythm": Ibid.

72   "The mothers were just as pushy": Ibid.

72   "I tried to make them feel comfortable": Ibid.

73   "Alan, I don't think": Ibid.

73   "I'm locked in my hotel room": Alan Pakula, "All Those Shirley Temples," *New York Herald Tribune,* July 15, 1962.

73   "a gamine haircut": Boatwright, interview with the author, November 1, 2016.

73   "Hmmm . . . definitely not a Shirley Temple clone": Ibid.

73   "We don't think nice people": Ibid.

73   "If you speak to even one person": Ibid.

74   "What could be the possible harm?": Barbara Hoffman, "Scout's Honor," *New York Post,* July 14, 2005.

74   "something about chopping some wood": *Fearful Symmetry,* produced and directed by Charles Kiselyak, Universal Studios Home Video, 1998.

74   "How old are you?": Mary McDonagh Murphy, ed., *Scout, Atticus, and Boo* (New York: HarperCollins, 2010), 54.

74   "pronounced 'nine' in two syllables": Boatwright, interview with the author, November 1, 2016.

74 "I found Scout!": Ibid.

74 "had nixed acting as 'tacky'": Diane McWhorter, *Carry Me Home: Birmingham, Alabama: The Climactic Battle of the Civil Rights Revolution* (New York: Simon & Schuster, 2001), 322.

75 "an angel face": Ibid.

76 "They both had a quality I was looking for": Marion Castleberry, *Blessed Assurance: The Life and Art of Horton Foote* (Macon, GA: Mercer University Press, 2014), 220.

76 "The only one they had to deal with was me": Robert Mulligan, "Feature Film Commentary," *To Kill a Mockingbird*, 50th Anniversary Edition, Universal Studios, 2012.

76 "It was just miraculous": Boatwright, interview with the author, November 1, 2016.

77 "I want to be in oil": Ibid.

77 "a very unaffected kid": Castleberry, *Blessed Assurance,* 220.

77 "Someday when I'm a big star": Boatwright, interview with the author, November 1, 2016.

77 "godlike quality": *Fearful Symmetry: Making of To Kill a Mockingbird*, Charles Kiselyak, director, Universal Home Video, 1998.

79 "you and I will have to have a clear understanding": Robert Mulligan, "Feature Film Commentary," *To Kill a Mockingbird*, 50th Anniversary Edition, Universal Studios, 2012.

79 "All the other girls": Dennis McLellan, "Collin Wilcox Paxton Dies at 74; actress was Mayella in 'To Kill a Mockingbird,'" *Los Angeles Times,* October 23, 2009.

8. FROM PULITZER PRIZE TO HOLLYWOOD DREAM TEAM

84 "an absolute wizard": Robert Mulligan, "Feature Film Commentary," *To Kill a Mockingbird*, 50th Anniversary Edition, Universal Studios, 2012.

84   "Henry Bumstead was a delightful man": Jeanine Basinger, interview with the author, February 16, 2017.

85   "a most charming person": Marja Mills, *The Mockingbird Next Door: Life with Harper Lee* (New York: Penguin, 2010), 17.

85   "Most of the houses are of wood": Ibid., 17–18.

86   "so we could do this sequence": Kerry Madden, *Up Close: Harper Lee* (New York: Viking, 2009), 146.

87   "My God Almighty!": Marion Castleberry, *Blessed Assurance: The Life and Art of Horton Foote* (Macon, GA: Mercer University Press, 2014), 222.

87   "They [the Finches] lived in the kind of house": Gerald C. Wood and Marion Castleberry, *The Voice of an American Playwright: Interviews with Horton Foote* (Macon, GA: Mercer University Press, 2012), 87.

88   "at least $100,000": "Film Crew Saves $75,000 on Shacks," *New York Times,* January 19, 1962.

89   "The reason that they were able to communicate": Elmer Bernstein, "On Film Music," *Journal of the University Film Association* 28, 4 (Fall 1976).

91   asking instead that the diner send food over: Charles J. Shields, *Mockingbird: A Portrait of Harper Lee* (New York: Henry Holt, 2006), 209.

91   "Isn't he delicious?": Mills, *The Mockingbird Next Door,* 199.

92   "in character and—the South has a good word for this": John K. Hutchens, "Life with Father," *New York Herald Tribune,* April 15, 1962.

92   "He was surprised," Madden, *Up Close: Harper Lee,* 129.

9. MAYCOMB COMES TO LIFE

93   "Always that warmth, that smile": "Scout Remembers," *To Kill a Mockingbird,* 50th Anniversary Edition, Universal Studios, 2012.

94   "It does not matter about the children being stars": Kerry Madden, *Up Close: Harper Lee* (New York: Viking, 2009), 155.

94   "Nothing empties a Southern movie house faster": "Gregory Peck:

The Seventeenth Annual American Film Institute Life Achievement Award Program," *American Film,* March 9, 1989, 11.

94   "one harmless indulgence": Ibid.

95   "It was the most amazing transformation": Lynn Haney, *Gregory Peck: A Charmed Life* (New York: Carroll & Graf, 2005), 308.

96   "The shooting, the editing, the use of music": "American Auteurs: Robert Mulligan," Lincoln Center Film Program Notes, March 18–25, 2009.

96   "If that man isn't really into my head": Terry Curtis Fox, "Interview with Robert Mulligan," *Boston Phoenix,* August 8, 1972.

97   "a glistening on her cheek": Haney, *Gregory Peck,* 308.

97   "everything would be fine without me": Harper Lee, as quoted at thebluegrassspecial.com/archive/2010/july10/harper-lee-interview.php, July 2010.

97   "How I delivered the lines was left to me": Mary Badham, as quoted in *Hey, Boo: Harper Lee & To Kill a Mockingbird,* a film by Mary McDonagh Murphy, First Run Features, 2011.

98   "Kids are marvelous at improvisation": Fox, "Interview with Robert Mulligan."

98   tan three-button suit: Thomas McDonald, "Bird in Hand," *New York Times,* May 6, 1962.

98   "not in the Dr. Spock sense": John C. Waugh, "Robert Mulligan's Aspirations," *Christian Science Monitor,* January 23, 1963.

98   "Children Will Listen": from *Into the Woods,* music and lyrics by Stephen Sondheim, 1987.

98   "How do you know to be afraid": Tom Goldrup and Jim Goldrup, *Growing Up on the Set: Interviews with 39 Former Child Actors of Classic Film and Television* (Jefferson, NC: McFarland, 2002), 30.

99   "My guardian angel": Ibid., 33.

99   "That's it guys": Ibid., 15.

99   "It never occurred to me that I couldn't do it": Ibid., 14.

100 "The world never seems as fresh and wonderful": "'Mockingbird' Film at 50," at www.cnn.com/2012/02/03/showbiz/to-kill-a-mockingbird-50/index.html.

100 "The man I see is still basically": Gary Fishgall, *Gregory Peck: A Biography* (New York: Scribner, 2002), 255.

100 "[a] great humanist": Ibid., 256.

100 "climbing into spare tires": Haney, *Gregory Peck,* 41.

100 "Acting with Mary and Phil is like living the part": Fishgall, *Gregory Peck,* 234.

101 "We tried to kill her": Barbara Hoffman, "Scout's Honor," *New York Post,* July 14, 2015.

101 The pond had been designated a reservoir: McDonald, "Bird in Hand."

102 "an heroic man": Waugh, "Robert Mulligan's Aspirations."

102 "to establish the kind of justice": Ibid.

102 "Think of something very, very sad": Robert Mulligan, "Feature Film Commentary," *To Kill a Mockingbird*, 50th Anniversary Edition, Universal Studios, 2012.

103 "I heard that there was real hostility": Ibid.

103 "malevolence that he carried around on his shoulders": *Fearful Symmetry,* produced and directed by Charles Kiselyak, Universal Studios Home Video, 1998.

103 "I was really afraid": Ibid.

103 "You don't show me shit!": Charles J. Shields, *Mockingbird: A Portrait of Harper Lee, from Scout to Go Set a Watchman* (New York: Henry Holt, 2016), 184.

103 "Jim despised me": *Fearful Symmetry.*

104 "That was not fake": Ibid.

104 "It was something I always wished my father": "Scout Remembers," *To Kill a Mockingbird*, 50th Anniversary Edition, Universal Studios, 2012.

105 "It's like getting back on the stage": Fishgall, *Gregory Peck,* 235.

105 "I had to stop myself": Haney, *Gregory Peck,* 310.

105 "There is nothing I can tell you": Robert Mulligan, "Feature

Film Commentary," *To Kill a Mockingbird*, 50th Anniversary Edition, Universal Studios, 2012.

106 "I've been kicked": *Fearful Symmetry*.

106 "The anger, the isolation": Ibid.

106 "All the colored atmosphere upstairs": Shields, *Mockingbird: A Portrait of Harper Lee, from Scout to Go Set a Watchman*, 183.

106 "Balcony atmosphere": Ibid.

106 "It gave the working actor": "Brock Peters Back at the Scene of Triumph," *New York Post*, October 13, 1963.

106 "We didn't know": Tom Weaver, "The Other Darth Vader," *Starlog*, January 1997.

106 "We need a knothole": "Gregory Peck: The Seventeenth Annual American Film Institute Life Achievement Award Program," *American Film*, March 9, 1989, 10.

107 "Horton's work is very delicate": *Fearful Symmetry*.

107 "As I touched the boy": Ibid.

107 "Just standing on the Radley porch," Harper Lee, *To Kill a Mockingbird* (1960) (New York: Harper Perennial Modern Classics, 2002), 321.

107 "I would never lead him home": Ibid., 319.

108 "the only way that satisfied": Robert Mulligan, "Feature Film Commentary," *To Kill a Mockingbird*, 50th Anniversary Edition, Universal Studios, 2012.

109 "staging long scenes and not being afraid of it": Ibid.

109 "I would tell actors": Alan Pakula, "Feature Film Commentary," *To Kill a Mockingbird*, 50th Anniversary Edition, Universal Studios, 2012.

109 "One of my favorite parts of the day": *Movietone News*, October 1973.

110 "I don't know what's going on with you": Mary McDonagh Murphy, ed., *Scout, Atticus, and Boo* (New York: HarperCollins, 2010), 49.

110 "Let's get this done and get it over with": Fishgall, *Gregory Peck*, 235.

110   "a man with a great passion for film": Robert Mulligan, "Feature Film Commentary," *To Kill a Mockingbird*, 50th Anniversary Edition, Universal Studios, 2012.

111   "[I was] so happy with the 'Hey, Boo' moment": Ibid.

111   "She could have easily been nominated": Ibid.

112   "Atticus has no chance to emerge": Fishgall, *Gregory Peck,* 236.

112   "In my opinion, the picture will begin to look better": Ibid.

112   In mathematical terms: Charles J. Shields, *Mockingbird: A Portrait of Harper Lee* (New York: Henry Holt, 2006), 218.

113   "quiet magic of the children's world": *WPAT Gaslight Revue Program Guide*, vol. 12, no. 10 (1967).

113   "The first time I heard the theme": Robert Mulligan, "Feature Film Commentary," *To Kill a Mockingbird*, 50th Anniversary Edition, Universal Studios, 2012.

114   "the trombones pursue her back": Kevin Mulhall, liner notes to *To Kill a Mockingbird,* Original Score, CD, Varese Sarabande Film Classics, 1997.

114   "one of my personal favorites": Ibid.

114   "I think he saved the picture": Gerald C. Wood and Marion Castleberry, *The Voice of an American Playwright: Interviews with Horton Foote* (Macon, GA: Mercer University Press, 2012), 165.

115   "a study in grays": Shields, *Mockingbird: A Portrait of Harper Lee,* 225.

116   "I think it's one of the best translations": Harper Lee, interview on WQXR, June 1964, as quoted at thebluegrassspecial.com /archive/2010/july10/harper-lee-interview.php, July 2010.

10. ON SCREENS AROUND THE WORLD

117   "I wish she could relax": Charles J. Shields, *Mockingbird: A Portrait of Harper Lee* (New York: Henry Holt, 2006), 183.

117   "Truman became very jealous": Mary McDonagh Murphy, ed., *Scout, Atticus, and Boo* (New York: HarperCollins, 2010), 25.

118   "I was his oldest friend": Letter from Harper Lee to Wayne Flynt,

March 10, 2006, in Wayne Flynt, *Mockingbird Songs: My Friendship with Harper Lee* (New York: HarperCollins, 2017), 60.

118 "dear little Nelle": Gerald Clarke, ed., *Too Brief a Treat: The Letters of Truman Capote* (New York: Random House, 2004), 317.

118 hung the Confederate Stars and Bars: Shields, *Mockingbird*, 220.

119 the use of fire hoses and police dogs: Murphy, ed., *Scout, Atticus, and Boo*, 143.

119 "By rooting for a black man": Diane McWhorter, as quoted in *Hey, Boo: Harper Lee & To Kill a Mockingbird*, a film by Mary McDonagh Murphy, First Run Features, 2011.

119 "I was upset about being upset": Kate McLaughlin, "'Mockingbird' Film at 50," www.cnn.com/2012/02/03/showbiz/to-kill -a-mockingbird-50/index.htm.

119 "I think other classmates": Diane McWhorter, interview with the author, January 15, 2017.

119 "For the first time, we came face-to-face": Diane McWhorter, *Carry Me Home: Birmingham, Alabama: The Climactic Battle of the Civil Rights Revolution* (New York: Simon & Schuster, 2001), 322.

119 "We saw the movie over and over": McWhorter, interview with the author, January 15, 2017.

120 "I think Reverend King and the NAACP": Harper Lee, as quoted in *Hey, Boo*.

121 "A major film achievement": "To Kill a Mockingbird," *Variety*, December 12, 1962.

121 "Peck . . . not only succeeds": Ibid.

121 "There is so much feeling for children": Bosley Crowther, "To Kill a Mockingbird," *New York Times*, February 15, 1963.

121 "remarkable figure of innate strength and nobility": Leo Mishkin, "To Kill a Mockingbird: Warm Moving Film Experience," *New York Morning Telegraph*, February 15, 1963.

121 "stature and lasting substance": Judith Crist, "To Kill a Mockingbird," *New York Herald Tribune*, February 15, 1963.

121 "A Tale of Three Tots": Leonard Mosley, "A Tale of Three Tots Delivers Real Childhood to the Screen," (London) *Daily Express,* May 9, 1963.

122 "[b]efore the intellectual confusion of the project": Andrew Sarris, "A Negro Is Not a Mockingbird," *Village Voice,* March 7, 1963.

122 "The Negro is less a rounded character": Ibid.

122 "there was a fair amount of derision": Pauline Kael, as quoted in Lynn Haney, *Gregory Peck: A Charmed Life* (New York: Carroll & Graf, 2005), 315.

123 "Neither *Great Expectations, King Lear,* nor *To Kill a Mockingbird*": *Life, The Enduring Power of To Kill a Mockingbird,* special issue, 2015, 63.

123 "It must be irritating for the American Negro": Brendan Gill, as quoted in Mark Harris, *Pictures at a Revolution: Five Movies and the Birth of the New Hollywood* (New York: Penguin, 2008), 160.

123 "an expert in the Negro condition": Sam Tanenhaus, "The Nat Turner Wars," *Vanity Fair,* September 2016.

123 "The moral of this can only be that": Brendan Gill, as quoted by Colin Nicholson, "Hollywood and Race: To Kill a Mockingbird," in *Cinema and Fiction: New Modes of Adapting, 1950–1990,* edited by John Orr and Colin Nicholson (Edinburgh: Edinburgh University Press, 1992), 97.

124 "a gross of $13,128,846": www.the-numbers.com/movie/To-Kill-A-Mockingbird#=tab-summary.

125 "I don't think there was any clue": Tom Goldrup and Jim Goldrup, *Growing Up on the Set: Interviews with 39 Former Child Actors of Classic Film and Television* (Jefferson, NC: McFarland, 2002), 33.

125 "Dear Harper, Congratulations": Lynn Haney, *Gregory Peck: A Charmed Life* (New York: Carroll & Graf, 2005), 311.

125 "An enormous amount of relief" and "Patty Duke was absolutely brilliant": Goldrup and Goldrup, *Growing Up on the Set,* 33.

126 "We were sitting in my son's room": Marion Castleberry, *Blessed Assurance: The Life and Art of Horton Foote* (Macon, GA: Mercer University Press, 2014), 225.

11. A STRAIGHT SHOT TO THE HEART

129 "It's very hard for film adaptations of popular books": Jeanine Basinger, interview with the author, February 16, 2017.

130 so realistic were the settings: Robert Mulligan, "Feature Film Commentary," *To Kill a Mockingbird,* 50th Anniversary Edition, Universal Studios, 2012.

131 "Stanley's voice doesn't sound like Harper Lee's": Diane Mc-Whorter, interview with the author, January 15, 2017.

131 "From that very voice I believe": *Fearful Symmetry,* produced and directed by Charles Kiselyak, Universal Studios Home Video, 1998.

133 "Why did I dissolve to that?": Robert Mulligan, "Feature Film Commentary," *To Kill a Mockingbird,* 50th Anniversary Edition, Universal Studios, 2012.

134 "Mary Badham is the antithesis": Basinger, interview with the author, February 16, 2017.

136 "Robert Mulligan is a very underrated director": Ibid.

137 "I know, if nobody else does": Gary Fishgall, *Gregory Peck: A Biography* (New York: Scribner, 2002), 235.

138 "He scared me": *Fearful Symmetry.*

139 "a morally towering": Alan Pakula, "Feature Film Commentary," *To Kill a Mockingbird,* 50th Anniversary Edition, Universal Studios, 2012.

141 "You knew you were in something special": Sandra McElwaine, "To Kill a Mockingbird Makes Its Mark 50 Years After the Film's Release," www.thedailybeast.com/to-kill-a-mockingbird-makes-its-mark-50-years-after-the-films-release, January 31, 2012.

142 "Russ Harlan was a joy to work with": Robert Mulligan, "Feature Film Commentary," *To Kill a Mockingbird,* 50th Anniversary Edition, Universal Studios, 2012.

143 "lyrical": Kevin Mulhall, liner notes to *To Kill a Mockingbird*, original score, CD, Varese Sarabande Film Classics, 1997.

144 "angelic": Alan Pakula, "Feature Film Commentary," *To Kill a Mockingbird*, 50th Anniversary Edition, Universal Studios, 2012.

144 "There are only two actors in America": Judith Slawson, *Robert Duvall: Hollywood Maverick* (New York: St. Martin's Press, 1985), 13.

145 "the way you tell a particular story" and "Critics talk about style": Sidney Lumet, *Making Movies* (New York: Vintage Books, 1996), 50–51.

12. IS *TO KILL A MOCKINGBIRD* RACIST?

148 "To the Negro in 1963": *Life, The Enduring Power of To Kill a Mockingbird*, special issue, 2015, 78.

148 "the strength of moral force": Ibid., 86.

148 "*To Kill a Mockingbird* is a book that inspires hope": Mary McDonagh Murphy, ed., *Scout, Atticus, and Boo* (New York: HarperCollins, 2010), 208.

149 "N word": Ibid., 191.

150 "a kind of moral Ritalin": Thomas Mallon, "Big Bird," *The New Yorker*, May 29, 2006.

150 "fatuous side porch sociology": "About Life and Little Girls," *Time*, February 22, 1963.

151 "living his own life as the passive participant": Monroe Freedman, "Atticus Finch, Esq., R.I.P.," *Legal Times*, March 24, 1992.

152 "another's mind, another's creation": Ryu Spaeth, as quoted at theweek.com/articles/566893/kill-mockingbird-racist, July 1, 2015.

153 "intellectual free agents": Sam Tanenhaus, "The Nat Turner Wars," *Vanity Fair*, September 2016.

153 "Who Lives, Who Dies, Who Tells Your Story": music and lyrics by Lin-Manuel Miranda, *Hamilton*, 2015.

153   "the enormous condescension of posterity": E. P. Thompson, as quoted in David A. Bell, "Rewriting History," at www.nytimes .com/2001/07/01/books/rewriting-history.html.

153   "a hall pass through history": Ta-Nehisi Coates, *Between the World and Me* (New York: Spiegel & Grau, 2015), 33.

153   "He would not be your morality": Ibid., 36.

154   "I'm a racist, a distorter of history": Tanenhaus, "The Nat Turner Wars."

154   "Bill's novel is a private act": Ibid.

154   "because no one can tell a writer what he can write": Ibid.

154   "It's a book I admire": Ibid.

13. THE LEGEND GROWS: HARPER LEE'S FIFTY-FIVE YEARS OF SILENCE

156   "I have my work cut out for me": "Harper Lee Planned More Novels, Letter Reveals," at bbc.com/news/entertainment-arts -33481898, July 10, 2015.

157   "sell this to the movies": Ibid.

157   "Can you feed and lodge me": Ibid.

157   "I can't tell you much about Nelle's new book": Gerald Clarke, ed., *Too Brief a Treat: The Letters of Truman Capote* (New York: Random House, 2004), 372.

157   "How do you feel" and "I'm scared": Charles J. Shields, *Mockingbird: A Portrait of Harper Lee, from Scout to Go Set a Watchman* (New York: Henry Holt, 2016), 193.

157   "My objectives are very limited": Harper Lee, as quoted at the bluegrassspecial.com/archive/2010/july10/harper-lee-interview .php, July 2010.

158   "I'm working on another novel": Ibid.

158   "You see, more than a simple matter of putting down words": Ibid.

158   Alice Lee seemed to contradict: William Grimes, "'Mockingbird' Author, Elusive Voice of the Small-Town South," *New York Times,* February 20, 2016.

158   Alice admitted that the second novel": Shields, *Mockingbird,* 248.

159   "Any time we work is time wasted": Harper Lee, as quoted at thebluegrassspecial.com/archive/2010/july10/harper-lee -interview.php, July 2010.

159   "I was exposed to seventeen years": Shields, *Mockingbird,* 191.

159   "Books are the things she cares about": Marja Mills, *The Mockingbird Next Door: Life with Harper Lee* (New York: Penguin, 2014), 26.

159   "she did value the opportunity to give bountiful sums": Ibid., 121.

160   "Instant information is not for me": Harper Lee, "Open Letter to Oprah Winfrey," *O, The Oprah Magazine,* July, 2006.

160   "I don't think any first-time author": Mills, *The Mockingbird Next Door,* 34.

161   "There is nowhere else to go but down": Harper Lee, as quoted in *Hey, Boo: Harper Lee & To Kill a Mockingbird,* a film by Mary McDonagh Murphy, First Run Features, 2011.

161   "[t]wo reasons": Mills, *The Mockingbird Next Door,* 210.

161   "Turning away from the church of fame": Mark Childress as quoted in *Hey, Boo.*

162   "She grows frustrated": Mills, *The Mockingbird Next Door,* 93.

14. LIFE AFTER TO KILL A MOCKINGBIRD

163   "That ramrod-straight quality of his": Jeanine Basinger, interview with the author, February 16, 2017.

164   "Do you like Negroes as you did in the film?" Gary Fishgall, *Gregory Peck: A Biography* (New York: Scribner, 2002), 243.

165   "equal parts Grant Wood and the Arrow Collar man": "Peck Epitomized Noble Heroes," *Variety,* June 16, 2003.

165   "There's only going to be one actor to be President": Lynn Haney, *Gregory Peck: A Charmed Life* (New York: Carroll & Graf, 2005), 338.

165 "You'll never be a good actor": James Bawden and Ron Miller, *Conversations with Classic Film Stars: Interviews from Hollywood's Golden Era* (Lexington: University Press of Kentucky, 2016), 57.

166 "Jonathan's greatest problem": Fishgall, *Gregory Peck,* 287.

166 "They did their dance": Haney, *Gregory Peck,* 353.

166 "benign neglect": Ibid.

166 "Whatever the causes were": Ibid., 364–65.

166 "show up for everything we did": *A Conversation with Gregory Peck*, directed by Barbara Kopple, Universal Studios, 1999.

166 "My father never let me down": Haney, *Gregory Peck,* 401.

167 "lofty manner": Vincent Canby, "MacArthur," *New York Times,* July 1, 1977.

167 "Peck, though he is generally excellent": "About Life and Little Girls," *Time,* February 22, 1963.

167 "When I read the script": Fishgall, *Gregory Peck,* 308.

168 "I was genuinely surprised": "American Film Institute Life Achievement Award," DVD extra, *To Kill a Mockingbird*, 50th Anniversary Edition, Universal Studios, 2012.

168 "Making millions is not the whole ball game": Ibid.

168 "and he was full of questions": Haney, *Gregory Peck,* 416.

169 "too much respect for other people": Cecilia Peck in *A Conversation with Gregory Peck.*

169 "just cancel everything": Goldrup and Goldrup, *Growing Up on the Set,* 32.

169 "quite a bit about you": Blake Green, "An Evening with the Leading Man," *Newsday,* February 27, 1997.

170 "when I saw this photo": Morrison Buck, "Harry Lee Coe 1932–2000," http://digital.lib.usf.edu.

170 "The movie is my little pipeline": Fishgall, *Gregory Peck,* 237.

170 "Having won": Ibid., 241.

170 "I hated myself": Caryn James, "Gregory Peck Enters the 'Tribute Stage," *New York Times,* April 12, 1992.

170   "One good thing about the bad movies": *American Legends: The Life of Gregory Peck* (Cambridge MA: Charles River Editors, 2014), 32.

170   "I have made a handful of pictures": Philip French, "A Born Leader, a Liberal Conscience—and Mount Rushmore," *The Observer* (London), June 15, 2003.

170   "When Veronique and I are in New York": Susan King, "How the Finch Stole Christmas," *New York Post,* December 12, 1997.

170   "Oh God, no!": Ibid.

171   "When he died Gregory Peck took": Richard Corliss, "Gregory Peck," *Time,* June 23, 2003.

171   "When he played Atticus Finch": *American Legends: The Life of Gregory Peck,* 30.

171   "In art there is compassion": Haney, *Gregory Peck,* 420.

171   "To my friend Gregory Peck": Marja Mills, *The Mockingbird Next Door: Life with Harper Lee* (New York: Penguin, 2014), 201.

172   "Mary's an actress": *Fearful Symmetry,* produced and directed by Charles Kiselyak, Universal Studios Home Video, 1998.

172   "I wouldn't want to live in Hollywood": Vernon Scott, "The Badham Way," *Newark Evening News,* January 27, 1963.

172   "It was a tough transition": Goldrup and Goldrup, *Growing Up on the Set,* 33.

172   "The attitude was": Dale Russakoff, "The Atticus We Always Knew," *The New Yorker,* July 17, 2015.

172   "I learned it was real work": Goldrup and Goldrup, *Growing Up on the Set,* 34, 36.

173   "an angel of mercy": Ibid., 36.

173   "felt cut off": Mary McDonagh Murphy, ed., *Scout, Atticus, and Boo* (New York: HarperCollins, 2010), 49.

173   "He remained a big, big influence": *Life, The Enduring Power of To Kill a Mockingbird,* special issue, 2015, 57.

173   "That same gentle guidance": "Scout Remembers," DVD extra, *To Kill a Mockingbird*, 50th Anniversary Edition, Universal Studios, 2012.

173   "I've always tried to live up to": www.thedailybeast.com/to-kill -a-mockingbird-makes-its-mark-50-years-after-the-films -release, January 31, 2012.

174   "The film has so much to give": Ray Nielsen, "To Kill a Mockingbird: An Interview with Mary Badham," *Classic Images*, February 1997.

174   "Mommy, you were so cute!": Ibid.

174   "What a wonderful business": Goldrup and Goldrup, *Growing Up on the Set*, 37.

174   "No, leave your memories where they are": Ibid., 31.

174   "How does it feel to be home?": Ibid.

175   "They had brought in other buildings": Ibid.

175   "family reunion": Tom Weaver, "The Other Darth Vader," *Starlog*, January 1997.

175   "Now apparently he has relented": Ibid.

175   "She and I are very close now": Goldrup and Goldrup, *Growing Up on the Set*, 14.

175   "As soon as I heard her voice": Ibid., 32.

176   "This is God's picture": Ibid., 37.

176   "I didn't do drugs": Ibid., 18.

176   "That business is not real": Ibid., 19.

176   "By then they don't know": Ibid.

176   "the two most wonderful children": Ibid.

177   "This man had a tremendous influence on my life": Ibid., 15.

177   a film version of John Cheever's acclaimed: Murray Schumach, "Two Cheever Novels to Make One Film," *New York Times*, February 28, 1964.

178   "Somehow for me": John Culhane, "Pakula's Approach," *New York Times Magazine*, November 21, 1982.

178   "passion, enthusiasm, and conviction": *Variety*, July 6, 1988.

178   "For a lot of people the idea of mental illness": Elisabeth Bumiller,

"A Filmmaker's Family Faces Mental Illness," *New York Times,* May 13, 1998.

179   "spectacular, eccentric, complicated": *New York Post,* November 23, 1998.

179   "I enjoyed working on it a lot": Gerald C. Wood and Marion Castleberry, *The Voice of an American Playwright: Interviews with Horton Foote* (Macon, GA: Mercer University Press, 2012), 300.

179   "the theater's great chronicler of existential sadness": Ben Brantley, "Heart of a Small Town, Vast in Its Loneliness," *New York Times,* November 19, 2009.

180   "disappearing before our eyes": Marion Castleberry, *Blessed Assurance: The Life and Art of Horton Foote* (Macon, GA: Mercer University Press, 2014), 307.

180   "You're on your own now": Horton Foote, *The Orphans' Home Cycle, Part One: The Story of a Childhood* (New York: Dramatists Play Service, Inc.), 2012.

180   "down here people called my cousins": Wood and Castleberry, *The Voice of an American Playwright,* 201.

181   "This cut of the film dehumanizes": "Rape Intact, Black Rapist's Remorse Cut; Peters in Plea to Actors Guild," *Variety,* July 21, 1970.

182   "Eddie Murphy, Richard Pryor, Whoopi Goldberg": *Telegram and Gazette* (Worcester, MA), October 27, 1989.

183   "the redeeming power of love": Judith Slawson, *Robert Duvall: Hollywood Maverick* (New York: St. Martin's Press, 1985), 87.

184   "If there were French directors as lucid as Mulligan": François Truffaut, *The Films in My Life* (Cambridge, MA: Da Capo Press, 1994), 203.

185   "Bummy was one of a kind": "Henry Bumstead," *Variety,* June 5–11, 2006.

187   "The irony is": Charles J. Shields, *Mockingbird: A Portrait of Harper Lee* (New York: Henry Holt, 2006), 244.

188   "I . . . do not know how to answer it": Letter from Harper Lee

to Wayne Flynt, February 20, 2006, in Wayne Flynt, *Mocking-bird Songs: My Friendship with Harper Lee* (New York: HarperCollins 2017), 55.

188 "If you know Boo": Murphy, ed., *Scout, Atticus, and Boo,* 204.

188 "It took inner wisdom": Oprah Winfrey, as quoted in *Hey, Boo: Harper Lee & To Kill a Mockingbird,* a film by Mary McDonagh Murphy, First Run Features, 2011.

188 "hell no!": Mills, *The Mockingbird Next Door,* 6.

188 "ridiculous": Shields, *Mockingbird: A Portrait of Harper Lee,* 193.

189 "Alice is truly and without a doubt": letter from Harper Lee to Wayne Flynt, February 18, 2005, in Flynt, *Mockingbird Songs,* 38.

189 "unhappily in love": Gerald Clarke, ed., *Too Brief a Treat: The Letters of Truman Capote* (New York: Random House, 2004), 332.

189 "One thing about us": Mills, *The Mockingbird Next Door,* 94.

189 name new subdivisions: Ibid., 39.

189 waited with a friend until the courthouse closed: Serge Kova-leski and Jennifer Crossley Howard, "Fond Recollections in an Alabama Town for Its Celebrated Literary Resident," *New York Times,* February 20, 2016.

189 "I wish I'd never written the damn thing": Mills, *The Mocking-bird Next Door,* 252.

190 "as the event drew closer": Ibid., 202.

190 "Nowadays I follow a mantra": letter from Harper Lee to Wayne Flynt, September 26, 2006, in Flynt, *Mockingbird Songs,* 102.

190 "They always see new things in it": Paul Harris, "Harper Lee Sues Agent Over Copyright to To Kill a Mockingbird," *The Observer* (London), May 5, 2013.

190 "It's better to be silent": Dwight Garner, "To Kill a Friend-ship," *New York Times,* July 17, 2014.

190 "Mary acts like that book is the Bible": Charles J. Shields, *Mockingbird: A Portrait of Harper Lee, from Scout to Go Set a Watchman* (New York: Henry Holt, 2016), 245.

191   on the rare occasions when she and Paley ran into each other: Gerald Clarke, *Capote* (New York: Carroll & Graf, 1988), 462.

192   "It struck me as the flip side of her lust for life": Mills, *The Mockingbird Next Door,* 177.

192   "Truman was a psychopath, honey": Ibid., 169.

192   "If there was a premiere and a party in New York": Ibid., 247.

192   "*Capote* had my name": Kerry Madden, *Up Close: Harper Lee* (New York: Viking, 2009), 179.

192   "I never wore socks": Ibid.

192   "That was uncanny": Mills, *The Mockingbird Next Door,* 248.

193   "You don't know how Hollywood works": Ibid., 245.

193   "Well, it was an interesting experience": Ibid., 250.

193   "You have a creature of such sweetness and light": Ibid., 251.

193   "like God, but clean-shaven": Ginia Bellafante, "Harper Lee: Gregarious for a Day," *New York Times,* January 30, 2006.

193   "I'll say it again": "Rare Sighting of Mockingbird Author," *New York Times,* May 23, 2005.

194   "Alice and Nelle became more conservative politically": Flynt, *Mockingbird Songs,* 45.

195   Eventually the novel's copyright: Paul Harris, *The Observer* (London), May 5, 2013.

195   "the personification of the exemplary lawyer": Madden, *Up Close: Harper Lee*, 181.

195   "We three sisters": Flynt, *Mockingbird Songs,* 179–80.

196   "[Nelle's] surprised at anything that she hears": Shields, *Mockingbird: A Portrait of Harper Lee, from Scout to Go Set a Watchman,* 257.

196   "The good Lord Himself couldn't get to her": Karen Crouse, "A Quest's Unwritten Final Chapter," *New York Times,* February 25, 2016.

197   "This level of involvement": Serge F. Kovaleski and Alexandra Alter, "Another Drama in Hometown of Harper Lee," *New York Times,* August 24, 2015.

197 "that Miss Lee is not in control": Shields, *Mockingbird: A Portrait of Harper Lee, from Scout to Go Set a Watchman*, 262.

15. *GO SET A WATCHMAN*

198 "Nelle's safe-deposit box": Alison Flood, "Harper Lee May Have Written a Third Novel, Lawyer Suggests," *The Guardian*, U.S. edition, July 13, 2015.

199 "several hundred pages": Ibid.

199 "I thought, That's another short story": Tonja Carter, as quoted in *From Mockingbird to Watchman*, a film by Mary McDonagh Murphy, First Run Features, 2015.

199 "preposterous claim": Joe Nocera, "The Harper Lee 'Go Set a Watchman' Fraud," *New York Times*, July 24, 2015.

199 "I went back to the safety-deposit box another day": Tonja Carter as quoted in *From Mockingbird to Watchman*.

199 "I immediately went to Nelle": Tonja B. Carter, "How I Found the Harper Lee Manuscript," *Wall Street Journal*, July 12, 2015.

199 "very wary": Andrew Nurnberg as quoted in *From Mockingbird to Watchman*.

200 "first submission . . . not edited": Tonja Carter, as quoted in Ibid.

200 "a couple of other people": Ibid.

200 "I was blown away": Michael Morrison, as quoted in Ibid.

200 "my dear friend and lawyer": Charles J. Shields, *Mockingbird: A Portrait of Harper Lee, from Scout to Go Set a Watchman* (New York: Henry Holt, 2016), 264.

200 "I thought it a pretty decent effort": Danika Fears and Leonard Greene, "Harper Lee's Mockingbird Surprise," *New York Post*, February 4, 2015.

200 "I am looking forward to reading the book": Ibid.

200 "I was a first-time writer": Diane McWhorter, "Harper Lee, the National Antidote," *The Slate Book Review*, April 8, 2016.

201   weighed in on the controversy: Anita Singh and David Millward, "To Kill a Mockingbird Editor Would Be Dismayed at Decision to Publish New Harper Lee Novel," *The Telegraph,* July 13, 2015.

201   "[Nelle] will take suggestions": Tonja Carter as quoted in *From Mockingbird to Watchman.*

201   "visited her several times": Joy Brown, as quoted in Ibid.

201   Flynt: "You could be King Lear": Wayne Flynt, as quoted in Ibid.

201   "It is completely finished": Russell Berman, "How Harper Lee's Long-Lost Sequel Was Found," www.theatlantic.com /entertainment/archive/2015/02/how-the-long-Sequel-to -Harper-Lee-To-Kill-A-mockingbird-was-found/385131, February 4, 2015.

201   "If an editor had come in now": Joy Brown as quoted in *From Mockingbird to Watchman.*

202   determined that Lee had not been forced: Serge F. Kovaleski and Alexandra Alter, "Another Drama in Hometown of Harper Lee," *New York Times,* August 24, 2015.

202   "hurt and humiliated": *Life, The Enduring Power of To Kill a Mockingbird,* special issue, 2015, 95.

202   "became angry at": Wayne Flynt, *Mockingbird Songs: My Friendship with Harper Lee* (New York: HarperCollins, 2017), 69.

202   "It is sort of strange": Alexandra Alter and Serge F. Kovaleski, "After Harper Lee Novel Surfaces, Plots Arise," *New York Times,* February 9, 2015.

202   "sharp as a tack": Ibid.

202   "I have no doubt": Diane McWhorter, interview with the author, January 15, 2017.

203   "He asked her multiple times": Flynt, *Mockingbird Songs,* 194–95.

203   "We asked Nelle": Michael Morrison, as quoted in *From Mockingbird to Watchman.*

203   "a gift that she didn't reread": McWhorter, interview with the author, January 15, 2017.

203 "Allegedly": Maureen Corrigan, *Fresh Air,* National Public Radio, July 13, 2015.

204 "was easy to look at": Harper Lee, *Go Set a Watchman* (New York: HarperCollins, 2015), 13.

204 "[She] sat there in front of me": Ibid., 161.

204 "Aunty . . . truly": Ibid., 29.

204 "You can't go back home to your family": Thomas Wolfe, *You Can't Go Home Again* (1934) (New York: Scribner, 2011), 602.

205 "Every time I come home": Lee, *Go Set a Watchman,* 75–76.

205 "churched to death": Ibid., 173.

205 "You may reach out and embrace all of Manhattan": Ibid., 180.

205 "the gift of loneliness and the gift of privacy": E. B. White, *Here Is New York* (1949) (New York: Little Bookroom, 1999), 19.

206 "Playing golf is the best way I know": Karen Crouse, "A Quest's Unwritten Final Chapter," *New York Times,* February 25, 2016.

206 "It had never fully occurred to Jean Louise": Lee, *Go Set a Watchman,* 116.

206 "failed her . . . had betrayed her": Ibid., 113.

206 "Don't you ever call me that again": Ibid., 151.

206 "The pleasure in suffering": David Brooks, *The Road to Character* (New York: Random House, 2015), 94.

207 venue for promoting salvation: Charles J. Shields, *Mockingbird: A Portrait of Harper Lee* (New York: Henry Holt, 2006), 121.

207 "Get off the 'social justice'": Ibid., 123.

207 "Like most of his generation": Ibid., 121.

207 "It's got to be done": Ibid., 125.

207 "His Methodist upbringing had persuaded him": Flynt, *Mockingbird Songs,* 5.

207 "By the time *To Kill a Mockingbird* was published": Shields, *Mockingbird: A Portrait of Harper Lee,* 125.

208   "it's very difficult to accurately capture": McWhorter, interview with the author, January 15, 2017.

208   "I need a watchman to tell me": Lee, *Go Set a Watchman,* 181–82.

208   "Jean Louise, every man's watchman is his conscience": Ibid., 265.

208   "He was letting you reduce him to the status of a human being": Ibid., 266.

209   "[P]rejudice, a dirty word": Ibid., 270–71.

209   "Do you want Negroes by the carload in our schools": Ibid., 245–246.

209   "If you're good and mind us": Ibid., 252.

209   "You may be sorry": Ibid., 277.

209   "I think I love you very much": Ibid., 278.

209   "As she welcomed him silently to the human race": Ibid.

210   "the importance of trying harder": Hillary Rodham Clinton, *What Happened* (New York: Simon & Schuster, 2017), 177.

210   "might even be described as a gentleman bigot": Isabel Wilkerson, "Our Racial Moment of Truth," *New York Times,* July 19, 2015.

211   Atticus, in fact, seems to resemble: Joseph Crespino, "Harper Lee's History," *New York Times,* July 16, 2015.

211   "standing around like buzzards": Lee, *Go Set a Watchman,* 149.

211   "Jeffersonian Democrat": Ibid., 244.

211   "manage my own affairs": Ibid., 245.

211   "Well sir, there they were": Ibid., 239.

211   "The sobering answer is yes": Crespino, "Harper Lee's History."

211   "Does *Watchman* cast doubt": McWhorter, "Harper Lee, the National Antidote."

212   "The answer is both": McWhorter, interview with the author, January 15, 2017.

212   "transport Scout to our own time"; Corrigan, *Fresh Air.*

212   "nonconforming tomboys": Ibid.

16. THEME AND VARIATIONS: EVERYTHING OLD IS NEW AGAIN

215   a figure that far outstrips: Mary McDonagh Murphy, ed., *Scout, Atticus, and Boo* (New York: HarperCollins, 2010), 7.

215   forty million copies: William Grimes, "'Mockingbird' Author, Elusive Voice of the Small-Town South," *New York Times,* February 20, 2016.

215   bestselling book of 2015: Ibid.

215   By some estimates: Charles J. Shields, *Mockingbird: A Portrait of Harper Lee, from Scout to Go Set a Watchman* (New York: Henry Holt, 2016), 241.

215   even if: Tracey O'Shaughnessy, *Put the Kettle On and Other Cultural Disconnections* (Cheshire, CT: Equa Press, 2016), 142.

216   "part literary idealism": Maureen Corrigan, *So We Read On: How The Great Gatsby Came to Be and Why It Endures* (New York: Little, Brown, 2014), 7.

216   The character those prisoners most identified with?: Kerry Madden, *Up Close: Harper Lee* (New York: Viking, 2009), 172.

216   "culturally, historically, and aesthetically significant": Donald Liebenson, "Cinematic Legends Take Their Place in National Film Registry," *Chicago Tribune,* January 4, 1996.

216   "[It] reverberates with memories of [my] own past": Roger Fristoe, "Party Politics and Movies: The Introduction," www.tcm.com/this-month/article/83306%7C0/Party-Politics-The-Movies-introduction.html, October 2004.

217   "A half century later": President Barack Obama, youtube.com/watch?v-qsynkk-qqtk, April 30, 2012.

217   "If our democracy is to work": President Barack Obama, www.theatlantic.com/entertainment/archive/2017/01/obamas-atticus-finch/512789, January 10, 2017.

218   "Let no man": Dr. Martin Luther King, Jr., as qoted in Isaac Chotiner, "What Is Malcolm Gladwell Talking About?" www

.thenewrepublic.com/article/51326/what-is-malcolm-gladwell -talking-about, August 4, 2009.

218   20 percent of Monroeville residents: Shields, *Mockingbird: A Portrait of Harper Lee, from Scout to Go Set a Watchman,* 258.

219   "Without wonder, we do not dare": O'Shaughnessy, *Put the Kettle On,* 148.

220   transformed into characters: Lindsay Bahr, "'Broken': Tim Roth on Film Inspired by 'To Kill a Mockingbird,'" www.ew.com /article2013/07/22/broken-exclusive-video, July 22, 2013.

220   "an adult children's tale": Ibid.

221   For the museum, which counted on the play: Serge F. Kovaleski and Alexandra Alter, "Another Drama in Hometown of Harper Lee," *New York Times,* August 24, 2015.

221   "Oh my God": Madden, *Up Close: Harper Lee,* 171.

221   "I found my inspiration": Marion Castleberry, *Blessed Assurance, The Life and Art of Horton Foote* (Macon, GA: Mercer University Press, 2014), 454.

222   "she finally decided that Scott": Alexandra Alter, "'To Kill a Mockingbird' Is Headed to Broadway," *New York Times,* February 10, 2016.

222   "As daunting a prospect": Ibid.

222   "*To Kill a Mockingbird* lives a little bit differently": Ibid.

222   "I was naïve": Ruthie Fierberg, "The Greatest Challenge with Broadway-Bound *Mockingbird,*" www.playbill.com/sorkin-mockingbird, July 31, 2016.

223   "He is in denial": Kyle Buchanan, "How Aaron Sorkin's *To Kill a Mockingbird* Will Surprise You," www.vulture.com /2017/09/how-aaron-sorkin-to-kill-a-mockingbird-will -surprise-you.html, September 13, 2017.

223   "memory play": Fierberg, "The Greatest Challenge with Broadway-Bound *Mockingbird.*"

223   "You won't have to worry": Ibid.

223   "I didn't write their language": Buchanan, "How Aaron Sorkin's *To Kill a Mockingbird* Will Surprise You."

223 "You can't just wrap the original": Alter, "'To Kill a Mockingbird' Is Headed to Broadway."

223 "not to blow it": Ibid.

223 "There's not much upside": Fierberg, "The Greatest Challenge with Broadway-Bound *Mockingbird*."

17. AT PEACE

224 "The Monroeville Walmart Supercenter": Adam Gopnik, "Sweet Home Alabama: Harper Lee's 'Go Set a Watchman,' *The New Yorker*, July 27, 2015.

225 "graffiti": Charles J. Shields, *Mockingbird: A Portrait of Harper Lee* (New York: Henry Holt, 2016), 244.

225 "There's not a blessed thing historic": letter from Harper Lee to Wayne Flynt, February 18, 2005, in Wayne Flynt, *Mockingbird Songs: My Friendship with Harper Lee* (New York: Harper-Collins, 2017), 37.

225 "This room was used as a model": Marianne M. Moates, *Bridge of Childhood: Truman Capote's Southern Years* (New York: Henry Holt, 1989), 4.

225 "I think she's a brilliant writer": *Hey, Boo: Harper Lee & To Kill a Mockingbird*, a film by Mary McDonagh Murphy, First Run Features, 2011.

226 "The book was part of my decision": James Roth, as quoted in Sona Patel, "How 'To Kill a Mockingbird' Changed Their Lives," *New York Times*, February 19, 2016.

226 "On a warm night in 1966": Lynn Haney, *Gregory Peck: A Charmed Life* (New York: Carroll & Graf, 2005), 396.

226 rewarding for adult readers in a way J. D. Salinger's *The Catcher in the Rye*: Mary McDonagh Murphy, ed., *Scout, Atticus, and Boo* (New York: HarperCollins, 2010), 165.

227 "instructive function, an instructive moral function": Ibid., 196.

227 "This is not a black-and-white": Ibid., 50.

227 "We're still grappling with these issues": Karen Nicoletti, "To Kill a Mockingbird at 50," movieline.com/2012/01/26

/to-kill-a-mockingbird-at-50-cecilia-peck-and-mary-badham-on
-its-legacy-lessons-and-life-with-gregory-peck, January 26,
2012.

227   "a permanent amphitheater of American adolescence": Adam
Gopnik, "Sweet Home Alabama."

227   "seem more meaningful and death less frightening": John Tierney, "Fond Remembrances," *New York Times,* July 9, 2013.

228   "Nostalgia makes us a bit more human": Ibid.

228   "Nostalgia serves a crucial existential function": Ibid.

228   "[s]ome of our research shows": Ibid.

228   "had removed the walls of distance": Paul Tillich as quoted in
Hillary Rodham Clinton, *What Happened* (New York: Simon
& Schuster, 2017), 431.

231   "I've met two in my lifetime": Michael Cieply and Brooks
Barnes, "Film Version of 'Watchman'? First, Untangling the
Rights," *New York Times,* July 17, 2015.

232   "There's a lot of ugly things": *To Kill a Mockingbird,* 50th Anniversary Edition, Universal Studios, 2012.

232   "He would be there all night": Harper Lee, *To Kill a Mockingbird* (1960) (New York: Harper Perennial Modern Classics,
2002), 323.

232   "He was real nice" and "Most people are, Scout": Ibid.

233   "The film made me realize": Oprah Winfrey, as quoted in *Hey,
Boo: Harper Lee & To Kill a Mockingbird.*

233   "What kind of man are you?": *To Kill a Mockingbird,* 50th Anniversary Edition, Universal Studios, 2012.

233   "the line separating good and evil": Aleksandr Solzhenitsyn, as
quoted in David Brooks, *The Road to Character* (New York:
Random House, 2015), xvii.

234   "When it counted, Harper Lee did what was necessary": James
McBride, as quoted in Murphy, ed., *Scout, Atticus, and Boo,*
133.

234   requested her ashes be scattered: Flynt, *Mockingbird Songs,*
100.

235 "Go the f— back": Joe Heim, "Recounting a Day of Rage, Hate, Violence and Death," *Washington Post,* August 14, 2017.

235 "Dylann Roof was a hero": Ibid.

235 "many sides": statement made by President Donald Trump on August 12, 2017.

235 "Racism is evil": statement made by President Donald Trump on August 14, 2017.

235 "torn the national fabric": Graydon Carter, "Editor's Letter," *Vanity Fair,* October 2017.

236 "where have you gone Joe DiMaggio": "Mrs. Robinson," music and lyrics by Paul Simon, 1968.

236 "Keep cool": B. H. Liddell Hart, as quoted in John F. Kennedy, "Books in the News," a review of *Deterrent or Defense,* by B. H. Liddell Hart, *Saturday Review,* September 3, 1960.

236 "People who have made peace with themselves": Charles J. Shields, *Mockingbird: A Portrait of Harper Lee* (New York: Henry Holt, 2006), 288.

237 "I think the journey is": Gerald C. Wood and Marion Castleberry, *The Voice of an American Playwright: Interviews with Horton Foote* (Macon, GA: Mercer University Press, 2012), 306.

237 "I have a few [movies] like that": *A Conversation with Gregory Peck,* directed by Barbara Kopple, Universal Studios, 1999.

237 "Perhaps they'll carry a thought away with them": Scott McGee, Kerryn Sherrod and Jeff Stafford, "To Kill a Mockingbird," tcm.com/this-month/article/71650%7C0/Behind--the-camera .html.

BIBLIOGRAPHY

BOOKS

American Legends: The Life of Gregory Peck. Cambridge, MA: Charles River Editors, 2014.

Arnold, Jeremy. *The Essentials: 52 Must-See Movies and Why They Matter*. Philadelphia: Perseus, 2016.

Brooks, David. *The Road to Character*. New York: Random House, 2015.

Brown, Jared. *Alan J. Pakula: His Films and His Life*. New York: Back Stage Books, 2005.

Brown, Jerry Elijah, ed. *Clearings in the Thicket: An Alabama Humanities Reader*. Macon, GA: Mercer University Press, 1985.

Castleberry, Marion. *Blessed Assurance: The Life and Art of Horton Foote*. Macon, GA: Mercer University Press, 2014.

Childress, Mark. *Looking for Harper Lee: Two Essays*. New York: Overture Books, 2015.

Clarke, Gerald. *Capote*. New York: Carroll & Graf, 1988.

———, ed. *Too Brief a Treat: The Letters of Truman Capote*. New York: Random House, 2004.

Clinton, Hillary Rodham. *What Happened*. New York: Simon & Schuster, 2017.

Coates, Ta-Nehisi. *Between the World and Me*. New York: Spiegel & Grau, 2015.

Corrigan, Maureen. *So We Read On: How The Great Gatsby Came to Be and Why It Endures*. New York: Little, Brown, 2014.

Eby, Margaret. *South Toward Home: Travels in Southern Literature*. New York: W. W. Norton, 2015.

Fishgall, Gary. *Gregory Peck: A Biography*. New York: Scribner, 2002.

Flynt, Wayne. *Mockingbird Songs: My Friendship with Harper Lee*. New York: HarperCollins, 2017.

Foote, Horton. *Three Screenplays*. New York: Grove Press, 1989.

Foster, Thomas C. *Reading the Silver Screen*. New York: Harper-Collins, 2016.

Freedland, Michael. *Gregory Peck*. New York: William Morrow, 1980.

Goldrup, Tom, and Jim Goldrup. *Growing Up on the Set: Interviews with 39 Former Child Actors of Classic Film and Television*. Jefferson, NC: McFarland, 2002.

Griggs, John. *The Films of Gregory Peck*. New York: Citadel Press, 1984.

Hamill, Pete. *Why Sinatra Matters*. New York: Little, Brown, 1998.

Haney, Lynn. *Gregory Peck: A Charmed Life*. New York: Carroll & Graf, 2005.

Harris, Mark. *Pictures at a Revolution: Five Movies and the Birth of the New Hollywood*. New York: Penguin, 2008.

Isenberg, Nancy. *White Trash: The 400-Year Untold History of Class in America*. New York: Viking, 2016.

Johnson, Claudia Durst. *To Kill a Mockingbird: Threatening Boundaries*. New York: Twayne, 1994.

Lee, Harper. *Go Set a Watchman*. New York: HarperCollins, 2015.

———. *To Kill a Mockingbird*. Philadelphia: J. P. Lippincott, 1960; New York: Harper Perennial Modern Classics, 2002.

Lumet, Sidney, *Making Movies*. New York: Vintage, 1996.

Madden, Kerry. *Up Close: Harper Lee*. New York: Viking, 2009.

McWhorter, Diane, *Carry Me Home: Birmingham, Alabama: The Climactic Battle of the Civil Rights Revolution.* New York: Simon & Schuster, 2001.

Mills, Marja. *The Mockingbird Next Door: Life with Harper Lee.* New York: Penguin, 2014.

Moates, Marianne M. *A Bridge of Childhood: Truman Capote's Southern Years.* New York: Henry Holt, 1989.

Murphy, Mary McDonagh, ed. *Scout, Atticus, and Boo: A Celebration of Fifty Years of To Kill a Mockingbird.* New York: HarperCollins, 2010.

Orr, John, and Colin Nicholson, eds. *Cinema and Fiction: New Modes of Adapting, 1950–1990.* Edinburgh: Edinburgh University Press, 1992.

O'Shaughnessy, Tracey. *Put the Kettle On and Other Cultural Disconnections.* Cheshire, CT: Equa Press, 2016.

Plimpton, George. *Truman Capote.* New York: Doubleday, 1997.

Shields, Charles J. *Mockingbird: A Portrait of Harper Lee.* New York: Henry Holt, 2006.

———. *Mockingbird: A Portrait of Harper Lee, from Scout to Go Set a Watchman.* New York: Henry Holt, 2016.

Slawson, Judith. *Robert Duvall: Hollywood Maverick.* New York: St. Martin's Press, 1985.

Thomson, David. *Moments That Made the Movies.* New York: Thames & Hudson, 2013.

Truffaut, François. *The Films in My Life* (1978) Cambridge, MA: Da Capo Press, 1994.

Wasson, Sam. *Fifth Avenue, 5 A.M.: Audrey Hepburn, Breakfast at Tiffany's, and the Dawn of the Modern Woman.* New York: HarperCollins, 2010.

White, E. B. *Here Is New York* (1949) New York: Little Bookroom, 1999.

Wolfe, Thomas. *You Can't Go Home Again* (1934) New York: Scribner, 2011.

Wood, Gerald C., and Marion Castleberry. *The Voice of an American Playwright: Interviews with Horton Foote.* Macon, GA: Mercer University Press, 2012.

PERIODICALS

"American Auteurs: Robert Mulligan." Lincoln Center Film Program Notes, March 18–25, 2009.

Alter, Alexandra. "A Collaboration in Mischief and More." *New York Times,* August 10, 2015.

———. "'To Kill a Mockingbird' Is Headed to Broadway." *New York Times,* February 10, 2016.

———. "While Some Are Shocked by 'Go Set a Watchman,' Others Find Nuance in a Bigoted Atticus Finch." *New York Times,* July 11, 2015.

———, and Serge F. Kovaleski. "After Harper Lee Novel Surfaces Plots Arise." *New York Times,* February 9, 2015.

Bellafante, Ginia. "Harper Lee: Gregarious for a Day." *New York Times,* January 30, 2006.

Bernstein, Elmer. "On Film Music." *Journal of the University Film Association* 28, 4 (Fall 1976).

Brantley, Ben. "Heart of a Small Town, Vast in Its Loneliness." *New York Times,* November 19, 2009.

"Brock Peters Back at Scene of Triumph." *New York Post,* October 13, 1963.

"Brock Peters of 'To Kill a Mockingbird' Is Dead at 78." *New York Times,* August 24, 2005.

Bumiller, Elisabeth. "A Filmmaker's Family Faces Mental Illness." *New York Times,* May 13, 1998.

Campbell, Bob. "Gregory Peck." *Sunday Star-Ledger,* October 20, 1991.

Canby, Vincent. "MacArthur." *New York Times,* July 1, 1977.

Carroll, Kathleen. "New Movies Are Mirrors of Today's Skepticism." New York *Daily News,* July 7, 1974.

Carter, Graydon. "Editor's Letter." *Vanity Fair,* October 2017.

Carter, Richard. "Remembering Brock Peters." *New York Amsterdam News,* September 15–21, 2005.

Carter, Tonja B. "How I Found the Harper Lee Manuscript." *Wall Street Journal,* July 12, 2015.

Champlin, Charles. "For Pakula It's Falling in Love with Love and Being in Love." *Los Angeles Times,* March 5, 1989.

———. "Mr. Peck After All These Years." *Los Angeles Times,* October 20, 1991.

"Chicago Press Call." *Rogue,* March 1963.

"Children Caught in Adult Dramas." *Life,* February 8, 1963.

Cieply, Michael, and Brooks Barnes. "Film Version of 'Watchman'? First Untangling the Rights." *New York Times,* July 17, 2015.

Corliss, Richard. "Gregory Peck." *Time,* June 23, 2003.

Crespino, Joseph. "Harper Lee's History." *New York Times,* July 16, 2015.

Crist, Judith. "To Kill a Mockingbird." *New York Herald Tribune,* February 15, 1963.

Crouse, Karen. "A Quest's Unwritten Final Chapter." *New York Times,* February 25, 2016.

Crowther, Bosley. "To Kill a Mockingbird." *New York Times,* February 15, 1963.

Culhane, John. "Pakula's Approach." *New York Times Magazine,* November 21, 1982.

Culligan, Glendy. "Listen to That Mockingbird." *Washington Post and Times-Herald,* July 3, 1960.

Dreher, Rod. "Pakula in Fine Detail." *New York Post,* November 21, 1998.

Fears, Danika, and Leonard Greene. "Harper Lee's Mockingbird Surprise." *New York Post,* February 3, 2015.

Film Comment 8, 2 (Summer 1972).

Film Quarterly, Spring 1963.

Films in Review, March 1963.

Film Society of Lincoln Center. "The Impeccable Gregory Peck: A Film Society Tribute," April 1992.

Fink, Mitchell. "Elite Bid Fond Farewell to Director Alan Pakula." New York *Daily News,* February 3, 1999.

Flood, Alison. "Harper Lee May Have Written a Third Novel, Lawyer Suggests." *The Guardian,* U.S. edition, July 13, 2015.

Focus on Film, 1 (1970).

———, 13 (1973).

Ford, Richard. "Runaway American Dream." *New York Times Book Review.* September 25, 2016.

Fox, Margalit. "Robert Mulligan, Director, Is Dead at 83." *New York Times.* December 23, 2008.

Fox, Terry Curtis. "Interview with Robert Mulligan." *Boston Phoenix,* August 8, 1972.

Freedman, Monroe. "Atticus Finch, Esq., R.I.P." *Legal Times,* March 24, 1992.

French, Philip. "A Born Leader, a Liberal Conscience—and Mount Rushmore Jaw." *The Observer* (London), June 15, 2003.

Gaffney, Adrienne. "The Real Story Behind 'To Kill a Mockingbird.'" *Wall Street Journal,* May 11, 2011.

Gao, Gordon. "Gregory Peck Interview." *Films and Filming,* June 1974.

Gardella, Kay. "Peck Reels in Memories." New York *Daily News,* August 14, 1988.

Garner, Dwight. "To Kill a Friendship." *New York Times,* July 17, 2014.

Gladwell, Malcolm. "The Courthouse Ring." *The New Yorker,* August 10 and 17, 2009.

Godfrey, Lionel. "The Music Makers." *Films and Filming,* September 1966.

Gopnik, Adam. "Sweet Home Alabama; Harper Lee's 'Go Set a Watchman.'" *The New Yorker,* July 27, 2015.

Green, Blake. "An Evening with the Leading Man." *Newsday,* February 27, 1997.

"Gregory Peck: The Seventeenth Annual American Film Institute Life Achievement Award Program," *American Film,* March 9, 1989.

Grimes, William. "Gregory Peck Is Dead at 87; Film Roles Had Moral Fiber." *New York Times,* June 3, 2003.

———. "Mockingbird Author, Elusive Voice of the Small-Town South." *New York Times,* February 20, 2016.

Gross, Jane. "Looking Beyond Controversy as Readers in Manhattan Welcome Lee's 'Watchman.'" *New York Times,* July 15, 2015.

Harmetz, Aljean. "Reflections by and Plaudits for Gregory Peck." *New York Times,* March 11, 1989.

Harris, Paul. "Harper Lee Sues Agent over Copyright to To Kill a Mockingbird." *The Observer* (London), May 5, 2013.

Heim, Joe. "Recounting a Day of Rage, Hate, Violence and Death." *Washington Post,* August 14, 2017.

Hendrick, Kimmis. "Brock Peters: Hope and Some Variations on a Theme." *Christian Science Monitor,* December 29, 1969.

"Henry Bumstead." *Variety,* June 5–11, 2006.

"Henry Bumstead, 91, Production Designer for Noted Films." *New York Times,* May 30, 2006.

Hoffman, Barbara. "Scout's Honor." *New York Post,* July 14, 2015.

Hoffman, Roy. "Harper Lee, My Daughter and Me." *New York Times,* July 9, 2015.

Holcomb, Mark. "The World in His Arms." *Village Voice,* June 18, 2003.

Hollywood Reporter, February 3, 1993.

Howard, Jennifer Crossley. "Where a Literary Favorite Is a Guaranteed Stage Hit." *New York Times,* April 15, 2015.

———, Katherine Webb, and Serge F. Kovaleski, "Mockingbird Author Is Memorialized as She Lived: Quietly and Privately." *New York Times,* February 21, 2016.

Hutchens, John K. "Harper Lee: On Life with Father." *New York Herald Tribune Books Review,* April 15, 1962.

———. "Gregory Peck: Snippets of 40 Years." *New York Times,* August 24, 1988.

James, Caryn. "Gregory Peck Enters the 'Tribute Stage.'" *New York Times,* April 12, 1992.

Kakutani, Michiko. "Kind Hero of 'Mockingbird' Is Cast as Racist in New Book." *New York Times,* July 11, 2015.

———. "The Loss of Innocence, First as Children, Then Again as Adults." *New York Times,* February 20, 2016.

Katzman, Lisa. "DeMille to Scorsese, He's Scored Them All." *New York Times,* November 3, 2002.

Kennedy, John F. "Books in the News." Review of *Deterrent or Defense,* by B. H. Liddell Hart. *Saturday Review,* September 3, 1960.

Kennedy, Randall. "Harper Lee's 'Go Set a Watchman.'" *New York Times Book Review,* July 14, 2015.

King, Susan. "How the Finch Stole Christmas." *New York Post,* December 12, 1997.

Klein, Elinor. "To Kill a Mockingbird." *New York Standard,* February 15, 1963.

Kovaleski, Serge F., and Alexandra Alter. "Another Drama in Hometown of Harper Lee." *New York Times,* August 24, 2015.

———, and Alexandra Alter. "'Mockingbird' Author's Will Is Unsealed but the Mystery of Her Life Only Deepens." *New York Times,* February 28, 2018.

———, and Jennifer Crossley Howard. "Fond Recollections in an Alabama Town for Its Celebrated Literary Resident." *New York Times,* February 20, 2016.

Lee, Harper. "Christmas to Me." *McCall's,* December 1961.

———. "Love—In Other Words." *Vogue,* April 1961.

———. "Open Letter to Oprah Winfrey." *O, The Oprah Magazine,* July 2006.

———. "When Children Discover America." *McCall's,* August 1965.

Liebenson, Donald. "Cinematic Legends Take Their Place in National Film Registry." *Chicago Tribune,* January 4, 1996.

Life. The Enduring Power of To Kill a Mockingbird, New York: Time Inc. Books, 2015.

Lumenick, Lou. "Harper's Bizarre Choice." *New York Post,* May 13, 2011.

Lyman, Rick. "A Movie Becomes Music to His Ears." *New York Times,* January 22, 1998.

———. "Watching Movies with Sissy Spacek; In the Arms of Memory." *New York Times,* February 1, 2002.

Mahler, Jonathan. "The Invisible Hand Behind Harper Lee's 'To Kill a Mockingbird.'" *New York Times,* July 12, 2015.

Maloney, Jennifer and Laura Stevens. "Harper Lee's Lawyer Expands Role." *Wall Street Journal,* July 28, 2015.

Mallon, Thomas. "Big Bird." *The New Yorker,* May 29, 2006.

Manners, Dorothy. "Performer You Liked Was Probably Peters." New York *Daily News,* October 25, 1964.

Maslin, Janet. "Finding Depth in Society's Shallow End." *New York Times,* November 23, 1998.

McDonald, Thomas. "Bird in Hand." *New York Times,* May 6, 1962.

McDonough, John. "Funny Music Maestro Gets Serious." *Wall Street Journal,* November 8, 1990.

McLellan, Dennis. "Collin Wilcox Paxton Dies at 74; Actress Was Mayella in 'To Kill a Mockingbird.'" *Los Angeles Times.* October 23, 2009.

McWhorter, Diane. "Harper Lee, the National Antidote." *The Slate Book Review,* April 8, 2016.

Micklin, Bob. "Bernstein." *Newsday,* March 18, 1967.

Mishkin, Leo. "To Kill a Mockingbird: Warm Moving Film Experience." *New York Morning Telegraph,* February 15, 1963.

Mitgang, Herbert. "Books of the Times." Review of *To Kill a Mockingbird,* by Harper Lee. *New York Times,* July 13, 1960.

Mosley, Leonard. "A Tale of Three Tots Delivers Real Childhood to the Screen." *Daily Express,* May 9, 1963.

"Movie Mockingbird," *New York Times Magazine,* August 5, 1962.

Movietone News, October 1973.

"Mulligan: Auteur or Sieve." *Village Voice,* July 27, 1972.

Nashawty, Chris. "In Honor of Atticus." *Entertainment Weekly,* June 16, 2017.

New York Times, May 12, 1961.

———, February 5, 1999.

Nichols, Peter. "Time Can't Kill Mockingbird." *New York Times,* February 27, 1998.

Nielsen, Ray. "To Kill a Mockingbird: An Interview with Mary Badham." *Classic Images,* February 1997.

Nocera, Joe. "The Harper Lee 'Go Set a Watchman' Fraud." *New York Times,* July 24, 2015.

O'Toole, Fintan. "Elmer Bernstein Finds Himself in Tune with Movies." *New York Times,* October 28, 1990.

Pakula, Alan. "All Those Shirley Temples." *New York Herald Tribune,* July 15, 1962.

———. "Pakula Switched and Hit Right Track." *Louisville Courier,* February, 2001.

Patel, Sona. "How 'To Kill a Mockingbird' Changed Their Lives." *New York Times,* February 19, 2016.

"Peck a Real-life Hero and True Class Act." *Variety,* June 12, 2003.

"Peters Was Mockingbird Star." *Variety,* August 29–September 4, 2005.

Pinkerton, Nick. "Films of Robert Mulligan at Walter Reade." *Village Voice,* March 18–24, 2009.

Pressley, Sue Anne. "Flocking In." *Newsday,* August 19, 1999.

"Rape Intact, Black Rapist's Remorse Cut; Peters in Plea to Actors Guild." *Variety,* July 21, 1970.

Risen, Clay. " 'Go Set a Watchman' Shatters the Myths of the White South." *New York Times,* July 24, 2015.

"Robert Mulligan." *Variety,* January 5–11, 2009.

Rogers, Katie. "How the Writer of 'Mockingbird' Doted on Opus the Penguin." *New York Times,* February 22, 2016.

Russakoff, Dale. "The Atticus We Always Knew." *The New Yorker,* July 17, 2015.

"Russell Harlan." *Variety,* March 6, 1974.

Sarris, Andrew. "A Negro Is Not a Mockingbird." *Village Voice,* March 7, 1963.

———. "Feel-good Fellas; Two Boys from the Bronx." *New York Observer,* March 22, 1999.

Schumach, Murray. "Film Crew Saves $75,000 on Shacks." *New York Times,* January 19, 1962.

———. "Two Cheever Novels to Make One Film." *New York Times,* February 18, 1964.

Scott, Vernon. "Film Version of First Novel Pleases Author." *Newark Evening News,* January 27, 1963.

Severo, Richard. "Elmer Bernstein, a Composer of Scores Capable of Outshining Their Films, Dies at 82." *New York Times,* August 20, 2004.

Seymour, Gene. "A Movie Icon for His Roles of Resolute Virtue." *Newsday,* June 13, 2003.

Shep. "Know Your Director." *Motion Picture Exhibitor,* March 24, 1971.

Singh, Anita, and David Millward. "To Kill a Mockingbird Editor Would Be Dismayed at Decision to Publish New Harper Lee Novel." *The Telegraph,* July 30, 2015.

Sisario, Ben. "Rare Sighting of Mockingbird Author." *New York Times,* May 23, 2005.

Sterritt, David. "Good Yarns Appeal to Director Mulligan." *Christian Science Monitor,* February 8, 1979.

Sterngold, James. "Alan J. Pakula, Film Director, Dies at 70." *New York Times,* November 20, 1998.

Tallmer, Jerry. "He's a Peck of a Guy." *New York Post,* April 15, 1992.

Tanenhaus, Sam. "The Nat Turner Wars." *Vanity Fair,* September 2016.

Teachout, Terry. "'To Kill a Mockingbird' Review: Changing Its Tune." *Wall Street Journal,* February 27, 2015.

"The Real Story Behind 'To Kill a Mockingbird.'" *Wall Street Journal,* May 11, 2011.

Tierney, John. "Fond Remembrances." *New York Times,* July 9, 2013.

"To Kill a Mockingbird." *Variety,* December 12, 1962.

TWA Ambassador, March 1988.

"Two Chosen for Mockingbird." *New York Times,* February 2, 1962.

Variety, July 6, 1988.

———, August 23, 2004.

Villager, February 14, 1963.

Voland, John. "Film Music's Master Chameleon." *Variety,* July 16, 1996.

Wahls, Robert. "Brock's Message." New York *Daily News,* April 30, 1972.

Warner, Alan. "Records." *Films and Filming,* March 1971.

Waugh, John C. "Robert Mulligan's Aspirations." *Christian Science Monitor,* January 23, 1963.

Weaver, Tom. "The Other Darth Vader." *Starlog,* January 1997.

Weber, Bruce. "Family Ties Bind Pakula to His 'Morning'." *New York Times,* April 16, 1989.

Wilkerson, Isabel. "Our Racial Moment of Truth." *New York Times,* July 19, 2015.

Wilmington, Michael. "Love of Literature Made Peck and Cronyn Special." *Chicago Tribune,* June 23, 2003.

Women's Wear Daily, February 28, 1977.

Worcester, MA. *Telegram & Gazette,* October 27, 1989.

WPAT Gaslight Revue Program Guide 12, no. 10 (1967).

CD

Bernstein, Elmer. *To Kill a Mockingbird* (original score). Varese Sarabande Film Classics, 1997. Liner Notes by Kevin Mulhall.

DVD

A Conversation with Gregory Peck. Directed by Barbara Kopple. Universal Studios, 1999.

Fearful Symmetry. Produced and directed by Charles Kiselyak. Universal Studios Home Video, 1998.

"American Film Institute Lifetime Achievement Award." DVD extra, *To Kill a Mockingbird*, 50th Anniversary Edition. Universal Studios, 2012.

From Mockingbird to Watchman. A Film by Mary McDonagh Murphy. First Run Features, 2015.

Hey, Boo: Harper Lee & To Kill a Mockingbird. A Film by Mary McDonagh Murphy. First Run Features, 2011.

"Scout Remembers." DVD extra, *To Kill a Mockingbird*, 50th Anniversary Edition. Universal Studios, 2012.

To Kill a Mockingbird, 50th Anniversary Edition. Universal Studios, 2012.

RADIO

Corrigan, Maureen. *Fresh Air,* National Public Radio, July 13, 2015.

Newquist, Roy. *Counterpoint,* June 5, 1964.

WEBSITES

Anderson, Nancy. "Harper Lee," www.encyclopediaofalabama.org /article/h-1126. March 19, 2007, updated November 17, 2016.

Bahr, Lindsey. "'Broken': Tim Roth on Film Inspired by To Kill a Mockingbird." www.ew.com/article/2013/07/22/broken-exclusive -video.

Bell, David. "Rewriting History." www.nytimes.com/2001/07/01/books /rewriting-history.html.

Berman, Russell. "How Harper Lee's Long-Lost Sequel Was Found." www.theatlantic.com/entertainment/archive/2015/02/how -the-lost-sequel-to-Harper-Lee's-To-Kill-A-Mockingbird-Was -Found/385131.

Buchanan, Kyle. "How Aaron Sorkin's To Kill a Mockingbird Will Surprise You." www.vulture.com/2017/09/how-aaron-sorkins-to -kill-a-mockingbird-will-surprise-you.html.

Buck, Morrison. "Harry Lee Coe 1932–2000." http://digital.lib.usf.edu.

Chotiner, Isaac. "What Is Malcolm Gladwell Talking About?" www .thenewrepublic.com/article/51326/what-is-malcolm-gladwell -talking-about. August 4, 2009.

Fierberg, Ruthie. "The Greatest Challenge with Broadway-Bound *Mockingbird.*" www.playbill.com/sorkin-mockingbird. July 31, 2016.

"50 Facts About To Kill a Mockingbird." www.liveforfilm.com /2012/02/09/50-facts-about-to-kill-a-mockingbird/. February 9, 2012.

Flynt, Wayne. "To Kill a Mockingbird." www.encyclopediaofalabama .org/article/h-1140. March 26, 2007, updated November 14, 2016.

Fristoe, Roger. "Party Politics and Movies: The Introduction." www
    .tcm.com/this-month/article/83306%7C0/Party-Politics-the
    -Movies-Introduction.html/. October 2004.

"Harper Lee Planned More Novels, Letter Reveals." bbc.com/news
    /entertainment-arts-33481898. July 10, 2015.

Herbert, Daniel, "To Mock a Killingbird: Martin Arnold's Passage a
    L'Acte and the Dyssemtrics of Cultural Exchange," mfj-online
    .org/journalPages/MFJ45/Herbertpage.html. Fall 2006.

Leerhsen, Charles. "Harper Lee's Novel Achievement." www.smith
    sonianmag.com/arts-culture/harper-lees-novel-achievement
    -141052/. June 2010.

McElwaine, Sandra. "To Kill a Mockingbird Makes Its Mark 50
    Years After the Film's Release." www.thedailybeast.com/to-kill-a
    -mockingbird-makes-its-mark-50-years-after-the-films-release.
    January 31, 2012.

McGee, Scott, Sherrod, Kerryn, Stafford, Jeff. "To Kill a Mockingbird."
    www.tcm.com/this-month/article/71650%7C0/Behind
    -the-camera.html.

McLaughlin, Katie. "'Mockingbird' Film at 50: Lessons on Toler-
    ance, Justice, Fatherhood Hold True." www.cnn.com/2012/02
    /03/showbiz/to-kill-a-mockingbird-50/index.html.

Nicoletti, Karen. "To Kill a Mockingbird at 50: Cecilia Peck and
    Mary Badham on Its Legacy, Lessons and Life with Gregory
    Peck." movieline.com/2012/01/26/to-kill-a-mockingbird-at-50
    -cecilia-peck-and-mary-badham-on-its-legacy-lessons-and-life-with
    -gregory peck/.

Nielsen, Karla. "Go Set a Watchman in the Papers of Harper Lee's
    Literary Agents." https://blogs.cul.columbia.edu/rbml/go-set-a
    -watchman-in-the-papers-of-harper-lees-literary-agents/.

"Raymond Chandler Talks About F. Scott Fitzgerald." https://
    silverbirchpress.wordpress.com/2012/09/13/raymond-chandlers
    -view-of-f-scott-fitzgerald/.

Seal, Mark. "To Steal a Mockingbird?" www.vanityfair.com/culture
    /2013/08/harper-lee-dispute-royalties/.

Spaeth, Ryu. "Is To Kill a Mockingbird Racist?" theweek.com/articles /566893/kill-mockingbird-racist.

"To Kill a Mockingbird." www.tcm.com/tcmdb/title/20116/To-Kill -A-Mockingbird/.

"To Kill a Mockingbird." www.the-numbers.com/movie/To-Kill-A -Mockingbird#tab = summary.

"To Kill a Mockingbird Film Locations." www.movie-locations.com /movies/t/To_Kill_a_Mockingbird.html#.Wk1kpT0ZM6U.

"To Kill a Mockingbird Turns 50." thebluegrassspecial.com/archive /2010/july10/harper-lee-interview.php.

Vlastelica, Ryan. "To Kill a Mockingbird Found Two Paths to Master-piece Status." https://aux.avclub.com/to-kill-a-mockingbird-found -two-paths-to-masterpiece-st-1798282021.

INDEX